Balkan Yearbook of European and International Law

Volume 2019

Balkans Yearbook of European and International Law publishes peer-reviewed scholarly articles, notes, comments and book reviews on private and public European and International Law. The yearbook contains summaries and analyses of recent decisions by national and international courts and arbitral or other tribunals. The yearbook has one section with a special hot topic or focus as well as sections about European and international law in each volume. Moreover, it presents book reviews to recent publications from the region or with a major impact for the region. The yearbook focuses on recent developments of European and International Law and presents a forum for scholarly discourse on European and International Law from the perspective of the region of South-East Europe. However, the publication is not exclusive in that regard: contributions from the perspective of the wider world are also strongly encouraged and welcomed.

More information about this series at http://www.springer.com/series/16247

Zlatan Meškić • Ivana Kunda •
Dušan V. Popović • Enis Omerović
Editors

Balkan Yearbook of European and International Law 2019

Springer

Editors
Zlatan Meškić
College of Law
Prince Sultan University
Riyadh, Saudi Arabia

Ivana Kunda
Faculty of Law
University of Rijeka
Rijeka, Croatia

Dušan V. Popović
Faculty of Law
University of Belgrade
Belgrade, Serbia

Enis Omerović
Faculty of Law
University of Zenica
Zenica, Bosnia and Herzegovina

ISSN 2524-8715 ISSN 2524-8723 (electronic)
Balkan Yearbook of European and International Law
ISBN 978-3-030-33057-6 ISBN 978-3-030-33058-3 (eBook)
https://doi.org/10.1007/978-3-030-33058-3

This Springer imprint is published by the registered company Springer Nature Switzerland AG.
The registered company address is: Gewerbestrasse 11, 6330 Cham, Switzerland

Editorial

The legal systems of South-East Europe are in transition for over three decades. Following the profound political and economic changes in the early 1990s, they took their own ways of development, sharing not only their legal history but also the continuous influences deriving from the European and International Law. The intensity by which the EU law affects the regional developments is very strong in all national legal systems of South-East Europe, while the variances depend largely on the progress each country has made towards the EU membership. In addition, legal obligations under international law are the continuous challenges for the countries in transition.

The *Balkan Yearbook of European and International Law* (BYEIL) aims at providing insights into recent developments in European and International Law and presents a forum for scholarly discourse on these areas of law from the perspective of South-East Europe. While the BYEIL's focus is on the South-East European region, its scope is not limited to that region, and contributions concerning the issues in European or International Law in general are welcomed as well. This policy is reflected in the contents of the first issue of the BYEIL. Besides these two sections, each issue of the BYEIL is devoted to a particular topic.

The first issue of the BYEIL is devoted in particular to International Commercial and Investment Arbitration as one of the fastest developing fields of law in South-East Europe. The thematic framework for contributions on this topic ranges from national to EU and international ones. The papers published in the permanent sections on European Law and International Law explore contemporary challenges in public and private law disciplines putting some old concepts in the new perspectives.

Riyadh, Saudi Arabia	Zlatan Meškić
Rijeka, Croatia	Ivana Kunda
Belgrade, Serbia	Dušan V. Popović
Zenica, Bosnia and Herzegovina	Enis Omerović

Contents

Editors and Contributors

About the Editors

Zlatan Meškić College of Law, Prince Sultan University, Riyadh, Saudi Arabia

Ivana Kunda University of Rijeka, Rijeka, Croatia

Dušan V. Popović University of Belgrade, Belgrade, Serbia

Enis Omerović University of Zenica, Zenica, Bosnia and Herzegovina

Contributors

Jasmina Alihodžić Faculty of Law, University of Tuzla, Tuzla, Bosnia and Herzegovina

Andrés E. Alvarado Garzón Saarland University, Saarbrücken, Germany

Marc Bungenberg Saarland University, Saarbrücken, Germany

Janet C. Checkley Singapore Management University School of Law, Singapore International Dispute Resolution Academy, Singapore, Singapore

Almir Gagula Law Faculty of the University in Zenica, Zenica, Bosnia and Herzegovina
Law Office Gagula, Sarajevo, Bosnia and Herzegovina

Nataša Hadžimanović GABRIEL Arbitration AG and University of Zurich, Zurich, Switzerland

Aliz Káposznyák Eötvös Loránd University, Faculty of Law, Department of Civil Procedure, Budapest, Hungary

Ilma Kasumagić Attorney at Law in Cooperation with Wolf Theiss, Sarajevo, Bosnia and Herzegovina

Adnan Mahmutovic Prince Mohammad Bin Fahd University, Khobar, Kingdom of Saudi Arabia

Nermina Memic-Mujagic University of Sarajevo, Sarajevo, Bosnia and Herzegovina

Emilia Mišćenić Faculty of Law, University of Rijeka, Rijeka, Croatia

Anna Piszcz Faculty of Law, University of Białystok, Białystok, Poland

One Size Fits All? Transparency in Investment and Commercial Arbitration

Marc Bungenberg and Andrés E. Alvarado Garzón

Contents

1 Introduction

Transparency has acquired a growing role in international economic law and international arbitration. It is the 'buzzword *du jour* (...) oft invoked and seldom defined'.[1] In spite of the lack of a comprehensive definition, transparency is usually

[1]Maupin (2013), p. 142.

M. Bungenberg (✉) and A. E. Alvarado Garzón (✉)
Saarland University, Saarbrücken, Germany
e-mail: marc.bungenberg@uni-saarland.de; alvarado@europainstitut.de

Z. Meškić et al. (eds.), *Balkan Yearbook of European and International Law 2019*,
Balkan Yearbook of European and International Law (2020) 2019: 1–22,
https://doi.org/10.1007/16247_2019_1, Published online: 19 December 2019

associated with legitimacy, accountability, democracy and good governance. Notably, calls for more transparency in international economic law touch upon different fields, such as international trade, financial law and international investment law. Particularly, the lack of transparency during the proceedings has been one of the criticisms to investment arbitration. Civil society is reluctant to accept a dispute settlement mechanism entitled to judge on the exercise of regulatory powers of the state behind closed doors. Thus, several efforts towards greater transparency in investment arbitration have been revealed; the UNCITRAL Rules on Transparency in Treaty-Based Investor-State Arbitration (UNCITRAL Rules on Transparency) represent the most prominent example.

Understandably, the debate of increasing transparency in investment arbitration has opened the floor for arguing in favour of more transparency in international commercial arbitration. However, the business community and users of commercial arbitration in general have certain concerns towards transparency and the possibility of full disclosure of their business activities. In this context, this contribution will discuss whether recent developments on transparency in investment arbitration can be transferred to international commercial arbitration according to the following structure: firstly, the debate surrounding transparency in international economic law (Sect. 2); secondly, the reasons behind the increasing transparency in investment arbitration (Sect. 3); thirdly, the relation between international commercial arbitration and transparency (Sect. 4); and, finally, conclusions (Sect. 5).

2 Transparency in International Economic Law

The evolution of transparency within the confines of international economic law has different nuances. It has influenced various sectors, but it has also diverse connotations depending on the specific field of law. Generally, efforts to group transparency across international law have been made[2]; nevertheless, the debate seems to be focused on the openness of international institutions and states towards civil society.[3] In this sense, it is considered that transparency enhances the accountability of the governments and the participation of the public, and promotes due process in adjudication procedures.[4]

One example is portrayed in the negotiations of the Transatlantic Trade and Investment Partnership (TTIP) and the Comprehensive Economic and Trade Agreement (CETA), whereby issues such as access to negotiation documents and

[2]Zoellner (2006), pp. 580–581: "[transparency] (1) as a concept underlying obligations international law places on a state's internal legal regimes and procedures; (2) as a concept governing the relations between institutions and regimes of international law and member states; and (3) as a concept denoting the openness of institutions and procedures of international law, especially *vis-à-vis* international civil society" (footnotes omitted).

[3]Long (2002), pp. 259–268.

[4]Ala'i and D'Orsi (2014), p. 369.

participation of civil society in the diplomatic activities concerning the negotiation of those treaties have raised certain criticisms.[5] However, it must be highlighted that in treaty negotiations, where state representatives try to keep a room for manoeuvre, not everything can be subject to public access. To this point, open discussions and indiscriminate access to civil society may lead to the stagnation of the treaty negotiations.

In international trade law, it may be argued that transparency is of great importance in the World Trade Organization (WTO), given the focus on regulatory convergence and harmonisation.[6] Initially, transparency was an obligation ancillary and subsidiary to the substantive provisions of market access and non-discrimination under the General Agreement on Tariffs and Trade (GATT). Under the WTO, transparency obligations became central and substantive obligations.[7] Transparency finds its way into the WTO decision-making procedures, as well as in the WTO Dispute Settlement Mechanism.[8] In WTO decision-making procedures, transparency is vital for the legitimacy of the system.[9] Some documents circulating for meetings of the Ministerial Conference are publicly available.[10]

At the WTO Dispute Settlement Mechanism, documents initiating consultations, requests for establishment of panels and notices of appeal are made public.[11] The WTO has developed more transparent procedures in the last years, for instance, with the admissibility of *amicus curiae* briefs and by means of access of non-disputing WTO members to the written submissions (this allows that WTO members, particularly developing countries, become acquainted with WTO litigation).[12] In the *US—Shrimp/Turtle* case, the WTO Appellate Body decided that accepting non-requested information (by means of *amicus curiae* brief) is in line with the provisions under the DSU.[13] Although the *amicus curiae* briefs were rejected in the *US—Lead and*

[5] Another recent example is the negotiation process on Trade in Services Agreement (TiSA) initiated by a number of WTO members, who now receive critics for lack of transparency not only from the public but also from other WTO members. It is thus necessary to explore the issue from the point of view of the major international actors, the business community, NGOs, and, more generally, civil society.

[6] Ala'i and D'Orsi (2014), p. 368.

[7] Transparency provisions in GATT, SPS Agreement, TBT Agreement, SCM Agreement refer to the obligation to notify other WTO members of the intention to pass new legislation, allowing other WTO members to comment that legislation, see Ala'i and D'Orsi (2014), p. 371.

[8] Delimatsis (2013), p. 113.

[9] Transparency serves the purpose of the perceived legitimacy of the institution (WTO). See Rogers (2006), p. 1308. Similarly, Delimatsis (2013), p. 114.

[10] Delimatsis (2013), p. 115.

[11] Delimatsis (2013), p. 123.

[12] Delimatsis (2013), p. 124.

[13] *United States – Import Prohibition of certain Shrimp and Shrimp Products – Report of the Appellate Body* (12 October 1998) WT/DS58/AB/R, paras. 99 et seq.

Bismuth II case,[14] the WTO Appellate Body acknowledged the power to accept and consider such submissions when pertinent and useful.[15] Even further, in the *EC—Asbestos* case, the WTO Appellate Body set up a procedure to deal with *amicus curiae* submissions in the specific case.[16] Another aspect of transparency dealt with by the WTO Dispute Settlement Body pertains to public hearings. The WTO Panel and Appellate Body hearings are not open to the public; however, in particular cases, open access has been granted.[17]

In financial law, transparency has been deemed essential to create trust in the financial markets, enhancing legal certainty and confidence,[18] in general safeguarding the proper functioning of the financial system. Transparency touches on three dimensions of financial law: first, enactment of financial regulation; second, a clear and robust set of rules leading to more trust in the financial system and its actors; third, accountability of the actors of the financial system.[19]

At the EU level, Article 15 Treaty on the Functioning of the EU (TFEU) stipulates for all institutions to respect the principle of transparency.[20] Furthermore, the European Parliament meets in public, as does the Council when it deliberates or votes on legislation.[21]

Originally, transparency in the context of international investment law aimed at providing a clear regulatory framework of the host state for the potential foreign investors.[22] As put forward in the *Tecmed v. Mexico* case, the 'foreign investor expects the host State to act in a consistent manner, free from ambiguity and totally transparently in its relations with the foreign investor'.[23] Nevertheless, the debate of transparency in international investment law has its most pressing concern in investment arbitration.

---

[14] *United States – Imposition of Countervailing Duties on certain hot-rolled Lead and Bismuth Carbon Steel Products originating in the United Kingdom – Report of the Appellate Body* (10 May 2000) WT/DS138/AB/R.

[15] *United States – Imposition of Countervailing Duties on certain hot-rolled Lead and Bismuth Carbon Steel Products originating in the United Kingdom – Report of the Appellate Body* (10 May 2000) WT/DS138/AB/R, para. 42.

[16] *European Communities – Measures affecting Asbestos and Asbestos-containing Products – Report of the Appellate Body* (12 March 2001) WT/DS135/AB/R, paras. 50 et seq.

[17] Some examples are *US – Continued Suspension (Hormones), Canada – Continued Suspension (Hormones), EC – Bananas III* and *EC – and Certain Member States – Large Civil Aircraft*, see Delimatsis (2013), pp. 131–132.

[18] Kaufmann and Weber (2010), p. 780.

[19] Kaufmann and Weber (2010), pp. 781 et seq.

[20] Art. 15 para. 1 TFEU: "(1) In order to promote good governance and ensure the participation of civil society, the Union institutions, bodies, offices and agencies shall conduct their work as openly as possible."

[21] Art. 15 para. 2 TFEU: "(2) The European Parliament shall meet in public, as shall the Council when considering and voting on a draft legislative act."

[22] Fry and Repousis (2016), p. 800.

[23] *Técnicas Medioambientales Tecmed SA v. The United Mexican States,* ICSID Case No. ARB/(AF)/00/2, Award 29 May 2003, para. 154.

3 Transparency in Investment Arbitration

The public outcry against the current system of investor-state dispute settlement (ISDS) has called for reforms, including more transparency in the proceedings. It is argued that ISDS should be more 'transparent', in the sense of openness to the public, as a means of increasing the legitimacy of investment arbitration.[24] However, transparency in international arbitration may encompass various aspects: publication of documents arising from the arbitration proceedings, with the redaction of certain confidential information; hearings open to the public; access for non-disputing parties, who are contracting parties of the particular investment treaty; participation of non-state parties, such as NGOs or other organisations (*amicus curiae* submissions); among others.[25]

Within investment arbitration, transparency has been a piecemeal process. The involvement of the state in arbitration was urging more transparency in the proceedings; nevertheless, at the beginning, only the publication of awards was considered.[26] The need for more transparency became evident in investment arbitration involving public interest considerations, such as measures relating to public health, security or protection of the environment.[27] An early example of the debate regarding transparency in investment arbitration can be traced back to the *Methanex Corporation v. United States* case, whereby the tribunal allowed third-party submissions despite the lack of provisions either in the treaty (the North American Free Trade Agreement—NAFTA) or in the arbitration rules specifically addressing this issue.[28] Subsequently, the NAFTA Free Trade Commission issued two documents: first, the 'Notes of Interpretation of Certain Chapter 11 Provisions' on 31 July 2001,[29] stating that there is no obligation on confidentiality in arbitration under NAFTA Chapter 11 or anything preventing the disputing parties to provide public access to the documents submitted or issued during the arbitration proceedings. Moreover, the contracting parties agreed thereby to make all documents submitted or issued during the arbitral proceedings available to the public. The second document

[24]Hay (2018), p. 212.

[25]Fry and Repousis (2016), pp. 808–811.

[26]Cremades and Cortes (2013), p. 31.

[27]Fry and Repousis (2016), p. 804.

[28]Although neither NAFTA nor the UNCITRAL Arbitration Rules of 1976 had provisions on the admissibility of third party submissions, the arbitral tribunal based on Art. 15(1) of the Arbitration Rules to allow those submissions, see *Methanex Corporation v. United States,* UNCITRAL Case, Decision of the Tribunal on Petitions from Third Persons to intervene as 'amici curie' 15 January 2001.

[29]NAFTA Free Trade Commission issued the 'Notes of Interpretation of Certain Chapter 11 Provisions' on 31 July 2001 <http://www.sice.oas.org/tpd/nafta/commission/ch11understanding_e.asp> (accessed 23 March 2019).

is a statement in 2004 allowing non-disputing parties to participate in the investment arbitration proceedings subject to specific requirements.[30]

Against this background, this contribution advances that the core of the debate of increasing transparency in investment arbitration lies on the hybrid nature of investment arbitration, including characteristics of public law (Sect. 3.1). Further, the recent developments towards transparency in investment arbitration will be explained (Sect. 3.2). Finally, interim conclusions of this section are drawn (Sect. 3.3).

3.1 Public Law Dimensions in Investment Arbitration

Investment arbitration may arise from investment contracts, international investment agreements (IIAs) or domestic legislation, but states consent to submit disputes with foreign investors relating to the exercise of public authority only through IIAs and domestic legislation.[31] Therefore, investment treaty arbitration involves more public law than private law issues,[32] arguably a system analogous to domestic administrative law.[33] In this sense, this system for solving disputes may be compared to international judicial review, such as before the Court of Justice of the European Union (CJEU) or the European Court of Human Rights (ECtHR).[34] In contrast, investment arbitration arising from contracts contains the characteristics of a commercial relationship between the state and the foreign investor acting in private capacity; hence, it is framed in the context of party autonomy,[35] but nevertheless issues of transparency obligations overriding party autonomy might arise. Currently, most of the investment arbitration cases are based on IIAs.[36]

Consequently, it can be concluded that investment arbitration, whereby regulatory disputes between foreign investors and host states are decided, bears a resemblance to public law[37] or 'a manifestation of global administrative law'.[38] By means of IIAs, states consent that their laws, court decisions and administrative acts could

[30]NAFTA Free Trade Commission, statement on Non-disputing Party Participation on 7 October 2004 <http://www.sice.oas.org/tpd/nafta/Commission/Nondispute_e.pdf> (accessed 23 March 2019).

[31]Van Harten (2007), pp. 24–25.

[32]Schill (2011), pp. 75–76.

[33]Van Harten and Loughlin (2006), p. 143–144.

[34]Schill (2011), p. 78.

[35]Van Harten and Loughlin (2006), p. 143.

[36]The rise of investor-state arbitration based on IIAs is evidenced over the last 25–30 years. See Behn (2015), p. 365. Furthermore, for a comparison between treaty-based and contract-based investment arbitration see Langford et al. (2017), p. 307.

[37]Howard (2018), p. 16.

[38]Van Harten and Loughlin (2006), p. 127. Similarly, Wälde (2010), p. 15.

be judged under international standards set forth in the respective treaties.[39] As expressed by the arbitral tribunal in *CMS v. Argentina* regarding the international liability of the state, 'it also does not matter whether some actions were taken by the judiciary and others by an administrative agency, the executive or the legislative branch of the State'.[40] Following this line of reasoning, investment arbitration may be portrayed as a vertical or hierarchical relationship between the host state and the foreign investor, the latter subject to the exercise of public authority by the former.[41] There is a regulatory relationship between the host state and the foreign investor, in contrast to a reciprocal or horizontal relation in commercial arbitration.

As highlighted by Thomas Wälde in his dissenting opinion in *Thunderbird Gaming Corp v. Mexico*, foreign investors are not on an equal footing with states since they are exposed to the sovereignty, and the regulatory, administrative and other governmental powers of a state, which differs from international commercial arbitration.[42] Similarly, when criticising the use of the corporate structure to be covered by the IIA in *Tokios Tokéles v. Ukraine*, the dissenting arbitrator highlighted the nature of public international law of investment arbitration.[43] Further, the nature of investment treaty arbitration as similar to public international law was acknowledged in *Loewen v. United States*.[44]

Moreover, in the midst of the backlash against investment arbitration, the analogy between international investment law and national public law is stressed. Critics of ISDS argued that by means of investment arbitration, not only domestic courts but also legislators are displaced, affecting the public policy of the states and having a direct impact on their societies.[45] Similarly, it is considered that the pending threat of a claim under an IIA creates pressure to change domestic law or to abstain from enacting certain regulations, also known as 'regulatory chill'.[46]

The critical point lies on the possibility to submit to arbitration the decisions or actions of the state stemming from the exercise of public authority. Thus, investment

---

[39]Alvarez (2011), p. 442.

[40]*CMS Gas Transmission Company v. The Republic of Argentina*, ICSID Case No. ARB/01/8, Decision of the Tribunal on Objections to Jurisdiction 17 July 2003, para. 108. Similarly, *Loewen Group Inc and Raymond L Loewen v. United States of America*, ICSID Case No. ARB(AF)/98/3, Decisions on hearing of Respondent's objection to Competence and Jurisdiction, para. 70; *Nykomb Synergetics Technology Holding AB v. The Republic of Latvia*, SCC Award 16 December 2003, s. 4.2.

[41]Schill (2011), p. 77; Van Harten (2007), p. 45.

[42]*International Thunderbird Gaming Corporation v. The United Mexican States*, UNCITRAL Case, Separate Opinion of Thomas Wälde 1 December 2005, para. 12.

[43]*Tokios Tokéles v. Ukraine*, ICSID Case No. ARB/02/18, Dissenting Opinion Prosper Weil 29 April 2004, para. 24.

[44]*Loewen Group Inc and Raymond L Loewen v. United States of America*, ICSID Case No. ARB (AF)/98/3, Award 26 June 2003, para. 233.

[45]Leader (2006), p. 684; Van Harten (2010), p. 449. Alvarez (2011), pp. 56 et seq.; Katz (2016), p. 173.

[46]Butler and Subedi (2017), p. 58; Puig and Shaffer (2018), p. 366.

treaty arbitration can be framed as public law. Due to its nature of public law, transparency must be a guiding standard of investment arbitration, granting the necessary legitimacy so often demanded by the civil society. For instance, it is argued that public access—being one aspect of transparency—should govern investment arbitration proceedings as it is also the case regarding decision-making in domestic and international courts.[47]

This contribution puts forward that transparency is deduced from fundamental principles of public law, specifically democratic legitimacy and the rule of law. The role of these two principles in the development of transparency in investment arbitration will be discussed in the following.

3.1.1 Transparency Deduced from Democratic Legitimacy

The assertion of a 'legitimacy crisis' of investment arbitration seems to be ubiquitous in academic literature, as well as in the public policy debate.[48] Nowadays, protests have spread to new IIAs, especially their ISDS systems. This has led, for example, to the delay on the implementation of the ISDS chapter in CETA, given Belgium's request to the CJEU for an opinion on the compatibility of such chapter with EU law.[49]

A state is accountable to its people,[50] thus the proceedings wherein the state is involved should be open to the scrutiny of the public,[51] insofar as the dispute relates to the exercise of public power. Accordingly, the civil society may voice its disapproval over the state's actions through elections.[52] In this sense, it is suggested that decisions taken in investment treaty arbitration should be subject to public scrutiny, also as a precondition of accountability and independence of the adjudication process.[53] In light of the foregoing, transparency emerges as a possible legitimising element for investment arbitration.

---

[47]Van Harten (2007), p. 159.

[48]Franck (2004), p. 1523; Chung (2007), p. 955; Kaushal (2009), p. 522.

[49]Puig and Shaffer (2018), p. 398. Nevertheless, the CJEU has rendered its opinion on 30 April 2019 considering that the chapter on Settlement of Investment Disputes in CETA is compatible with EU law. See, CJEU, Opinion 1/17, Request for an opinion submitted by the Kingdom of Belgium ECLI:EU:C:2019:341.

[50]Howard (2018), p. 23.

[51]Buys (2003), p. 134.

[52]Buys (2003), p. 134.

[53]Van Harten (2007), p. 159. Stein (2001), p. 493.

3.1.2 Transparency Deduced from the Rule of Law

The rule of law engenders continuing controversy as regards its exact meaning or scope.[54] Nevertheless, in a more-or-less comprehensive approach, the rule of law may be framed in terms of the requirements of a well-ordered legal system, including the prohibition of arbitrary power; laws that are general, prospective, clear and consistent; and courts accessible and structured to judge legal claims.[55] In other terms, the rule of law does not place emphasis only on the exercise of power within the constraints of certain public norms but also stresses on the fact that a legal system is provided with legal certainty and predictability.[56] Furthermore, compliance with the rule of law also implies that an adjudication procedure functions properly.[57]

Despite the different aspects the rule of law may involve, it is undisputed that transparency is considered to be essential to achieve the rule of law.[58] In this context, considering investment arbitration as public law and that the legality of the exercise of the regulatory powers of a state is an issue of public concern,[59] the rule of law, especially transparency, must guide the whole procedure of investment arbitration.

3.2 Recent Developments Towards Transparency in Investment Arbitration

The major developments towards transparency in investment arbitration in the recent years are reflected in the UNCITRAL Rules on Transparency[60] in conjunction with the United Nations Convention on Transparency in Treaty-Based Investor-State Arbitration (Mauritius Convention). The Mauritius Convention has been signed by 23 states and ratified by five states. It only entered into force on 18 October 2017.[61] The UNCITRAL Rules on Transparency were developed to tackle some of the criticisms often raised against investment arbitration. In fact, it may be argued that transparency is expected to lead to more trust and acceptance of the arbitral process.[62]

In principle, the UNCITRAL Rules on Transparency apply to investor-state arbitrations under UNCITRAL Arbitration Rules based on IIAs concluded on or

---

54 Fallon (1997).

55 Stein (2001), fn. 21.

56 Waldron (2008), p. 6.

57 Waldron (2008), pp. 7 et seq.

58 Poorooye and Feehily (2017), p. 285. Similarly, Rogers (2006), p. 1337; Comrie-Thomson (2017), p. 280.

59 Howard (2018), p. 23.

60 Effective as of 1 April 2014.

61 <https://treaties.un.org/pages/ViewDetails.aspx?src=TREATY&mtdsg_no=XXII-3&chapter=22&lang=en> (accessed 23 March 2019).

62 Poorooye and Feehily (2017), p. 285.

after 1 April 2014.[63] By means of the Mauritius Convention, the coverage of the UNCITRAL Rules on Transparency is extended and those rules are applied to investor-state arbitrations, regardless of the arbitration rules chosen, based on IIAs concluded even before 1 April 2014.[64] The obligations set forth under the UNCITRAL Rules on Transparency may be grouped into three categories: publication of information and documents arising out of the investment proceedings, possibility for non-disputing parties to a treaty and third persons to present submissions to the arbitral tribunal, and public hearings.

Pursuant to Article 2 UNCITRAL Rules on Transparency, once a notice of arbitration is submitted, the name of the disputing parties, the economic sector involved and the specific IIA based upon must be made available to the public. Furthermore, according to Article 3 UNCITRAL Rules on Transparency, all written submissions and decisions and awards of the arbitral tribunal must be available to the public as well.

Under the label of transparency, the participation of 'interested third parties' has often been discussed in the past. Allowing submissions of interested parties could even serve as 'minority protection' in a broad sense. In any case, the UNCITRAL Rules on Transparency prescribe, on the one hand, that non-disputing parties to the treaty, whereon the arbitration was based, shall be allowed to present submissions to the arbitral tribunal.[65] On the other hand, third persons may be allowed to file written submissions, insofar as there is a significant interest of the third person and the submission may be useful for the arbitral tribunal.[66] The latter may be depicted as *amicus curiae* brief.

Concerning public hearings, according to Article 6 UNCITRAL Rules on Transparency, hearings for the presentation of evidence or oral arguments shall be, in principle, public. Nevertheless, it must be highlighted that the UNCITRAL Rules on Transparency contain certain exceptions for confidential or protected information, such as business and trade secrets.[67]

Furthermore, developments on transparency can also be evidenced in recent IIA practice. Some rules on transparency in arbitration proceedings have been sketched in different model IIAs, such as Article 29 US Model Bilateral Investment Agreement of 2012 and Article 20(11) Draft Netherlands Model Bilateral Investment Agreement of 2018. Moreover, Article 8.36 CETA and Article 3.46 EU-Vietnam Investment Protection Agreement (EU-Vietnam IPA) establish the application of the UNCITRAL Rules on Transparency with some additional specifications. A different approach was taken in Article 3.16 EU-Singapore IPA, which refers to Annex 8 thereof with tailor-made rules regarding transparency in the arbitration proceedings.

---

[63]UNCITRAL Rules on Transparency, Art. 1.

[64]Mauritius Convention, Art. 1–2.

[65]UNCITRAL Rules on Transparency, Art. 5.

[66]UNCITRAL Rules on Transparency, Art. 4.

[67]UNCITRAL Rules on Transparency, Art. 7.

3.3 *Interim Conclusions*

The asymmetrical relation between the host state and the foreign investor next to the possibility of submitting the exercise of regulatory powers to investment arbitration comes closer to public law, particularly administrative law. Therefore, it is explained that civil society demands that the proceedings in investment arbitration are conducted with transparency in order to safeguard democratic legitimacy of the system, as well as the rule of law in the decisions rendered. Recent developments, such as the UNCITRAL Rules on Transparency and IIA practice, aim to provide investment arbitration with more transparency; nonetheless, its effectiveness remains to be seen.

4 Transparency or Confidentiality in International Commercial Arbitration

The growing debate on transparency in international economic law and specifically investment arbitration is reaching the shores of international commercial arbitration. From the outset, transparency protects different interests, and it is not required in strictly commercial relations; however, reforms towards more transparency in international commercial arbitration have already taken place, which prompts a careful analysis.[68]

In this sense, transparency in arbitral proceedings confronts some of the purportedly basic characteristics of international commercial arbitration, namely privacy of the hearings and confidentiality. These two concepts have even been portrayed as 'two sides of the same coin'[69]; however, in spite of being interconnected, they may be distinguished from each other.

Privacy implies that only the disputing parties may attend the hearings and participate in the process, whereas confidentiality refers to the obligation of the parties of not disclosing information related to arbitration to third parties.[70] Confidentiality may concern all stages of arbitration, for instance, confidentiality regarding the existence of the arbitration case, confidentiality during the arbitral proceedings (including the evidence produced) and confidentiality of the award.[71] Although confidentiality covers more phases of the proceedings, it might overlap

[68]In this sense, see Poorooye and Feehily (2017), p. 286.

[69]*Esso Australia Resources Ltd. and others v. The Honourable Sidney James Plowman, The Minister for Energy and Minerals and others*, High Court of Australia, 95/014, 7 April 1995 (1996) XXI (21) Yearbook Commercial Arbitration 137, para. 59; See also *Ali Shipping Corporation v Shipyard Trogir* [1997] EWCA Civ 3054 (19 December 1997).

[70]Brown (2001), fn. 6; Born (2014), p. 2782; Hay (2018), p. 211; Similarly, Poorooye and Feehily (2017), p. 281.

[71]Smeureanu (2011), p. 27; Buys (2003), p. 124.

with privacy in the context of hearings without implying that all the information disclosed during the hearings is confidential.[72]

Generally, it may be argued that international commercial arbitration is private, but it does not mean that for the same reason, all information revealed during the arbitration is confidential.[73] With respect to the privacy during the proceedings, public access is normally restricted according to most of the arbitration rules, unless parties agree otherwise,[74] whereas confidentiality, as one characteristic of arbitration, is at least disputed.[75]

In this context, this contribution will focus on party autonomy as the cornerstone of commercial arbitration, with emphasis on confidentiality, given its importance in the transparency debates (Sect. 4.1). Furthermore, the developments in transparency in the midst of international commercial arbitration will be discussed (Sect. 4.2), following the analysis on the limits to the principle of party autonomy (Sect. 4.3). Finally, the interim conclusions of this section are stated (Sect. 4.4).

4.1 Party Autonomy as the Backbone of International Commercial Arbitration

Party autonomy is the backbone of international arbitration,[76] by which parties are free to decide, not only on the applicable law to the substance of the dispute but also on several aspects of the arbitral proceedings.[77] The principle of party autonomy is related to freedom of contract, which in some jurisdictions might be considered as a constitutional principle.[78] This means that the parties have the freedom to choose how and before whom their dispute would be settled.[79] In this sense, since 1923, through the Geneva Protocol on Arbitration Clauses, party autonomy was recognised: 'The arbitral procedure, including the constitution of the tribunal, shall

[72]Smeureanu (2011), p. 6.

[73]Schmitz (2006), p. 1211et seq.

[74]For instance, Art. 26(3) International Chamber of Commerce (ICC) Arbitration Rules (2017); Art. 19(4) London Court of International Arbitration (LCIA) Arbitration Rules (2014); Art. 32(3) Stockholm Chamber of Commerce (SCC) Arbitration Rules (2017); Art. 22(7) Hong Kong International Arbitration Centre (HKIAC) Arbitration Rules (2018).

[75]Contrasting court decisions on the nature of confidentiality in commercial arbitration can be found in: *Dolling-Baker v Merrett and Another* (England Court of Appeal) [1990] 1 WLR 1205; *Esso Australia Resources Ltd. and others v. The Honourable Sidney James Plowman, The Minister for Energy and Minerals and others*, High Court of Australia, 95/014, 7 April 1995 (1996) XXI (21) Yearbook Commercial Arbitration 137, para. 31.

[76]Fagbemi (2015), p. 224. In the same sense, Williams and Anna Kirk (2018), p. 87.

[77]Böckstiegel (1997), p. 25; Livingstone (2008), pp. 529–530.

[78]Böckstiegel (1997), p. 25.

[79]Comrie-Thomson (2017), p. 279.

be governed by the will of the parties and by the law of the country in whose territory the arbitration takes place' (emphasis added).[80]

It derives from most of national laws, but it can be deduced as well from the Convention on the Recognition and Enforcement of Foreign Arbitral Awards (NYC), whereby the parties' procedural autonomy is highlighted.[81] Furthermore, other international instruments such as the UNCITRAL Model Law on International Commercial Arbitration, in its Article 19(1), recognises that the parties to a dispute 'are free to agree on the procedure to be followed by the arbitral tribunal'.[82] At a national level, the UK Arbitration Act of 1996 underlines, for instance, that 'the parties should be free to agree how their disputes are resolved, subject only to such safeguards as are necessary in the public interest'.[83] Therefore, those instruments are considered to be based upon party autonomy as the cornerstone of international commercial arbitration.[84]

In this respect, party autonomy has been generally recognised and enforced regarding the applicable law to the substance of the dispute, as well as regarding the aspects of the arbitral procedure chosen by the parties.[85] Considering that the parties to arbitration can tailor their arbitral process,[86] confidentiality may also be subject to the parties' agreement, which in most of the cases would be upheld at national courts.[87] Nevertheless, party autonomy with regard to confidentiality may be expressed in three different ways: first, by explicitly agreeing on the confidentiality of the arbitral proceedings, second, by choosing arbitration rules with provisions on confidentiality; third, by choosing a jurisdiction where an implied obligation of confidentiality in international arbitration is upheld.

4.1.1 Choosing Confidentiality for Arbitral Proceedings

Confidentiality has been considered as one of the advantages for choosing international commercial arbitration.[88] Private enterprises regard confidentiality as crucial for their business operations; thus, they prefer that their disputes, as well as the possible negative outcomes of those disputes, remain undisclosed.[89] Moreover,

[80]Protocol on Arbitration Clauses in Commercial Matters, signed at Geneva 24 September 1923, s. 2, League of Nations Treaty Series No 278 (Vol. XXVII, p. 158).

[81]NYC Art. II(1) and V(1)(d).

[82]In conjunction with Art. 10(1) and Art. 28(1) UNCITRAL Arbitration Rules.

[83]UK Arbitration Act 1996, s. 1(b). In conjunction with s. 15(2), s. 16(1) and s. 46(1)(a) thereof.

[84]Livingstone (2008), p. 530.

[85]Böckstiegel (1997), p. 29.

[86]Livingstone (2008), p. 530.

[87]Hay (2018), p. 212; Comrie-Thomson (2017), p. 279.

[88]Blackaby et al. (2015), para. 2.196; Hay (2018), p. 211; Tung and Lin (2018), p. 77; Brown (2001), p. 972.

[89]Moses (2017), p. 4. See also Rogers (2006), p. 1326; Comrie-Thomson (2017), p. 290.

companies are drawn to international arbitration with the belief that their trade secrets, competitive practices or know-how are protected.[90]

As described by the case law of different jurisdictions, parties have the freedom to agree on confidentiality, but naturally such provisions would not bind third parties, such as witnesses.[91] In this sense, deriving from party autonomy, if the arbitration agreement expressly contemplates confidentiality, the states and domestic courts should respect such agreement.[92]

4.1.2 Choosing Arbitration Rules: Default Option for Confidentiality

The parties to arbitration may have overlooked confidentiality when drafting their arbitration clause.[93] This situation redirects the attention to the arbitration rules chosen by the parties, which might cover the confidentiality of the arbitral proceedings.[94] In this sense, a closer look to some of the most representative arbitration rules is necessary with emphasis on their confidentiality provisions.

Several arbitral institutions have engaged in reforms to their arbitration rules, making them more competitive by addressing new developments in arbitration as emergency arbitrator, third-party funding or security of costs. However, confidentiality provisions have remained identical or with slightly similar wording. The London Court of International Arbitration (LCIA) Arbitration Rules of 2014 oblige the parties to the arbitration to keep the awards and all materials revealed in the proceedings confidential unless disclosure is required.[95] The Stockholm Chamber of Commerce (SCC) Arbitration Rules of 2017 impose a confidentiality obligation on the SCC and the arbitral tribunal and its staff, without mentioning the parties.[96]

The Hong Kong International Arbitration Centre (HKIAC) Arbitration Rules of 2018 have a comprehensive and detailed provision on confidentiality whereby parties may not publish, disclose or communicate any information relating to the arbitral proceedings, although including certain cases where disclosure is allowed.[97] The *Deutsche Institution für Schiedsgerichtbarkeit* (DIS) (German Arbitration Institute) Arbitration Rules of 2018 impose an obligation on all people involved in the arbitral proceedings to not disclose any information relating to the arbitration unless

[90]Blackaby et al. (2015), para. 2.196; Hay (2018), p. 212; Tung and Lin (2018), p. 78.

[91]*Esso Australia Resources Ltd. and others v. The Honourable Sidney James Plowman, The Minister for Energy and Minerals and others*, High Court of Australia, 95/014, 7 April 1995 (1996) XXI (21) Yearbook Commercial Arbitration 137, para. 29.

[92]Regarding the arbitration agreements to be respected by the states and domestic courts, see Van Harten and Loughlin (2006), p. 141.

[93]Brown (2001), pp. 989–990.

[94]In this regard, see Smeureanu (2011), p. 10.

[95]LCIA Arbitration Rules of 2014, Art. 30.

[96]SCC Arbitration Rules of 2017, Art. 3.

[97]HKIAC Arbitration Rules of 2018, Art. 45.

disclosure is required by mandatory laws or for the purpose of recognition and enforcement, or for challenging the award.[98]

Other often-used arbitration rules, such as the International Chamber of Commerce (ICC) Arbitration Rules of 2017 and the UNCITRAL Arbitration Rules of 2010, do not specify obligations on confidentiality.

4.1.3 No Confidentiality Provisions: Is Confidentiality Implied?

The problem arises when the parties to the arbitration have not included any clauses regarding confidentiality of the arbitral proceedings and the arbitration rules do not provide any guidance in this respect. This situation has led to a theory of confiden tiality as an implied obligation for those choosing arbitration as a dispute settlement mechanism. The debate regarding an implied obligation is nevertheless far from being settled, and domestic courts in different jurisdictions have reached opposing conclusions.

Supporters of confidentiality as an implied obligation in international commercial arbitration follow the approach taken by English courts. As stated in the emblematic case *Ali Shipping Corporation v. Shipyard Trogir* 'as a matter of principle (...) the obligation of confidentiality, whatever its precise limits, arises as an essential corollary of the privacy of arbitration proceedings, the court is propounding a term which arises as the nature of the contract itself implicitly requires'.[99] In other words, it is advanced that the obligation of confidentiality arises from the privacy of arbitral proceedings. Courts in Singapore have followed suit, stating that the parties to arbitration do not need to agree upon confidentiality since this will apply nonetheless as a 'substantive rule of arbitration law'.[100]

The opposite position is to be found, for instance, in Australia, where the parties of the dispute must agree on confidentiality; otherwise, such obligation would not be upheld by the courts, as reasoned in *Esso Australia Resources v. Plowman*.[101] In the same line, courts in the US have decided, though tangentially, that parties to arbitration are not obliged to treat the proceedings as confidential unless otherwise agreed.[102] Similarly, the Swedish Supreme Court has put forward that the parties to

---

[98]DIS Arbitration Rules of 2018, Art. 44.

[99]*Ali Shipping Corporation v. Shipyard Trogir* (England Court of Appeal) [1999] 1 WLR 314. Similarly, *Dolling-Baker v. Merrett and Another* (England Court of Appeal) [1990] 1 WLR 1205.

[100]*AAY v. AAZ* (Singapore High Ct) [2011] 1 SLR 1093, para. 55; *International Coal Pte Ltd v. Kristle Trading Ltd and Another* [2008] SGHC 182, para. 82.

[101]*Esso Australia Resources Ltd and others v. The Honourable Sidney James Plowman, The Minister for Energy and Minerals and others*, 95/014, 7 April 1995 (High Court of Australia) (1996) XXI (21) Yearbook Commercial Arbitration 137, para. 24 et seq.

[102]*Industrotech Constructors v. Duke University*, 17 April 1984 (Court of Appeals of North Carolina) [1984] 314 S.E.2d 272.

an arbitration are not bound by a duty of keeping arbitral proceedings confidential, unless they had agreed upon such obligation.[103]

Some other states have preferred to regulate confidentiality by means of legislation. In Norway, confidentiality is addressed in the Arbitration Act of 2004. According to § 5 thereof, 'arbitral proceedings and the arbitral award shall not be subject to a duty of confidentiality, unless otherwise agreed by the parties'. France, on the other hand, has different provisions for confidentiality between domestic and international arbitration. Pursuant to Decree No. 2011-48, confidentiality of the arbitral proceedings applies by default unless the parties agree on lifting such confidentiality. However, confidentiality is not contemplated in international arbitration. Based on this difference, it is argued that, according to French law, the parties have to agree explicitly on confidentiality in international arbitration, otherwise, they would not be bound by it.[104]

A more detailed provision has been enacted in the Arbitration Ordinance of 1 June 2011 in Hong Kong. Pursuant to section 18 thereof, the parties' agreement on confidentiality prevails; nevertheless, in the absence of such agreement, the parties to the dispute are subject to strict rules on confidentiality of the arbitral proceedings and the awards similar to those embedded in the HKIAC Arbitration Rules.

4.2 Developments in Transparency: The Retreat of Party Autonomy?

Some efforts towards transparency in international commercial arbitration have been undertaken, although in a lesser degree than in investment arbitration. Publishing decisions on arbitrator challenges, press reports on pending cases or even publishing awards (fully or redacted) are some of the examples of increased transparency nowadays. For instance, the LCIA publishes the decisions on challenges of arbitrators on its website,[105] shedding some light on the reasoning and criteria applied in those cases, working as guidance for users and arbitrators. Other examples relate to the Finland Arbitration Institute, which publishes on its website redacted summaries of arbitral decisions,[106] or the ICC through its publication of the ICC Dispute Resolution Bulletin with case decisions.[107]

[103] *AI Trade Finance Inc v. Bulgarian Foreign Trade Bank Ltd*, 27 October 2000, Case No. T 1881-99 (Supreme Court of Sweden) [2000].

[104] Blackaby et al. (2015), fn. 284; Born (2014), p. 2799.

[105] <https://www.lcia.org/challenge-decision-database.aspx> (accessed 23 March 2019).

[106] <https://arbitration.fi/category/fai-cases/> (accessed 23 March 2019).

[107] <http://store.iccwbo.org/annual-subscription-icc-dispute-resolution-bulletin> (accessed 23 March 2019).

Similarly, some states have enacted reforms that provide for the publication of arbitral awards unless otherwise agreed by the parties.[108] In New Zealand, the Arbitration Act of 1996 provides for confidentiality as the default rule[109]; however, pursuant to section 14C thereof, a detailed list enumerates cases where disclosure is allowed. Such practices are meant to address the concerns regarding the lack of transparency in international arbitration. Furthermore, arbitral institutions may introduce these practices as competitive strategies among them to attract more users of the system as well.[110]

These developments towards transparency are deemed to promote a higher quality of the arbitral process since arbitrators would be subject to public scrutiny with regard to their decisions and efficiency.[111] In fact, it is argued that keeping awards confidential hinders the possibility of benefit from their content.[112] Even if not under a formal system of precedent, arbitral awards may provide guidance for future arbitral tribunals, domestic courts or users of arbitration in general.[113] Similarly, the publication of awards may promote legislation in international commercial arbitration in accordance with or in response to the practice developed by arbitral tribunals.[114]

Some authors put forward that given its similarity with judicial decision-making, the public is interested in the fact that arbitration functions properly, which requires certain degree of transparency.[115] As it concerns judicial decision-making, a balancing approach between transparency and confidentiality is taken in different national procedure laws and also in the European Convention on Human Rights (ECHR). For example, in Germany, § 169 *Gerichtsverfassungsgesetz* (GVG) (Courts Constitution Act) foresees general public access to all judicial proceedings (*Öffentlichkeitsgrundsatz* (public access principle)). The original purpose of this elementary procedural principle was supposed to be the control of the exercise of public powers, as well as the strengthening of judiciary's independence and trust of the general public into the third power.[116] The abovementioned general principle applies also to civil/commercial proceedings. Nevertheless, there is no access to documents in civil proceedings pursuant to §§ 299, 760 *Zivilprozessordnung* (ZPO) (Code of Civil Procedure).

---

[108] § 5 Norwegian Arbitration Act of 14 May 2004; Art. 38 Law No 8937 of 2011 Costa Rica (OG No. 100 of 25 May 2011).

[109] S. 14B Arbitration Act 1996 (New Zealand).

[110] Rogers (2006), p. 1314 et seq.

[111] Born (2014), p. 2822. See also Rogers (2006), p. 1316; Tung and Lin (2018), p. 83.

[112] Cremades and Cortes (2013), p. 35; Buys (2003), p. 136.

[113] Buys (2003), p. 135; Rogers (2006), p. 1320; Tung and Lin (2018), p. 84.

[114] Comrie-Thomson (2017), p. 289.

[115] Comrie-Thomson (2017), p. 280.

[116] Meissner and Schenk (2019), para. 10; Zimmermann (2017), para. 1; Meyer-Ladewig et al. (2017), para. 183–184.

However, these developments towards transparency do not imply a restriction to the principle of party autonomy since the parties to the dispute have always the possibility of stipulating different provisions and reaffirming the confidentiality of their arbitral proceedings.

4.3 Party Autonomy Far from Being an Absolute Right: Balancing Other Interests

Despite the ample freedom that the parties have regarding the tailoring of their arbitration proceedings, party autonomy is subject to certain limits.[117] For example, some jurisdictions might prohibit arbitration for specific fields of law (arbitrability)[118]; thus, should the parties conclude an agreement to arbitrate certain disputes, which are expressly excluded from arbitration by domestic legislation, such agreement would be overridden by the respective mandatory provisions of national law. Arguably, the limitations on party autonomy legitimise arbitration as a valid dispute settlement mechanism.[119]

To the same extent, confidentiality, which derives from party autonomy, is also subject to certain limits. In fact, even in jurisdictions where confidentiality is considered an implied obligation, courts are prompt to assert that confidentiality has exceptions.[120] In general terms, there are four cases where confidentiality can be lifted: first, by express or implied consent of the parties to the dispute; second, by a court's order; third, when necessary for the protection of interests of a party to the dispute; fourth, when required by public interest.[121]

A clear example consists of the obligation to disclose to the insurer matters involved in arbitration that are material to the risk insured against.[122] Another example is the disclosure required to publicly traded companies regarding material financial information, which might include legal disputes that are pending.[123]

---

[117]Mandatory laws regarding guaranteeing natural justice, protection of weaker parties or protection of the public good may outweigh party autonomy in arbitration. See Livingstone (2008), pp. 531 et seq.; Williams and Anna Kirk (2018), p. 88. In similar sense, Pryles (2007), p. 36

[118]Böckstiegel (1997), p. 27; Williams and Anna Kirk (2018), p. 91.

[119]Williams and Anna Kirk (2018), p. 89; Buys (2003), p. 135.

[120]Noussia (2010), p. 133.

[121]*John Forster Emmott v. Michael Wilson & Partners Limited* (England Court of Appeal) [2008] EWCA Civ 184.

[122]*Esso Australia Resources Ltd and others v. The Honourable Sidney James Plowman, The Minister for Energy and Minerals and others*, 95/014, 7 April 1995 (High Court of Australia) (1996) XXI (21) Yearbook Commercial Arbitration 137, para. 27.

[123]Rogers (2006), p. 1310. Similarly, Brown (2001), p. 1003; Noussia (2010), p. 22.

Confidentiality in arbitration might also be disregarded by domestic courts during the challenge of awards or by means of recognition and enforcement procedures.[124]

In this context, one might argue that when public interests are involved in international commercial arbitration, not only confidentiality must be lifted but also a higher degree of transparency throughout the arbitral proceedings is needed.[125] For instance, in a commercial arbitration where one of the parties is a state-owned enterprise, the award may have an impact on the public finances of the state, which is of interest of the public at large.[126] Nevertheless, reforms on transparency in international commercial arbitration targeting only cases where the public interest is involved face different problems. Not only the definition of public interest is unfeasible, but also the extent of transparency would be subject to discussions.[127]

The public interest should not be taken to the extreme in order to impose transparency obligations on every case of international commercial arbitration.[128] Such approach would be in clear detriment to the core principle of party autonomy, and parties to a dispute would be discouraged from using arbitration in the first place. In fact, even proponents of more transparency in international commercial arbitration recognise that any obligation towards transparency must not impinge party autonomy more than what is necessary.[129]

4.4 Interim Conclusions

Transparency in international commercial arbitration clashes with the traditional concepts of privacy and confidentiality, which are grounded on the principle of party autonomy. Privacy is generally accepted as a characteristic of international commercial arbitration, whereas confidentiality has been handled differently in many jurisdictions. However, even party autonomy is subject to certain limitations, and confidentiality in arbitration stemming from such principle is not the exception.

[124]Moses (2017), p. 57; Hay (2018), p. 227; Smeureanu (2011), p. 51; Buys (2003), p. 135; Noussia (2010), pp. 22–23.

[125]Hay (2018), pp. 218–219; Tung and Lin (2018), p. 81.

[126]Comrie-Thomson (2017), p. 281.

[127]The example of state-owned enterprises entering into commercial arbitration is enlightening. Not all commercial arbitrations involving a state-controlled enterprise touch upon public interests and not all commercial arbitrations dealing with public interests involve state-controlled enterprises. See Hay (2018), pp. 219–223.

[128]For a different opinion, arguing in favour of providing more transparency in international commercial arbitration, see Comrie-Thomson (2017), p. 280.

[129]Comrie-Thomson (2017), p. 296. In similar sense, Brown (2001), pp. 1019–1020; Buys (2003), p. 138.

5 Conclusion: Can We Transfer Developments in Transparency from Investment Arbitration to International Commercial Arbitration?

The crux of the matter consists in the relationship between the disputing parties and the possibility of submitting the exercise of public authority to arbitration. On the one hand, investment arbitration bears a resemblance to public law, given the possibility of bringing claims regarding regulatory measures of a state, as well as the asymmetrical relation between the host state and the foreign investor. Therefore, more transparency in investment arbitration is justified in order to safeguard the democratic legitimacy of the system, as well as the rule of law in the decisions rendered.

On the other hand, international commercial arbitration is rooted in the principle of party autonomy, whereby the parties are theoretically in a horizontal relationship. Furthermore, arbitrators are called to decide on commercial relations, occasionally breaches of statutory laws; however, international commercial arbitration does not judge the exercise of regulatory powers of the state. Therefore, this mechanism of dispute settlement remains in the field of private law, whereby transparency towards the civil society may be excluded by parties' agreement. Besides, there is no accountability of the managers of corporations towards the public in contrast to government officials.[130]

Be that as it may, issues of public interest might find their way into international commercial arbitration. The involvement of state-owned enterprises, for instance, may require a certain degree of transparency in the arbitral proceedings. Such transparency would never have the same extent as in investment arbitration, where transparency stems from its hybrid nature, including public law dimensions, whereas international commercial arbitration is based on the principle of party autonomy framed in private law. A 'one-size-fits-all' approach does not seem to reflect the purpose of transparency; thus, developments in this regard in investment arbitration should not be transferred to international commercial arbitration indiscriminately. Nevertheless, those developments may serve as guidance only in cases where the public interest might be involved.

References

Ala'i P, D'Orsi M (2014) Transparency in international economic relations and the role of the WTO. In: Ala'I P, Vaughn RG (eds) Research handbook on transparency. Edward Elgar, Northampton, pp 368–399

Alvarez JE (2011) The public international law regime governing international investment. Hague Academy of International Law, Leiden

[130] Buys (2003), p. 135.

Behn D (2015) Legitimacy, evolution and growth in investment arbitration: empirically evaluating the state-of-the-art. Georgetown J Int Law 46:363–416
Blackaby N et al (2015) Redfern and hunter on international arbitration, 6th edn. OUP, Oxford
Böckstiegel KH (1997) The role of party autonomy in international arbitration. Dispute Resolut J 52 (3):24–30
Born GB (2014) International commercial arbitration, 2nd edn. Kluwer Law International, The Netherlands
Brown AC (2001) Presumptions meets reality: an exploration of the confidentiality obligation in international commercial arbitration. Am Univ Int Law Rev 16:969–1026
Butler N, Subedi S (2017) The future of international investment regulation: towards a world investment organisation? Neth Int Law Rev 64(1):43–72
Buys CG (2003) The tensions between confidentiality and transparency in international arbitration. Am Rev Int Arbitr 14:121–138
Chung O (2007) The lopsided international investment law regime and its effect on the future of investor-state arbitration. Virginia J Int Law 47(4):953–976
Comrie-Thomson P (2017) A statement of arbitral jurisprudence: the case for a national law obligation to publish international commercial arbitral awards. J Int Arbitr 34(2):275–301
Cremades BM, Cortes R (2013) The principle of confidentiality in arbitration: a necessary crisis. J Arbitr Stud 23(3):25–38
Delimatsis P (2013) Institutional transparency in the WTO. In: Bianchi A, Peters A (eds) Transparency in international law. CUP, New York
Fagbemi SA (2015) The doctrine of party autonomy in international commercial arbitration: myth or reality? J Sustain Dev Law Policy 6(1):222–246
Fallon RH (1997) "The rule of law" as a concept in constitutional discourse. Columbia Law Rev 97 (1):1–56
Franck SD (2004) The legitimacy crisis in investment treaty arbitration: privatizing public international law through inconsistent decisions. Fordham Law Rev 73:1521–1626
Fry JD, Repousis OG (2016) Towards a new world for investor-state arbitration through transparency. NYUJ Int Law Polit 48:795–865
Hay E (2018) Winds of change? Confidentiality and in international commercial arbitration. In: González-Bueno C (ed) 40 under 40 international arbitration. Dykinson, Spain
Howard DM (2018) Creating consistency through a world investment court. Fordham Int Law J 41 (1):1–52
Katz RL (2016) Modeling an international investment court after the World Trade Organization dispute settlement body. Harv Negot Law Rev 22:163–188
Kaufmann C, Weber RH (2010) The role of transparency in financial regulation. J Int Econ Law 13 (3):779–797
Kaushal A (2009) Revisiting history: how the past matters for the present backlash against foreign investment regime. Harv Int Law J 50(2):491–534
Langford M, Behn D, Lie RH (2017) The revolving door in international investment arbitration. J Int Econ Law 20(2):301–332
Leader S (2006) Human rights, risks, and new strategies for global investment. J Int Econ Law 9 (3):657–705
Livingstone ML (2008) Party autonomy in international commercial arbitration. J Int Arbitr 25 (5).529–535
Long DE (2002) Democratizing globalization: practicing the policies of cultural inclusion. Cardozo J Int Comp Law 10:217–269
Maupin JA (2013) Transparency in international investment law: the good the bad and the murky. In: Bianchi A, Peters A (eds) Transparency in international law. CUP, New York
Meissner C, Schenk W (2019) VwGO § 55 (Ordnungsvorschriften des GVG). In: Schoch F, Schneider JP, Bier W (eds) Verwaltungsgerichtsordnung (VwGO) Kommentar. CH Beck, München

Meyer-Ladewig J, Harrendorf S, König S (2017) EMRK Artikel 6 Recht auf ein faires Verfahren. In: Meyer-Ladewig J, Nettesheim M, von Raumer S (eds) EMRK Europäische Menschenrechtskonvention Handkommentar, 4th edn. Nomos
Moses ML (2017) The principles and practice of international commercial arbitration, 3rd edn. CUP, Cambridge
Noussia K (2010) Confidentiality in international commercial arbitration: a comparative analysis of the position under English, US, German and French law. Springer, Heidelberg
Poorooye A, Feehily R (2017) Confidentiality and transparency in international commercial arbitration: finding the right balance. Harv Negot Law Rev 22:275–323
Pryles M (2007) Limits to party autonomy in arbitral procedure. J Int Arbitr 24(3):327–339
Puig S, Shaffer G (2018) Imperfect alternatives: institutional choice and the reform of investment law. Am J Int Law 112(3):361–409
Rogers CA (2006) Transparency in international commercial arbitration. Univ Kansas Law Rev 54 (5):1301–1337
Schill SW (2011) Enhancing international investment law's legitimacy: conceptual and methodological foundations of new public law approach. Virginia J Int Law 52:57–102
Schmitz AJ (2006) Untangling the privacy paradox in arbitration. Kans Law Rev 54:1211–1253
Smeureanu IM (2011) Confidentiality in international commercial arbitration. Kluwer Law International, The Netherlands
Stein E (2001) International integration and democracy: no love at first sight. Am J Int Law 95 (3):489–534
Tung S, Lin B (2018) Chapter II: the arbitrator and the arbitration procedure, more transparency in international commercial arbitration: to have or not to have? In: Klausegger C et al (eds) Austrian yearbook o international arbitration 2018. Manz'sche Verlags- und Universitätsbuchhandlung, Austria
Van Harten G (2007) Investment treaty arbitration and public law. OUP, Oxford
Van Harten G (2010) Perceived Bias in investment treaty arbitration. In: Waibel M et al (eds) The backlash against investment arbitration. Kluwer Law International
Van Harten G, Loughlin M (2006) Investment treaty arbitration as a species of global administrative law. Eur J Int Law 17(1):121–150
Wälde TW (2010) Procedural challenges in investment arbitration under the shadow of the dual role of the state: asymmetries and tribunal's duty to ensure, pro-actively, the equality of arms. Arbitr Int 26(1):3–42
Waldron J (2008) The concept and the rule of law. Georgia Law Rev 43(1):1–61
Williams DAR, Anna Kirk A (2018) Chapter 6: balancing party autonomy, jurisdiction and the integrity of arbitration: where to draw the line? In: Kaplan N, Moser MJ (eds) Jurisdiction, admissibility and choice of law in international arbitration: liber Amicorum Michael Pryles. Kluwer Law International, The Netherlands
Zimmermann (2017) § 169 GVG [Öffentlichkeit]. In: Rauscher T, Krüger W (eds) Münchener Kommentar zur Zivilprozessordnung mit Gerichtsverfassungsgesetz und Nebengesetzen, 5th edn. CH Beck, München
Zoellner CS (2006) Transparency: an analysis of an evolving fundamental principle in international economic law. Mich J Int Law 27:579–628

Cross-Border Enforcement of Mediated Settlement Agreements and Potential Impact on the Practice of International Arbitration

Observations from Singapore on the Adoption of the Singapore Convention on Mediation

Janet C. Checkley

Contents

J. C. Checkley (✉)
Singapore Management University School of Law, Singapore International Dispute Resolution Academy, Singapore, Singapore
e-mail: jcheckley@smu.edu.sg

Z. Meškić et al. (eds.), *Balkan Yearbook of European and International Law 2019*,
Balkan Yearbook of European and International Law (2020) 2019: 23–40,
https://doi.org/10.1007/16247_2019_2, Published online: 18 January 2020

1 Introduction: The View from Singapore

There is perhaps no better perch from which to observe the latest developments in international dispute resolution than from Singapore's ascending sphere. The country has carried out a sustained campaign to compete with the world's most favoured international dispute resolution centres and in the last several years has broken through the rankings to be listed among the top five choices in international user surveys.[1] It has achieved this by consistently leading the way in advancements in the field, offering an array of new technologies, developments, services and mechanisms through which to access international dispute resolution.[2]

Rising most prominently among the areas in which Singapore leads the way is the practice and development of mediation. Mediation as a primary form of dispute resolution in Singapore arose as a matter of necessity; the Singapore courts were experiencing unmanageable backlog of pending civil cases.[3] Between 1994 and 1998, several important reforms went into effect aimed at reducing the backlog by introducing mediation as a means of dispute resolution: the judiciary introduced court-based mediation procedures, the Singapore Mediation Centre (SMC) was established to manage commercial cases and the Ministry of Law established Community Mediation Centres (CMC).[4]

As a result of these measures, court backlogs were indeed reduced and Singapore launched into its progressive and practice-based approach to dispute resolution, which rested on close working relationships between the Singapore courts, judges and registrars with the SMC and the CMC.[5] Since then, the SMC has become a leading example for excellence in mediation services around the world. Today the Centre handles more than 500 cases per year and offers a range of services going beyond standard commercial mediation and that include collaborative family practice, neutral evaluation, mediation-arbitration, construction adjudication and domain name dispute resolution.[6] Most recently, the Centre has announced an ODR Protocol to resolve disputes online.[7] Meanwhile, CMC in Singapore have succeeded in reducing litigation and promoting a 'harmonious, civil and gracious community, where social conflicts can be resolved amicably'.[8] And in 2017, the Singapore Mediation Act went into effect, which regulates the practice of mediation in Singapore and the enforcement of agreements to mediate by the courts.[9]

[1]International Arbitration Survey (2018), p. 9.

[2]See, for example: Croft, Jane (2016), and Huang, Claire (2016). See also SIMC, A New Dawn for Mediation? (2014).

[3]Lim (2017), p. 3.

[4]Lim (2017), pp. 3–4.

[5]Lim (2017), p. 7.

[6]Lim (2017), p. 8.

[7]Singapore Mediation Centre Online Dispute Resolution Platform (2019).

[8]Lim (2017), p. 11; see also Community Mediation Centres, 2019.

[9]Singapore Mediation Act 2017.

Besides this impressive domestic framework for mediation, Singapore has also taken strong leadership in the international sector as well. With an eye on capturing business arising from ASEAN and Asian trade and commerce flows, Singapore established the Singapore International Mediation Centre in 2014. It was the first of its kind as a stand-alone international mediation service provider.[10] Among its offerings are the innovative SIAC-SIMC Arb-Med-Arb Protocol, which is a unique multi-tiered dispute resolution clause offered in collaboration with the Singapore International Arbitration Centre (SIAC).[11]

In addition to the establishment of the Singapore International Mediation Centre, Singapore undertook initiatives to professionalise the practice of mediation by establishing the Singapore International Mediation Institute (SIMI). The goal of SIMI is to implement a national framework by which to certify mediator competency in the resolution of international disputes,[12] thereby providing users of mediation services in Singapore with an extra trustmark of quality when selecting mediators and providing mediators with a valuable additional qualification.[13] In addition, SIMI administers a partnership program through which it accredits organisations as training providers qualified to train and certify SIMI mediators.

Last but not least, in 2016, the Singapore International Dispute Resolution Academy (SIDRA) was established. Conceived to be a thought leader and think tank in the field of international dispute resolution, the organisation was tasked with providing the practice and user community with leading, cutting-edge research and development and applicable solutions to cross-border conflict.[14] These three organisations, along with the SIAC, the SMC and the Singapore International Commercial Court (SICC), make up what has come to be called informally the Singapore Suite of international dispute resolution service providers and development organisations.

Given this context, it was fitting that Singaporean leadership figured prominently in the development of the latest international dispute resolution instrument to emerge from the UN Commission on International Trade Law (UNCITRAL) on mediation in cross-border disputes. Working Group II took up the work to develop an international instrument on the enforcement of international mediated settlement agreements in 2015.[15] During negotiations on the text of the document, sessions were

---

[10]Lim (2017), p. 18.

[11]The Protocol provides for arbitration to be commenced under the SIAC, immediately after which the Tribunal stays the proceedings for mediation to commence at the SIMC. If no resolution is reached, parties can return to arbitration at the SIAC. If resolution is achieved in mediation, parties may request the SIAC to issue a consent award. For more, see the Singapore International Mediation Centre website.

[12]Lim (2017), p. 20.

[13]The SIMI Credentialing Scheme aims to recognise mediator experience and credentials through a tiered system ultimately leading to international certification under the International Mediation Institute.

[14]Lim (2017), pp. 21–22.

[15]Schnabel (2018), p. 5.

chaired by Ms Natalie Morris-Sharma from the Singapore Ministry of Law, who was later recognised by the committee for her excellent leadership and facilitative role in bringing about the final text to be adopted.[16] And it was all the more appropriate to recognise the critical role that Singapore played by naming the new instrument after the country that is most representative of the aspirations it embodies. At the General Assembly meeting in December 2018, the UN formally adopted the Convention on the Enforcement of International Settlement Agreements Resulting from Mediation and, in the same session, determined to call the new convention after Singapore.[17] The Convention opened for signature on 7 August 2019 in Singapore, and at the time of publishing has 51 signatories.

Heralded as an exciting and important advancement in the field of international dispute resolution, the Singapore Convention's advocates and supporters hope that, if successful, it will help to achieve for cross-border mediation what the New York Convention[18] achieved for international arbitration.[19] Indeed, the primary purpose of the Singapore Convention is to promote the growth of stand-alone mediation procedures for the settlement of cross-border disputes.[20] This frank desire to promote mediation among a committed and enthusiastic community of cross-border dispute resolution experts and advocates naturally leads to the question of whether and how such potential success will impact the practice of international arbitration, which has long held pole position as the most favoured form of dispute resolution between international parties when compared to litigation in domestic courts.[21] It cannot be forgotten, however, that the practice of international arbitration is currently facing a number of other transformative trends, which are also changing the ways that parties in cross-border disputes select dispute resolution services. Where does the advent of the Singapore Convention fit into this evolving picture for international arbitration, and how might it impact the future of international dispute resolution?

In the following pages, this article will explore potential answers to this question by first reviewing a selection of the key international dispute resolution trends impacting the practice of international arbitration today. Then it will review the Singapore Convention's scope and main features, and finally it will offer several predictions about the future of international arbitration with the Singapore Convention figuring as the latest disruptor to the international dispute resolution landscape.

---

[16]Seow (2018).

[17]Schnabel (2018), p. 8.

[18]UN Convention on the Recognition and Enforcement of Foreign Arbitral Awards (New York, 1958).

[19]Chua (2019), p. 1.

[20]Schnabel (2018), pp. 2–3.

[21]International Arbitration Survey (2018), p. 5.

2 Key International Dispute Resolution Trends Impacting International Arbitration

As noted above, international arbitration is far and away the most favoured form of international dispute resolution among users.[22] Its popularity is largely due to the ease of enforceability of awards around the world, perceived flexibility and ability to avoid litigation in unfriendly jurisdictions or legal systems, among numerous other reasons.[23] These factors have held as the status quo for a number of years. International arbitration absolutely dominates the international dispute resolution landscape. But the practice of international arbitration is always being shaped by user preferences that have shifted and molded the field over the years.[24] Some of the recent trends are proving truly transformative to international arbitration's long-standing practice tenets. Outlined below are several transformative trends that may signal future directions and changes for the practice of international arbitration.

2.1 *Calls for Greater Transparency*

Users of international arbitration consistently rank confidentiality of arbitration as one of the features that attract users to it again and again.[25] The High Court in Australia in 1995 recognised confidentiality in arbitration as one of its 'essential attributes'.[26] For decades, confidentiality has been thought to be paramount in the consideration of whether to go to litigation or settle the dispute away from the eye of the public.[27]

But a global rise in the use of arbitration to settle investor-state dispute due to advancements in the use of investor-state dispute settlement (ISDS) clauses in bilateral investment treaties has led to questions about the sanctity of confidentiality in international arbitration, particularly in the investment context.[28] As a result, a number of measures to increase transparency in international investment arbitration have developed over the last several years.[29] These include the development of new international instruments aimed at increasing transparency in investor-state arbitration, such as the UNCITRAL Rules on Transparency in Treaty-Based Investor-State

---

[22]International Arbitration Survey (2018), p. 5.

[23]International Arbitration Survey (2018), p. 7.

[24]Chua (2019).

[25]International Arbitration Survey (2018), p. 7.

[26]Esso Australia Resources Ltd. and others v. The Honourable Sidney James Plowman, The Minister for Energy and Minerals and others (1995) 193 CLR 10.

[27]McDougall et al. (2018), p. 2.

[28]McDougall et al. (2018), pp. 4–5.

[29]Bassi and Newman (2016).

Arbitration[30] and the UN Convention on Transparency in Treaty-Based Investor-State Arbitration ('The Mauritius Convention').[31] Arbitration institutions, including ICSID, the PCA and the SIAC, have also taken measures to increase transparency in investment arbitration under their rules and procedures.[32]

In the context of international commercial arbitration that takes place between two private parties, calls for increased transparency have been met with greater resistance.[33] Even so, a number of measures have emerged among commercial arbitration service providers increasing transparency of the arbitration process. Some institutions have begun publishing data about the cases they manage.[34] Some have also begun publishing limited case information or redacted awards.[35] These measures have invited mixed reactions from international arbitration practitioners and commentators.[36] Many feel that while some increase in transparency in commercial arbitration is warranted, too much will simply drive users away from the practice and open providers and arbitrators to perhaps unwelcome scrutiny.[37]

2.2 *Third-Party Funding*

Another significant trend to disrupt the dispute resolution landscape for international arbitration has been the development of third-party funding in international arbitration.[38] In recent years, the practice of arbitration users securing capital provided by a disinterested third party has grown considerably, with some jurisdictions undertaking legal reforms to clear the way for third-party funding arbitration and to regulate its function.[39] Further regulatory reforms around the world are likely as concerns about the use of third-party funding has grown. Of principle concern is the identity of the funder and addressing any potential conflicts of interest related to the third-party funder.[40]

Some soft law instruments have been developed to address third-party funding concerns. These include the publishing of the 2004 IBA Guidelines on Conflicts of

---

[30]UNCITRAL Rules on Transparency in Treaty-based Investor-State Arbitration.

[31]UN Convention on Transparency in Treaty-based Investor-State Arbitration (New York, 2014).

[32]McDougall et al. (2018), pp. 5–6.

[33]Khanna and Power (2017), and Cosgrove and Hosking (2018).

[34]See for example the ICC Arbitration Tribunals and the LCIA Reports.

[35]International Chamber of Commerce Note to Parties and Arbitral Tribunals on the Conduct of the Arbitration under the ICC Rules of Arbitration (2019).

[36]See generally Tung and Lin (2018).

[37]Cosgrove and Hosking (2018).

[38]McDougall et al. (2018), p. 7.

[39]Secomb and Wallin (2018) and IMF Bentham Blog (2018).

[40]McDougall et al. (2018), p. 7.

Interest in International Arbitration[41] and the publication of the ICCA-Queen Mary Task Force Report on Third-Party Funding in International Arbitration.[42] Both documents contain a set of guidelines or principles designed to guide the practice of using third-party funding in international arbitration. They include measures such as disclosing the existence of third-party funding and, in some cases, disclosing the identity of the third-party funder.[43]

In addition, several prominent common law jurisdictions have undertaken significant legal and regulatory reform to clear the way for third-party funding and regulate its use. Singapore and Hong Kong have led the way in Asia, removing the major hurdles to third-party funding by abolishing the laws of champerty and maintenance and enacting corresponding civil law and regulatory reforms.[44] In 2018, the High Court in Singapore declared for the first time a third-party funding agreement under the new legal framework to be valid.[45] The third-party funding trend in international arbitration is likely to increase the use of international arbitration as a means of offsetting the sometimes prohibitive fees associated with the practice.

2.3 *Regional Shifts*

The world's centre of trade and commercial gravity is shifting inexorably towards Asia.[46] As investments in the region and from the region increase and economies boom, disputes follow course, and Asia is set to capture an increasing share of the global market for international arbitration.[47] Standing to benefit in particular are Hong Kong and Singapore as centres for dispute resolution, as Asian companies with growing bargaining power seek familiar environs for international arbitration and litigation.[48]

A key driver of this shift is China's ambitious Belt and Road Initiative (BRI), which seeks to revive and expand the ancient Silk Road trading routes, which connected China to African and European markets during the Han Dynasty.[49] So far, an estimated $1 trillion has been invested and committed as a result of BRI projects in development around the world, a breathlessly large figure that portends an increase in related disputes and an expanding need for dispute resolution services in

[41]IBA Guidelines on Conflicts of Interest in International Arbitration (2004).

[42]Report of the ICCA-Queen Mary Task Force (2018).

[43]See Report of the ICCA-Queen Mary Task Force (2018), p. 188; IBA Guidelines on Conflicts of Interest in International Arbitration (2004), Part II.

[44]Sun and Leng (2018).

[45]Gek (2018).

[46]Choong and Rosenberg (2018), pp. 11–12.

[47]Choong and Rosenberg (2018), pp. 11–12.

[48]Choong and Rosenberg (2018), pp. 11–12.

[49]See World Bank Group Belt and Road Initiative (2018) for an overview.

Asia.[50] Arbitrations with China as the seat or the choice of forum are therefore likely to rise, and rules in arbitration institutions in the region are likely to see innovative updates to capture the new type of public-private partnership disputes emerging out of BRI.[51] This trend also therefore likely means positive developments for international arbitration service providers and arbitrators based in Asia. It remains to be seen whether other regions will benefit in a similarly anticipated fashion or if international dispute resolution business will shift significantly away from the West to the Asia region as a result.

2.4 *International Commercial Courts*

In recent years, a number of specialised international commercial courts have emerged around the world.[52] These courts work in tandem with domestic courts and therefore retain important coercive powers, such as compelling production of evidence, issuing orders or injunctions and enforcing judgements.[53] The Singapore International Commercial Court, established in 2015, is one such example of a specialised international commercial court. More have been established or are under development such as in Frankfurt, Brussels, Dubai, the Netherlands and the recently announced Chinese International Commercial Court.

It is perceived by some prominent observers that the rise of international commercial courts is a response to the growing dissatisfaction with international arbitration as parties gravitate towards more transparency, security and relative familiarity of court proceedings.[54] International commercial courts as a choice of dispute resolution procedure have recently been made more viable by the introduction of the Hague Choice of Court Convention in 2005.[55] It is probably still too early to tell whether users will select international commercial courts in significant numbers of international commercial arbitration, but the growth of this service represents a significant new landmark in the shifting terrain.[56]

---

[50]Choong and Rosenberg (2018), p. 12.

[51]Choong and Rosenberg (2018), p. 11.

[52]Honorable Justice John Middleton (2018).

[53]Loh (2015), pp. 16–17.

[54]Bell (2018), p. 194.

[55]Hague Conference on Private International Law Convention on Choice of Court Agreements (2005).

[56]Bell (2018), p. 195.

3 Advent of the Singapore Convention on Mediation

As the most recent major development in the international dispute resolution landscape, the Singapore Convention on Mediation joins the key trends highlighted above as a potentially transformative event for the field. In this section, I will briefly discuss the origin of the Convention and its purpose, describe the Convention's scope and explore the Convention's main features.

3.1 Origin and Purpose

The Singapore Convention's purpose is to promote the practice of cross-border mediation as a stand-alone dispute resolution procedure in international disputes.[57] While mediation is widely practiced around the world in the domestic context,[58] cross-border mediation has not seen a significant uptake, and the lack of a clear enforcement mechanisms for international mediated settlement agreements has been understood to be one of the main barriers to participation in mediation.[59] The Convention's main goal is therefore not to provide a means of enforcement for agreements that would not have otherwise been enforceable; the main goal is, instead, to incentivise the use of mediation where parties would not have otherwise considered it.[60]

This stated purpose goes some way towards answering the question of whether a convention on enforcement is necessary when compliance rates with mediated settlement agreements are already naturally high. Indeed, compliance rates are high; the Convention therefore seeks to expand this form of dispute resolution to a new class of users by giving it the 'stamp of legitimacy' enjoyed by international arbitral awards under the New York Convention.[61]

3.2 Scope

The Convention facilitates the enforcement of what can be considered a new international instrument: the international mediated settlement agreement (iMSA).[62] The Convention defines several features of this instrument:

---

[57]Schnabel (2018), p. 2.

[58]See for example Chua (2015), pp. 20–21; see also Saul (2012).

[59]Schnabel (2018), pp. 2–3.

[60]Schnabel (2018), p. 4.

[61]Schnabel (2018), p. 3.

[62]Alexander (2018), and Schnabel (2018), pp. 9–10.

- an agreement resulting from mediation;
- commercial in nature; and
- international.[63]

The Convention does not apply to matters other than commercial disputes (such as family, inheritance, consumer or employment).[64] The Convention also explicitly excludes from its scope settlement agreements that result from court-annexed mediation enforceable as judgements or settlement agreements that are enforceable as an arbitral award.[65]

The Convention defines mediation broadly, whereby any process in which the parties attempt to reach a settlement with the assistance of a third party that lacks the authority to impose a solution upon the parties meets the standard.[66] This broad standard is intended to encompass the wide variety of approaches to mediation currently in practice around the world and constitutes a nod to the importance of cultural considerations in this form of dispute resolution.[67] In addition, the Convention does not define the extent to which a mediator is to be involved in the process in order for the settlement to 'result' from the mediation, creating another broad standard intended to capture settlement agreements regardless of what style or approach the mediator used.[68]

The iMSA must result from a dispute of a commercial nature under the Convention, and again this standard is to be interpreted broadly.[69] This means that it is feasible for agreements resulting from some types of investor-state disputes to be enforceable under the Convention.[70] But if the agreement results from a dispute under one of the excluded categories listed above (investor-state disputes are not included in that list), it will not fall within the scope of the Convention.[71]

The iMSA must result from a dispute that is international. This requirement eases the burden on adopting states to modify existing legal frameworks for domestic mediation.[72] The international characteristic is critical at the time the iMSA is concluded (not before, during the dispute or the mediation proceedings, and not after, during enforcement proceedings).[73] The identity of the parties determines whether the dispute is international, in that they have their places of business in different states or their places of business are in different states from where the

[63] Singapore Convention, Article 1(1).

[64] Singapore Convention, Article 1(2); Chua (2019), p. 3.

[65] Singapore Convention, Article 1(3).

[66] Singapore Convention, Article 2(3).

[67] Schnabel (2018), pp. 15–16.

[68] Schnabel (2018), pp. 15–16.

[69] Schnabel (2018), p. 23.

[70] Schnabel (2018), p. 23.

[71] Schnabel (2018), p. 23.

[72] Schnabel (2018), p. 20.

[73] Schnabel (2018), pp. 21–23.

obligations in the iMSA are to be performed or the subject matter of the dispute is most closely connected.[74]

In addition to determining the scope of the international mediated settlement agreement, the Convention applies several formality requirements as well. Under the Convention, iMSAs must be concluded in writing, but this is also to be interpreted broadly and the Convention does not specify that agreements must be distilled into one writing or one document (an agreement may be contained in a series of email exchanges, for example).[75] The writing must be signed by the parties, and this can be effected by electronic signature.[76] Parties seeking to enforce an iMSA must provide proof that the settlement resulted from mediation.[77] This requirement can be met a number of ways, including by providing the mediator's signature on the settlement agreement, a separate verifying document signed by the mediator, an attestation from the administering institution or 'any other evidence acceptable to the competent authority'.[78] These formality requirements are exhaustive, and therefore adopting states cannot promulgate additional requirements for the enforcement of an iMSA under the Convention.[79]

Last but certainly not least, the Convention does provide for limited reservations. Adopting states may declare that the Convention shall not be applied to settlement agreements to which it is itself a party or to which any government agency or agent of that state is a party, and adopting states are free to determine the extent of this reservation in the declaration.[80] And adopting states may declare that the Convention shall apply only to the extent that the parties to the settlement agreement have agreed to be subject to the Convention.[81] This reservation essentially permits adopting states to create a national opt-in regime for the Convention if they so desire.

3.3 Enforcement

The Singapore Convention requires adopting states to enforce iMSAs and to functionally recognise them as well.[82] Therefore, parties seeking relief may rely on the

---

[74]Singapore Convention, Article 1(1).

[75]Singapore Convention, Article 1(1) and Article 4(1)(a); Schnabel (2018), 29.

[76]Singapore Convention, Art. 4(2).

[77]Singapore Convention, Art. 4(1).

[78]Singapore Convention, Art. 4(1)(b).

[79]Schnabel (2018), pp. 33–34.

[80]Singapore Convention, Art. 8(1)(a).

[81]Singapore Convention, Art. 8(1)(b).

[82]There was much debate in the UNCITRAL WGII meetings about the functions of recognition and enforcement. For a detailed analysis and description of the compromise leading to the Conventions functional approach, see Schnabel (2018), pp. 34–39.

Convention as both a 'sword'[83] and as a 'shield',[84] as is to be determined under the relevant procedural rules of the enforcing court in the party state.[85] The Convention itself does not prescribe the procedure to be used in enforcement or recognition proceedings.[86]

There are exclusive grounds for the refusal of enforcement as well within the Convention.[87] In general, the grounds for refusal are comparable to the regime provided in the New York Convention.[88] The party seeking to block relief carries the burden of proof to raise and demonstrate that the grounds for refusal have been met.[89] The grounds for refusal under the Singapore Convention are permissive, in that courts may choose to provide relief or states may choose not to require that courts grant relief under specific grounds.[90] But this list is also exhaustive, in that adopting states may not establish additional grounds for refusal under the Singapore Convention. Enforcement or recognition may be refused where it has been established as follows:

- a party was under some incapacity[91];
- the settlement is invalid[92];
- the settlement is not binding or not final[93];
- the settlement has been subsequently modified[94];
- obligations in the settlement agreement have already been performed[95];
- obligations in the settlement agreement are not clear or comprehensible[96];

[83]SCM Art. 3(1): 'Each Party to the Convention shall enforce a settlement agreement in accordance with its rules of procedure and under the conditions laid down in this Convention.'

[84]SCM Art. 3(2): 'If a dispute arises concerning a matter that a party claims was already resolved by a settlement agreement, a Party to the Convention shall allow the party to invoke the settlement agreement in accordance with its rules of procedure and under the conditions laid down in this Convention, in order to prove that the matter has already been resolved.'

[85]Schnabel (2018), p. 40.

[86]Schnabel (2018), p. 41.

[87]Singapore Convention, Art. 5.

[88]New York Convention, Article V.

[89]Schnabel (2018), p. 43.

[90]Schnabel (2018), p. 43.

[91]Singapore Convention Art. 5(1)(a). This may include elements such as one party was a minor at the time the settlement was executed, was intoxicated, or was not in his or her right mind.

[92]Singapore Convention Art. 5(1)(b)(i). This may include instances where there has been fraud or misrepresentation.

[93]Singapore Convention Art. 5(1)(b)(ii). This relief may be granted only where the settlement agreement is not final or binding 'according to its terms,' meaning by the language of the agreement itself (thus presenting a four-corner rule and barring reliance on extrinsic evidence to meet the burden of proof).

[94]Singapore Convention Art. 5(1)(b)(iii).

[95]Singapore Convention Art. 5(1)(c)(i).

[96]Singapore Convention Art. 5(1)(c)(ii). This would only be met if the settlement agreement is so confusing that the competent authority could not confidently issue the relief sought if it found that the requesting party was entitled to relief.

- granting relief would be contrary to the terms of the settlement[97];
- there has been 'serious' mediator misconduct or failure by the mediator to disclose circumstances that raise justifiable doubts as to the mediator's impartiality or independence[98];
- granting relief would be contrary to public policy where relief is sought;[99] or
- the subject matter of the dispute is not capable of settlement by mediation.[100]

Thus, the Singapore Convention does in significant ways replicate for international mediated settlement agreements what the New York Convention regime provides for international arbitration awards. This instrumental innovation does indeed represent the latest disrupter in the international dispute resolution space and appears poised to eventually elevate cross-border mediation to equal stature with international arbitration. Does it therefore threaten international arbitration's position as the leading choice for users in cross-border disputes?

4 Predictions and Impact on International Arbitration

The answer to the question posed above and elsewhere in the preceding paragraphs, drawn from a review of the current trends impacting international arbitration within the dispute resolution landscape, is most likely in the negative. International arbitration is undoubtedly experiencing transformational and perhaps turbulent changes during this time in its history. But the advent of the Singapore Convention is unlikely to be one of the causes of any potential decline in use or popularity of international arbitration. In other words, users who are satisfied with international arbitration are not likely to begin selecting mediation procedures for dispute settlement instead simply because of the new enforcement regime for iMSAs under the Singapore Convention. Rather, this article anticipates that the Singapore Convention will increase the use of cross-border mediation without a corresponding reduction in the use of international arbitration, for the following reasons.

[97]Singapore Convention Art. 5(1)(d). This would apply if the relief sought directly contradicts the intentions stated by the parties in the settlement agreement. Therefore, if a settlement agreement restricts the parties' abilities to seek relief, the competent authority must give effect to those intentions. This ground for refusal is also broad enough to allow parties to opt out of the Convention's applicability to their settlement altogether.

[98]Singapore Convention Art. 5(1)(e) and (f). This would only apply in cases where applicable existing codes of conduct on mediator practices proscribe certain behaviors, those codes of conduct have been breached, and without such breach the party seeking relief would not have entered into the settlement agreement; or where the failure to disclose circumstances raising justifiable doubts as to the mediator's independence or impartiality was so material that had the disclosure been made the party seeing relief never would have entered into the settlement agreement.

[99]Singapore Convention Art. 5(2)(a).

[100]Singapore Convention Art. 5(2)(b).

4.1 Taking the Best, Leaving the Rest

Surveys of international dispute resolution users show that international arbitration is the preferred method of dispute resolution[101] but not that it is considered a panacea. On the one hand, respondents in the 2018 White & Case and Queen Mary International Arbitration Survey listed enforceability of awards, avoiding specific legal systems and/or national courts, flexibility of the process, ability to select arbitrators, and confidentiality and privacy, neutrality, finality, speed and cost as among the most valuable characteristics of international arbitration, in that order.[102] But users also identified the worst characteristics of international arbitration in that survey, pointing to cost, lack of effective sanctions during arbitration proceedings, lack of power in relation to third parties, lack of speed, lack of insight into the arbitrator's efficiency, national court intervention, lack of insight into institutional appointments, lack of appeals on the merits, other characteristics and lack of flexibility, in that order.[103]

A glance at these results reveals a simple conclusion regarding the advent of the Singapore Convention on Mediation. The Singapore Convention preserves the characteristics that users most appreciate about arbitration, thereby adding no significant additional advantage to mediation other than *perhaps* a lower cost and a speedier resolution (depending on the complexity of the dispute). Given that respondents to the 2018 International Arbitration Survey are already arbitration users and that 99% of them responded 'yes' when asked whether they would choose or recommend international arbitration to resolve cross-border disputes in the future, it is unlikely that the marginal difference presented to such satisfied users would sway their opinion away from international arbitration.

Another recent survey provides additional insight for why the use of international arbitration is unlikely to decline under the iMSA enforcement regime. The 2016–2017 Global Pound Conference Series[104] identified 'global interest in the use of pre-dispute protocols and mixed-mode dispute resolution (combining adjudicative and non-adjudicative processes)' as a key global theme drawn from the data collected around the world.[105] Likewise, the 2018 International Arbitration survey results indicated that a growing number of users prefer the use of international arbitration combined with other ADR methods to resolve cross-border disputes.[106]

[101]International Arbitration Survey (2018), p. 5. Ninety-seven per cent of respondents indicate that international arbitration is their preferred method of dispute resolution.

[102]International Arbitration Survey (2018), p. 7.

[103]International Arbitration Survey (2018), p. 8.

[104]Global Pound Conference Series (2017), p. 13.

[105]Global Pound Conference Series (2017), p. 13.

[106]International Arbitration Survey (2018), p. 5.

These findings jointly indicate that users prefer to mix their dispute resolution methods in cross-border disputes, and the Singapore Convention excludes from its scope settlement agreements that result from combined dispute resolution proceedings, such as court-annexed mediation, or mediation agreements that are enforceable as judgments or arbitral awards.[107] Thus, users may find themselves unable to take advantage of the Singapore Convention enforcement mechanism due to standing negotiated dispute resolution clauses, which combine international arbitration with other ADR methods such as mediation. Many are therefore unlikely to turn to mediation for stand-alone proceedings simply in order to capitalise on the new iMSA enforcement regime, when they may use mediation in tiered or escalating procedures and receive the same enforcement benefit under the New York Convention.

4.2 *Increased Access to Justice for MSMEs*

Rather than draw satisfied users away from arbitration proceedings, this article predicts that new users that are currently unrepresented in the international dispute resolution marketplace will see stand-alone mediation proceedings as a new, affordable and viable product for their use, thanks to the Singapore Convention. Small and medium enterprises (SMEs) and micro, small and medium enterprises (MSMEs) account for an increasingly large share of the global supply chain.[108] The OECD estimates that SMEs are the predominant form of enterprise around the world, accounting for 99% of firms, about 70% of employment, and adding between 50% and 60% of value in the global supply chain.[109] Yet MSMEs can rarely afford to pursue legal claims or defend themselves against legal claims arising from their cross-border transactions. More often, MSMEs choose to absorb the loss of terminated contracts or deals gone wrong because pursuing litigation or arbitration overseas is simply out of the question for what amount to small claims in comparison to the main share of the international dispute resolution market.[110]

However, MSMEs may be more inclined to pursue legal claims across borders through an affordable means of dispute resolution, such as mediation under the new, lower-risk enforcement regime provided by the Singapore Convention. Combined

---

[107] Singapore Convention Art. 1(3).

[108] The OECD defines SMEs as firms employing up to 249 people: micro enterprises are defined as having between 1 and 9 employees, small enterprises are defined as having between 10 and 49 employees, and medium anywhere between 50 and 249.

[109] OECD (2017), p. 6.

[110] Butler and Herbert (2014), p. 187. See also Clay and Harvey (2017) and Gliddon and Harrison (2019).

with online dispute resolution (ODR) methods for resolving disputes, made available thanks to a boom in ODR providers[111] and affordable high-speed internet being more and more widely accessible, the Singapore Convention may help providers capture a currently underserved population of users seeking access to commercial justice.[112]

4.3 More Choice for IDR Users

Finally, the Singapore Convention will serve to expand the suite of services available to dispute resolution users in the international dispute resolution landscape for whom international arbitration does not present the most appropriate form of dispute resolution. Mediation is generally a less adversarial, less formal and more collaborative dispute resolution process than arbitration.[113] For disputes involving close business partners, small claims, sensitive subject matter or where parties are willing to forgo findings of fact and law, mediation may represent a far more suitable form of dispute resolution than international arbitration proceedings.[114]

5 Conclusion

In conclusion, the Singapore Convention on Mediation is indeed poised to usher in a new era of peaceable international dispute resolution, but it will not do so at the expense of international arbitration. The scope of the Convention itself will limit the new enforcement regime for international mediated settlement agreements to only stand-alone mediation proceedings, and users who are currently happy with their selection of international arbitration or mixed ADR proceedings are unlikely to switch to stand-alone mediation. However, the Singapore Convention does have the potential to open up access to potential dispute resolution users, such as MSMEs, which represent an underserviced population in the international dispute resolution landscape. And the Singapore Convention is likely to expand the suite of services available to dispute resolution users that feel that arbitration is not the most suitable form of dispute resolution for their purposes.

The view from Singapore, therefore, on the future of international dispute resolution under the new enforcement regime, is looking bright.

---

[111] See for example Fairway Resolution (2019), Portable (2019), and SettleTech (2019).

[112] See generally Roberge and Fraser (2018).

[113] Chua (2019), p. 9.

[114] Chua (2019), p. 9.

References

Alexander N (2018) The Singapore convention on mediation. Kluwer Mediation Blog. http://mediationblog.kluwerarbitration.com/2018/07/24/singapore-convention-mediation/. Accessed Mar 15 2019

Bassi R, Newman J (2016) Increased transparency in international commercial arbitration. Financier Worldwide. https://www.financierworldwide.com/increased-transparency-in-international-commercial-arbitration#.XeSL5ZMzbjA. Accessed 15 Mar 2019

Bell GF (2018) The new international commercial courts—competing with arbitration? The example of the Singapore international commercial court. Contemp Asia Arbitr J 11(2):193–216

Butler P, Herbert C (2014) Access to justice for small and medium sized enterprises: the case for a bilateral arbitration treaty. NZULR 26(2014):186–221

Choong J, Rosenberg K (2018) China's belt and road initiative: opportunities and risks. Freshfield Bruckhaus Deringer, International Arbitration, illuminating the top trends in 2018

Chua E (2015) Singapore: reflecting on the development of the domestic mediation scene. ADR World 1(1):20–21

Chua E (2019) The Singapore convention on mediation - a brighter future for Asian dispute resolution. Asian J Int Law. Research Collection School of Law. https://ink.library.smu.edu.sg/cgi/viewcontent.cgi?article=4827&context=sol_research. Accessed 28 Mar 2019

Clay C, Harvey N (2017) Why the current system of dispute resolution is stacked against SMEs. SME Guidance for Global Growth. http://www.smeweb.com/2017/04/10/current-system-dispute-resolution-stacked-smes/. Accessed 28 Mar 2019

Cosgrove E, Hosking A (2018) Open up! How far should transparency in international arbitration go? King & Wood Mallesons Insights. https://www.kwm.com/en/knowledge/insights/how-far-should-transparency-in-international-commercial-arbitration-go-20180412. Accessed 15 Mar 2019

Croft J (2016) Singapore is becoming a world leader in arbitration. Financial Times. https://www.ft.com/content/704c5458-e79a-11e5-a09b-1f8b0d268c39#axzz4AUrfZCHD. Accessed 28 Mar 2019

Gek TP (2018) Landmark ruling lets Triksomel unit liquidators tap commercial claims funder. The Business Times. https://www.businesstimes.com.sg/companies-markets/landmark-ruling-lets-trikomsel-unit-liquidators-tap-commercial-claims-funder. Accessed 15 Mar 2019

Gliddon J, Harrison R (2019) A changing battlefield for SME disputes. Financier Worldwide. https://www.financierworldwide.com/a-changing-battlefield-for-sme-disputes#.XeSeXJMzbjA. Accessed 28 Mar 2019

Global Pound Conference Series (2016–2017) Global data trends and regional differences

Huang C (2016) Singapore's newest international commercial court set to thrive. Business Times. https://www.businesstimes.com.sg/government-economy/singapores-newest-international-commercial-court-set-to-thrive. Accessed 28 Mar 2019

IMF Bentham Blog (2018) Milestone decision on third party funding in Singapore. https://www.imf.sg/newsroom/blog/blog-full-post/imf-bentham-asia-blog/2018/09/12/milestone-decision-on-third-party-funding-in-singapore. Accessed 28 Mar 2019

International Council for Commercial Arbitration (2018) Report of the ICCA-Queen Mary Task Force on third-party funding in international arbitration. The ICCA Reports No. 4

Khanna D, Power R (2017) Transparency in international arbitration – striking the right balance. Clyde&Co Insight and Knowledge. https://www.clydeco.com/insight/article/transparency-in-international-arbitration-striking-the-right-balance. Accessed 15 Mar 2019

Lim G (2017) Development of mediation in Singapore. In: McFadden D, Lim G (eds) Mediation in Singapore, a practical guide, 2nd edn. Sweet and Maxwell, Singapore, pp 1–24

Loh Q (2015) Perspectives on harmonising transnational commercial law. Thirty-five years of uniform sales law: trends and perspectives. In: Proceedings of the high level panel held during the forty-eighth session of the UN Commission of International Trade Law

McDougall AL et al (2018) Recent trends in International Arbitration. White & Case Publications. https://www.whitecase.com/publications/article/recent-trends-international-arbitration. Accessed 15 Mar 2019
Middleton J (2018) The rise of the international commercial court. Speech to the 2018 Hong Kong International Commercial Law Conference. http://www.austlii.edu.au/au/journals/FedJSchol/2018/18.html
OECD (2017) Meeting of the OECD Council at Ministerial Level 2017: enhancing the contributions of SMEs in a global and digitalised economy
Roberge J-F, Fraser V (2018) Access to commercial justice: a roadmap for Online Dispute Resolution (ODR) Design for Small and Medium-Sized Businesses (SMEs) disputes, Ohio State Journal on Dispute Resolution (Forthcoming). Available at SSRN: https://ssrn.com/abstract=3299246. Accessed 28 Mar 2019
Saul J (2012) The legal and cultural roots of mediation in the United States. Opinio Juris in Comparatione, No. 1/2012, Paper No. 8
Schnabel T (2018) The Singapore convention on mediation: a framework for the cross-border recognition and enforcement of mediated settlements. Pepperdine Dispute Resol Law J 19:1–61
Secomb M, Wallin A (2018) Singapore: third party litigation funding law review, 2nd edn
Seow BY (2018) UN treaty on mediation to be named after Singapore. The Straights Times. https://www.straitstimes.com/singapore/un-treaty-on-mediation-to-be-named-after-singapore. Accessed 28 Mar 2019
Sun C, Leng SC (2018) Third-party funding – taking stock. Singapore Law Gazette. https://lawgazette.com.sg/feature/third-party-funding-taking-stock/. Accessed 15 Mar 2019
Tung S, Lin B (2018) More transparency in international commercial arbitration: to have or not to have? Contemp Asia Arbitr J 11(1):21–44
White & Case, Queen Mary University of London School of International Arbitration (2018) International arbitration survey: the evolution of international arbitration

Third-Party Funding in Arbitration: A Case for Mandatory Disclosure?

Nataša Hadžimanović

Contents

1 Third-Party Funding as a Typical Scenario Triggering Requests for Disclosure

The problem of transparency/disclosure is an ongoing issue in international arbitration. Disclosure of third-party funding is a replay of this topic, which is gaining more recognition with time as there is a growing industry of arbitration funding.[1]

[1]See http://third-party-funding.org/list-of-funders/.

N. Hadžimanović (✉)
GABRIEL Arbitration AG and University of Zurich, Zurich, Switzerland
e-mail: n.hadzimanovic@gabriel-arbitration.ch; natasa.hadzimanovic@uzh.ch

Z. Meškić et al. (eds.), *Balkan Yearbook of European and International Law 2019*,
Balkan Yearbook of European and International Law (2020) 2019: 41–52,
https://doi.org/10.1007/16247_2019_3, Published online: 3 December 2019

The essence of third-party funding is the use of legal capital to fund the realisation of assets that depend on the resolution of some sort of legal proceedings.[2] If the assets that are to be realised are sufficiently attractive, third-party funding can (also) be used to fund other things than legal costs, including, for instance, corporate expenses.[3] Third-party funding was originally developed as a way to fund impecunious parties. Today, more and more companies use third-party funding to be able to use their assets for other things than to fund arbitration proceedings. Usually, legal capital is invested on the basis that the funded party is without recourse other than to the proceeds of the legal asset whose realisation is being pursued. The recovery is therefore limited to what can be realised from the legal asset itself.[4] Third-party funding transfers the risk of the dispute to the funder, who, in exchange, obtains a portion of the potential value of the claim.[5] The funded party is, unless there is a breach of contract, not personally liable to the funder.[6] This is why a third-party-funded investment cannot be described as a loan.[7] However, third-party funding takes a variety of forms[8]: it can, for instance, be provided by a company in the same group of companies or by a professional third-party funder (see also Sect. 2.2.2). The process of applying for third-party funding is relatively clear, but it is time-consuming (which can be a problem in case a claim is going to be time-barred soon): It can take many weeks or even months to go through a tough application process. An application will only be successful if the funder is persuaded that the claim has a good or very good prospect of success. This also explains why rather big than small claims are funded: if it takes the same amount of time to evaluate the success chance of a claim, the (successful) big rather than the small claim is going to be financed.

Issues on transparency/disclosure typically arise in connection with third-party funding for the following reasons:

(a) Third-party funders may in some way be connected to arbitrators and, therefore, impair their impartiality and independence.
(b) Third-party funders are no parties to the procedure and can therefore not become liable for the payment of costs ordered in the award to the opponent of an impecunious funded party—but if the arrangement and the concealed impecuniosity were revealed, the opponent could request a security for costs.

---

[2]Perrin (2017), p. v.

[3]Perrin (2017), p. v.

[4]Perrin (2017), p. v.

[5]The decision Essar Oilfields Services Ltd v. Norscot Rig Management Pvt Ltd [2016] EWHC 2361 (Comm) (15 September 2016) illustrates such arrangements well: The litigation funder had made an agreement with Norscot, whereby it advanced to it the sum of around £647,000 to fund Norscot's arbitration. That agreement entitled the funder, in the event of Norscot's success, to a fee of 300% of the funding or 35% of the recovery.

[6]Perrin (2017), p. v.

[7]Perrin (2017), p. v.

[8]See Livschitz (2018), p. 2615 et seqq.

(c) In some cases, a party is fiercely opposing a security for costs order by painting a picture of being a poor David oppressed by a wealthy Goliath when in fact this party is just as strong financially due to third-party funding.

There is, therefore, an ongoing debate whether at the outset of the arbitration proceedings (or at a later stage if such an arrangement is made later on) a funded party should be required to disclose a third-party funding agreement and even its terms to the arbitral tribunal and the opponent. Because (a) this could prevent a challenge of an arbitrator at too late a stage of the proceedings or of setting aside actions after the award has been rendered, (b) it would allow the opponent of the funded party to ask for a security for costs at the earliest possible time and (c) it would allow the arbitral tribunal to better assess whether a security for costs shall be ordered. Disclosure would, however, be a problem insofar as third-party funding agreements usually contain a confidentiality clause.

In the following, it shall be discussed whether it would make sense to require disclosure from the parties at the outset of the arbitration proceedings. The pros and cons will be displayed and then weighed up.

2 Shall a Party Be Under a Duty to Disclose Third-Party Funding?

2.1 Pros

2.1.1 Important Element When Deciding on Security for Costs

It has been argued that the existence of third-party funding is an important element when an arbitral tribunal has to decide whether it shall comply with a respondent's application for security for costs.[9] If it is, for instance, revealed that an apparently *impecunious David*, who is fighting hard against an order for security by *painting a picture of financial oppression by a wealthy Goliath*, in fact has just as deep a purse through third-party funding, the case which in the beginning looked like a case of commercial oppression radically changes its complexion.[10]

Information would also be helpful to identify the 'arbitral hit and run scenario', where the claimant's arbitration fees and expenses are being covered by, e.g., a third-party funder who is gaining if the claimant wins but who would not become liable to meet any award of costs that may be rendered against the claimant if the case is lost.[11] For such situations, it has been held that information on third-party funding should be disclosed because this would enable the counterparty to request a security for costs.[12]

---

[9]Stone (2015), p. 65 et seq.

[10]Stone (2015), p. 66.

[11]Kirtley and Wietrzykowski (2013), p. 26.

[12]Stone (2015), p. 70.

2.1.2 Impartiality and Independence of Arbitrators Are at Risk Without Mandatory Disclosure

Parties to arbitration have a legitimate interest in being fully informed of all facts or circumstances that, in their view, will prove whether a (prospective) arbitrator is and remains independent and impartial.[13] Mandatory disclosure is held to be necessary to assess any potential conflict of interest between arbitrators and the funder (see IBA Guidelines on Conflicts of Interest in International Arbitration 2014, '**IBA Guidelines**', General Standards 6b and 7a).[14]

To warrant the independence and impartiality of arbitrators, the name of the funder and the key terms of the third-party contract would have to be displayed. It has been held that parties and arbitrators shall be under a duty to disclose these pieces of information at the earliest possible moment as only this could prevent the disruption of the arbitration proceedings.[15] If a funder's involvement were only revealed at a later stage in the proceedings, this could have serious if not disastrous consequences, especially at the stage of the award enforcement.[16] This would endanger the efficiency and integrity of an arbitral process.[17] And this, in turn, would turn arbitration into an unattractive conflict resolution mechanism.[18]

The Report of the ICCA-Queen Mary Task Force on Third-Party Funding in International Arbitration, April 2018, ICCA Report No. 4,[19] contains the following principles in Chapter 4, *Disclosure and Conflicts of Interest*:

A.1. A party and/or its representative should, on their own initiative, disclose the existence of a third-party funding arrangement and the identity of the funder to the arbitrators and the arbitral institution or appointing authority (if any), either as part of a first appearance or submission, or as soon as practicable after funding is provided or an arrangement to provide funding for the arbitration is entered into.

A.2. Arbitrators and arbitral institutions have the authority to expressly request that the parties and their representatives disclose whether they are receiving support from a third-party funder and, if so, the identity of the funder.

However, the question is how to implement coherent rules on the disclosure of third-party funding that would apply uniformly to international arbitration. Such rules could (apart from specifically being included in the arbitration agreement itself) be contained in (a) a treaty or (b) soft law, as are the IBA Guidelines, which would, however, have to be made applicable or (c) the rules of arbitration institutions.[20]

---

[13]Darwazeh and Leleu (2016), p. 132 et seqq.

[14]Darwazeh and Leleu (2016), p. 132 et seqq.

[15]Mansinghka (2017), p. 110 et seq.; Osmanoglu (2015), p. 339 et seqq.

[16]Darwazeh and Leleu (2016), p. 134 et seqq.

[17]Stone (2015), p. 66.

[18]Stone (2015), p. 66.

[19]The Report of the ICCA-Queen Mary Task Force on Third-Party Funding in International Arbitration, April 2018, The ICCA Report No. 4, 81.

[20]Darwazeh and Leleu (2016), p. 137 et seq.

This trend towards disclosure has been followed not only through the adaptation of the IBA Guidelines but also by arbitration institutions. Arbitration rules are slowly being adapted to the existence of third-party funding in international arbitration. The trend seems to be to establish the principle of disclosure of third-party funding—either indirectly, i.e. via the arbitrators, or directly, via the funded party or its counsel.

2.1.2.1 Disclosure by Arbitrators

On 12 February 2016, the ICC published a *Guidance Note* ('**Note**') for the disclosure of conflicts by arbitrators. This Note was updated on 19 December 2018 and entered into force on 1 January 2019. It aims at ensuring that arbitrators are forthcoming and transparent in their disclosure of potential conflicts. The Note clarifies that disclosures should be made with respect to not only the parties and their affiliates but also the non-parties having an interest in the outcome of the arbitration (para. 24). In this regard, the Note highlights the practice of the Secretariat to identify, at the outset of the arbitration, a list of *relevant entities*.

The Note specifically states that arbitrators should consider, when evaluating whether to make a disclosure, relationships with any entity having a direct economic interest in the dispute or an obligation to indemnify a party for the award (para. 28). This definition of third-party funding is the one contained in the General Standard 7a of the IBA Guidelines, which requires the funded party to disclose any such entity at the earliest opportunity.

However, the Note does not mandatorily require the disclosure by each party at the outset of the arbitration of *any entity having direct economic interest in the dispute or an obligation to indemnify a party for the award.* But only if such disclosure were provided, the arbitrators would be in the position to consider whether they have any form of relationship with a revealed funder that may require disclosure on the part of the arbitrator. And only such disclosure at the outset would enable the institution to know what it wishes to know. The developments in Hong Kong and Singapore have taken such an approach, as will be shown further below.

2.1.2.2 Disclosure by Party or Counsel

Third-party funding has been allowed in Hong Kong since 1 February 2019. With this legislation, Hong Kong has imposed a statutory requirement that the funded party shall notify all parties involved in the arbitration, as well as the arbitral tribunal, about the existence of a funding arrangement (Hong Kong Arbitration and Mediation Legislation [Third-Party Funding] 2017, Art. 98U[21]).

[21]https://www.gld.gov.hk/egazette/pdf/20172125/es1201721256.pdf.

Third-party funding is now also permitted in Singapore.[22] However, also Singapore has imposed a disclosure duty. The parties involved, as well as the tribunal, have to be informed. The rule can be found in the Legal Profession (Professional Conduct) Rules 2015 (Art. 49A). The duty is imposed on Singapore counsel only[23]; unregistered foreign counsel representing parties in arbitrations seated in Singapore are not strictly bound by the Singapore Legal Profession Rules.[24]

The Hong Kong legislation requires disclosure (a) on the commencement of the arbitration if the third-party funding agreement has been entered into on or before the commencement of the arbitration (b) and within 15 days after the funding agreement has been entered into if it has been entered into later on.[25]

Timing is not as clear under the Singapore Legal Profession Rules. Counsel is under a strict obligation to make the disclosure *as soon as practicable after the third-party funding contract is entered into.*

These disclosure rules are only a very soft reminder of the ancient common law doctrines of maintenance and champerty, which historically prevented third parties from intervening in litigation in which they were not already directly involved as parties.[26] The disclosure rules have also found their way into the institutional arbitration rules of Hong Kong and Singapore. Third-party funding has been taken care of also in the 2017 Investment Arbitration Rules of the China International Economic and Trade Arbitration Commission ('**CIETAC 2017 IA Rules**') (see Art. 27 CIETAC 2017 IA Rules).

Article 44 HKIAC 2018 Rules requires disclosure of third-party funding. Also, the SIAC Rules require disclosure: the SIAC 2017 IA Rules provide the arbitral tribunal with the power to order the disclosure of third-party funding (Art. 24 lit. l SIAC 2017 IA Rules) and so does the Practice Note 01/17 SIAC ('Practice Note SIAC') in its Arts. 5-8, applying to commercial arbitration. The CIETAC 2017 IA Rules contain a similar rule (Art. 27.2 CIETAC 2017 IA Rules). Moreover, Arts. 33 and 35 of the SIAC 2017 IA Rules respectively provide that the arbitral tribunal is entitled to *take into account any third-party funding arrangements in apportioning the costs of the arbitration* (similar to Art. 34.4 HKIAC 2018 Rules and Art. 27.3 CIETAC 2017 IA Rules) and *shall have the authority to order in its Award that all or a part of the legal or other costs of a Party be paid by another Party. The Tribunal may take into account any third-party funding arrangements in ordering in its Award that all or a part of the legal or other costs of a Party be paid by another Party*. Such provisions are also contained in Arts. 10-11 of the Practice Note SIAC.

---

[22]Henderson et al. (2019), p. 68, on Singapore.

[23]https://sso.agc.gov.sg/SL/LPA1966-S706-2015#pr49A-; Sim (2018): http://arbitrationblog.kluwerarbitration.com/2018/05/22/third-party-funding-asia-whose-duty-disclose/.

[24]Sim (2018), http://arbitrationblog.kluwerarbitration.com/2018/05/22/third-party-funding-asia-whose-duty-disclose/.

[25]Hong Kong Arbitration and Mediation Legislation (Third-Party Funding) 2017 Art. 98U: https://www.gld.gov.hk/egazette/pdf/20172125/es1201721256.pdf; Sim (2018), http://arbitrationblog.kluwerarbitration.com/2018/05/22/third-party-funding-asia-whose-duty-disclose/.

[26]Perrin (2017), p. v.

2.1.3 Sanctions for Non-disclosure

Infringement of a right must have consequences. In arbitration, consequences would either be procedural or substantive. Whether there is a claim for compensation depends on the parties creating a corresponding substantive basis in their agreement. Not all contractual provisions create a basis for substantive claims, especially not in the context of arbitration agreements. This is because such agreements are primarily concluded to regulate an issue of procedure, namely the tribunal's jurisdiction to decide the parties' dispute on the merits. Furthermore, the parties frequently include provisions that simply regulate the (arbitral) procedure itself. These procedural rules bind the parties, as well as any other contractual provision, but they do not create substantive claims. If a party fails to comply with procedural provisions, it will suffer consequences only according to the procedural rules (if at all), such as procedural disadvantages.[27]

This triggers the question what the consequence of non-disclosure would be if it were a mandatory obligation. The following consequences are, in principle, possible—there is and can be, however, no such thing as a general sanction,[28] and there is no direct way to force a party or its counsel to disclose a third-party funding arrangement (just as there is no direct way to force a party or its counsel to disclose any other fact covered by a document production order—no obligation to do something can be enforced directly—this being a general problem in civil law: who could force a painter to paint the promised portrait or the builder to build the promised street? There are only indirect ways to obtain the desired result)[29]:

(a) Non-disclosure of a potential conflict arising from a connection between an arbitrator and a funder may result in the recusal of the arbitrator or successful challenge of the award.[30]
(b) Failure to provide relevant information in connection with a funding agreement may lead the arbitral tribunal to draw adverse inferences assuming an unfavourable content of the funding agreement for the funded party.[31]
(c) The party who did not make the disclosure could be ordered to carry the costs[32] that were caused by its conduct, i.e. the extra costs that were incurred in case certain procedural steps in which the challenged arbitrator participated would have to be repeated.[33]

[27]Gabriel (2018), para. 25.
[28]von Goeler (2016), p. 157.
[29]von Goeler (2016), p. 157.
[30]von Goeler (2016), p. 157.
[31]von Goeler (2016), p. 157.
[32]von Goeler (2016), p. 157.
[33]Berger and Kellerhals (2015), para. 917.

(d) If a funded party requests-for the decision on costs-an uplift payable to its funder[34] but without mentioning why this is necessary, the arbitral tribunal may disregard the funded party's request.

(e) In case such a decision on costs could no longer be made because the arbitration proceedings have ended, non-disclosure could, if certain prerequisites were met, give rise to a claim for damages: a legal basis for such a claim would be needed. As has been explained, this would have to be a substantive law obligation.[35] Furthermore, there would have to be jurisdiction to award such damages in a different proceeding but under the same arbitration agreement.[36] For arbitration agreements that are governed by the Swiss *lex arbitri*[37] or comparable *leges arbitri*, it is held that the arbitration agreement typically provides for arbitral jurisdiction for substantive disputes arising out of the arbitration agreement, unless this is expressly excluded by the agreement itself.[38] One could theoretically argue that the arbitration agreement does not refer to itself to the extent that it is a separate contract under some *leges arbitri* (such as the Swiss).[39] However, such an understanding appears to be too dogmatic and even artificial. Arbitral jurisdiction must exist for all kinds of substantive disputes concerning arbitration agreements with the typical language (such as all disputes *arising out of the contract* or *in connection with the contract*).

2.2 *Cons*

2.2.1 Disclosure Duties Are Unnecessary

It has been argued that mandatory disclosure is unnecessary. The following reasons have been given for this approach.

First, the economics behind most litigation funding provides a key safeguard against conflicts of interest, bad faith and any other misconduct that could endanger or prolong the arbitration process[40]:

[34] The decision Essar Oilfields Services Ltd v. Norscot Rig Management Pvt Ltd [2016] EWHC 2361 (Comm) (15 September 2016) shows what is meant by an uplift: The litigation funder had made an agreement with Norscot, whereby it advanced to it the sum of around £647,000 to fund Norscot's arbitration. That agreement entitled the funder, in the event of Norscot's success, to a fee of 300% of the funding or 35% of the recovery.

[35] Gabriel and Hadžimanović (2017), p. 40.

[36] Gabriel and Hadžimanović (2017), p. 37 et seq.

[37] To international arbitration Chapter 12 of the Swiss Private International Law Act applies and to domestic arbitration the Third Part of the Swiss Procedural Act applies.

[38] In 2013, the Swiss Federal Tribunal specifically held that, under the Swiss *lex arbitri*, arbitral tribunals have jurisdiction to decide on claims for damages for breach of an arbitration agreement: Decision of the Swiss Federal Tribunal, BGer. 30.9.2013, 4A_232/2013 para. 3.4.2.

[39] Berger and Kellerhals (2015), paras. 679 et seqq. on the autonomy of arbitration agreements.

[40] Bogart (2017), p. 322.

(a) There is no need for mandatory disclosure duties because it is in the best interest of the funder and the funded party to disclose any conflict of interest with an arbitrator as they do not wish the award to be set aside or not enforced.[41]
(b) It also seems that good funders provide security for costs *sua sponte*,[42] which the funded party can then voluntarily offer because it wishes the arbitration proceedings to be conducted as efficiently as possible.
(c) It is, furthermore, likely that chances of settlement would increase if the financial strength and soundness of the case were demonstrated *sua sponte* to the opposing party early on.[43] So it may be in the interest of both the funder and the funded to make the disclosure.

Second, in many cases, it is in the funded party's own interest to make a spontaneous disclosure: where the prevailing funded party would like to recover more than its normal legal costs from the losing party (i.e. where a success-based cost element is payable to the funder, a so-called uplift) by not disclosing the corresponding funding-related facts in the cost submission, the funded party would risk the dismissal of the cost claim for lack of substantiation or for claiming an unreasonably high amount.[44] The HKIAC 2018 Rules, the SIAC 2017 IA Rules, the Practice Note SIAC, as well as the CIETAC 2017 IA Rules allow an arbitral tribunal to take into account any third-party funding arrangement when fixing and apportioning the costs of the arbitration.

Third, even though there may be situations where there is no interest on the side of the funder and the funded to make a spontaneous disclosure, the opponent does not necessarily have to suffer from this.

The opponent of the funded party has often alternative means to obtain information giving rise to suspicion concerning a claim being funded by a third-party funder. It may have obtained such information from the parties' previous dealings or from other sources[45]; it can also attempt to obtain information as to the latter's financial condition by requesting the production of documents in the context of a security for costs—however, without intending a fishing expedition[46]: where due attention is paid, the opponent of the funded party will most probably grow suspicious of the funded party's financial situation and funding and will be able to react adequately.[47]

Finally, it is important to note that in international arbitration, third-party funding alone does not entitle the requesting party to obtain a security for costs.[48] This is because third-party funding does not necessarily mean that the funded party is

[41]von Goeler (2016), p. 155.

[42]Kirtley and Wietrzykowski (2013), p. 17.

[43]Bernet and Hoffmann-Nowotny (2017), p. 161; Livschitz (2018), para. 52.

[44]von Goeler (2016), p. 155.

[45]Livschitz (2018), para. 53.

[46]See also von Goeler (2016), p. 155.

[47]von Goeler (2016), p. 155.

[48]Redfern and O'Leary (2016), p. 407 et seq.

impecunious. It may well be that the funded party wishes to diversify its litigation risk or to regulate its budgetary requirements.[49]

2.2.2 Disclosure Duties are Impractical

It has, furthermore, been argued that mandatory disclosure would be impractical. The following reasons have been given for this approach.

First, disclosure would be impractical because it is difficult to separate third-party funding from other financial arrangements.[50] This, in turn, would mean that a broad understanding of third-party funding would have to be applied to cover it all. And this would have as a consequence that a funded party would have to disclose (almost) any kind of financial arrangement (with lawyers,[51] insurers, banks, parent companies, equity investors, corporate financers and other stakeholders) and possibly also its exact terms just to exclude any potential conflict.[52]

This, however, would unnecessarily consume time and money as (a) in the vast majority of cases, there would be no conflict[53]; (b) funded parties would possibly try and raise privilege defences, which would further increase time and costs spent on this matter[54]; and (c) the opponent of the funded party would possibly try to further delay the proceedings by unnecessarily using the obtained information against the funded party or an arbitrator.[55]

Second, it is unclear when one could speak of a perceived conflict of interest. If an arbitrator is connected to the third-party funder by an investment (through shareholding), the question is how substantial the arbitrator's investment in the third-party funder and how substantial the third-party funder's involvement in the arbitration proceedings should be to raise potential concerns of a conflict of interest.[56] It seems that this would be a question of degree to be resolved on a case-by-case basis. This, again, would use time as the arbitral tribunal could not make a quick assessment.

2.2.3 No Possibility to Directly Force A Party to Disclose

Finally, it has been argued that the fact that there is no possibility to force parties to disclose third-party funding turns an obligation to disclose illusory.[57]

[49]Livschitz (2018), para. 73.

[50]von Goeler (2016), p. 151 et seq.; Livschitz (2018), para. 60.

[51]Wehrli (2008), p. 241 et seqq.

[52]von Goeler (2016), p. 153.

[53]von Goeler (2016), p. 152 et seq.; Livschitz (2018), para. 61.

[54]von Goeler (2016), p. 140.

[55]See Waterhouse v. Contractors Bonding Limited SC 66/2012 [2013] NZSC 89; von Goeler (2016), p. 155 et seq. on the "*Waterhouse saga*".

[56]Livschitz (2018), para. 62.

[57]von Goeler (2016), p. 157 et seq.

One may find merits in this position. However, this argument is at odds with the universal principles of the law of obligations. As stated above, no obligation that consists of a duty to do something can be enforced *in natura*. This does not turn such an obligation automatically into a duty of a lesser kind. It just means that there will be a pecuniary compensation in case of breach.

2.2.4 Protection of Sensitive Information

One could also argue that the information on how a party obtains financing should in principle stay confidential. It is not for the public to know, e.g., which entity in a group of companies is financing the others or to speculate on the reasons why a company engages a third-party funder instead of using funds of its own. Such information if displayed may, for instance, have adverse effects on the stock market.

3 Discussion and Conclusion

There seems to be a trend in international arbitration towards the imposition of a mandatory disclosure obligation:

(a) Soft law like the IBA Guidelines contains rules on third-party funding to prevent conflict of interests with arbitrators—albeit by imposing duties only on the arbitrators, not on the parties, which is also the ICC's approach.
(b) The two main arbitration hubs in Pacific Asia, Singapore and Hong Kong, have recently created legislation to impose a duty on the funded party and its counsel respectively to reveal third party funding. However, these countries used to be hostile to third-party funding due to an old common law rule. It is understandable that the recognition of third-party funding as a new phenomenon comes at a certain price. The arbitration rules of the institutions have been adapted to reflect this change. The CIETAC 2017 IA Rules in mainland China (PRC) has contained similar provisions since 2017.

The positive effects of an imposition of a duty to disclose—if the funded party were to comply with it—would be the early revelation of potential interest conflicts of arbitrators and a higher awareness for situations in which a security for costs shall be requested and such an order rendered respectively.

On the other hand, there is the position that self-regulation is sufficient and the more cost-effective way to deal with third-party funding—especially as there is no way to force a funded party or its counsel to make disclosure. Furthermore, the information on how a party has obtained financing may be sensitive information, worth being protected. There are, therefore, also merits for advocating this position.

Weighing up the arguments behind these positions, the following solution shall be proposed:

For the time being instead of including into more institutional arbitration rules an obligation for parties and counsel to disclose third-party funding, it would rather be prudent (a) to closely watch the developments in Hong Kong, Singapore and mainland China (PRC) to see (as far as that is possible, see, e.g., Art. 45.5 HKIAC) whether or not a disclosure duty produces undesirable results, such as in Waterhouse v. Contractors Bonding Limited SC 66/2012 [2013] NZSC 89 and (b) to suggest to arbitral institutions to provide the parties with an information leaflet on third-party funding with a list of recommendations and short explanations as to the consequences of too late a revelation of third-party funding. This would possibly motivate parties (and funders) to make revelations in their own interest.

References

Berger B, Kellerhals F (2015) International and domestic arbitration in Switzerland, 3rd edn. Bern

Bernet M, Hoffmann-Nowotny U (2017) The third party litigation funding law review. Chapter 16, Switzerland, pp 154–164

Bogart CP (2017) Third-party financing of international arbitration. b-Arbitra, pp 315–325

Darwazeh N, Leleu A (2016) Disclosure and security for costs or how to address imbalances created by third-party funding. J Int Arbitr 33:125–150

Gabriel S (2018) Chapter 18, Part XVIII: damages for breach of arbitration agreements. In: Arroyo M (ed) Arbitration in Switzerland, The Practitioner's Guide, 2nd edn, Kluwer, Alphen aan den Rijn

Gabriel S, Hadžimanović N (2017) Consequences of the breach of arbitration agreements. Slovenska arbitražna praksa, pp 37–48

Henderson A, Waldek D, Chua E (2019) Singapore. In: Friel S, Barnes J (eds) Litigation funding, pp 68–71, Law Business Research, London

Kirtley W, Wietrzykowski K (2013) Should an arbitral tribunal order security for costs when an impecunious claimant is relying upon third-party funding? J Int Arbitr 30:17–30

Livschitz T (2018) Chapter 18, Part VI: third party funding in arbitration. In: Arroyo M (ed) Arbitration in Switzerland: the practitioner's guide, 2nd edn, Kluwer, Alphen aan den Rijn

Mansinghka V (2017) Third-party funding in international commercial arbitration and its impact on independence of arbitrators: an Indian perspective. Asian Int Arbitr J 13:97–112

Osmanoglu B (2015) Third-party funding in international commercial arbitrator and arbitrator conflict of interest. J Int Arbitr 32:325–350

Perrin L (2017) The third party litigation funding law review. Preface, v–vi

Redfern A, O'Leary S (2016) Why is it time for international arbitration to embrace security for costs? Arbitr Int 32:397–413

Sim C (2018) Third Party Funding in Asia: whose duty to disclose? Kluwer Arbitration Blog, 22 May 2018. http://arbitrationblog.kluwerarbitration.com/2018/05/22/third-party-funding-asia-whose-duty-disclose/. Accessed 13 Mar 2019

Stone W (2015) Third party funding in international arbitration: a case for mandatory disclosure? Asian Dispute Rev 17:62–70

The Report of the ICCA-Queen Mary Task Force on Third-Party Funding in International Arbitration, April 2018, The ICCA Report No. 4

von Goeler J (2016) Third-party funding in international arbitration and its impact on procedure. Kluwer Law International

Wehrli D (2008) Contingency Fees/Pactum de Palmario 'civil law approach'. ASA Bull 2008:241–258

Arbitrability of Shareholder Disputes in Bosnian Law

Almir Gagula

Contents

1 Introduction

The Bosnian legal system still applies as a main option the classical model of judicial review of legality of the decision of shareholders in limited liability companies (ltd). This means that the Bosnian legal system, on purely legislative level, accepts only one of the possible forums for resolution of disputes regarding the legality of shareholders' decision, i.e. civil courts. Such model is not quite an adequate solution due to certain negative characteristics of the Bosnian court system. Those characteristics are partly the usual negatives of any civil court system.

Civil court procedures in Bosnia and Herzegovina are well known for their long duration, which is publicly proclaimed by high judicial and other relevant authorities. In contrast to that, there is a modern business that requests fast resolution of disputes.

A. Gagula (✉)
Law Faculty of the University in Zenica, Zenica, Bosnia and Herzegovina

Law Office Gagula, Sarajevo, Bosnia and Herzegovina
e-mail: almir.gagula@gagula.ba

Z. Meškić et al. (eds.), *Balkan Yearbook of European and International Law 2019*,
Balkan Yearbook of European and International Law (2020) 2019: 53–68,
https://doi.org/10.1007/16247_2019_4, Published online: 13 December 2019

Not less important issue is an issue of legal certainty. In case a civil court after several years of deliberation decides in favour of the annulment of the disputed shareholders' decision, a question on the effects of such decision on later decisions of shareholders is raised. The question is: what is the effect of the decision regarding the annulment on new decisions? What will happen when a decision regarding the appointment of the supervisory board is annulled? Is it possible that all decisions of the supervisory board in question be treated null and void?

This issue is clearly and closely connected with speedy resolution of disputes. Legal certainty and the speedy resolution of disputes in civil procedure are two faces of the same coin. Having in mind the aforementioned, this article investigates the possibility of using arbitration as an alternative and better-suited mechanism for dispute resolution, between shareholders in particular.

2 Legal Boundaries on the Control of the Legality of Shareholders' Decisions

When we take a close look at the current legislation in Bosnia and Herzegovina, we shall be faced with two different solutions in two entities of Bosnia and Herzegovina. Bosnia consists of two entities: Federation of the Bosnia and Herzegovina (FBIH) and Republic of Srpska (RS). Under the Constitution of Bosnia and Herzegovina, civil procedure and commercial and company law fall under the constitutional competence of the entities. This constitutional division of powers between the state and its entities results in different legal frameworks and opens space for further differentiations. Both entities have a different company law legal framework and almost the same civil procedure legal framework.

Law on Companies in FBIH[1] constitutes the right of a shareholder to request the annulment of the decision of the General Assembly against which it voted. The procedure can be initiated within a strict 30-day deadline after the proclamation of the decision.[2] The exact forum for the initiation of such procedure is left undefined, making this type of disputes potentially arbitrable.[3]

Law on Companies in FBIH does not have any additional provisions regarding the issue at hand, therefore making possible the question of application of the rules contained in the same law that are applicable to stock companies.[4] The law regulated certain aspects of the annulment procedure for stock companies. Several issues are directly covered by provisions of the law. It is clearly regulated when a decision of the General Assembly is to be considered null and void: (a) the General Assembly was not convened in accordance with the law, (b) the decision of the General

[1]Official Gazette FBiH No. 81/2015.

[2]Bikić and Gagula (2019), p. 164.

[3]Article 338 of the Law on Companies of FIBH.

[4]Article 303 of the Law on Companies of FIBH.

Assembly is not registered in the minutes of the meeting in accordance with Article 241 of the law or (c) the nullity of the decision is confirmed by the final decision of the court in the procedure following the legal action for the nullification of the decision. However, the law does not define this issue in great detail. We must bear in mind that an analogous application of the rules of the law for stock companies to issues of ltd companies might be arguable at some level. Limited liability companies in Bosnian law are to be considered as a more flexible form of the capital societies, hence making it possible to implement more flexible options of decision-making within the company. One example is a written voting process of the shareholders.[5] Written voting as well as form of circular decisions exclude formal process of convening of the general assembly in ltd companies. In this scenario of voting, it is not necessary to prepare the minutes or to register the decision in the minutes, unless otherwise explicitly requested by the foundation act or the statute of the company.

It is of great importance for our topic how issue of competent forum for annulment procedure of the decision is defined on legislative level. The legislator does it in arbitration friendly manner. Law on Companies in Article 338 defines the right of the shareholder to initiate the annulment procedure with following wording:

> Shareholder has a right to initiate procedure of annulment of decision of the General Assembly that he voted against, within 30 days, before the competent court.

It is obvious on its face that this provision does not call for an exclusive civil court jurisdiction. The law does not request that the annulment procedure be initiated only before the civil courts, without the possibility of referring the dispute to other types of dispute resolution mechanisms. In other words, the law did not establish an exclusive jurisdiction of the civil courts. This is of great importance for conclusion regarding arbitrability of the issue at hand.

The Law on Companies in the Republic of Srpska, although following a different direction, establishes a similar rule for the annulment procedure. By the provision of the law, it is regulated that rules regarding the annulment of decisions of a general assembly in stock companies shall be *mutatis mutandis* applied for ltd companies. The law defines in great detail general and special grounds and conditions for the annulment of the general assembly's decision.[6] But the same with the Law on Companies in FBIH, the law in the Republic of Srpska does not also explicitly exclude arbitrability this type of dispute or define the exclusive competence of the civil state courts. The law mentions that an action may be submitted to a 'competent court' and also stipulates different procedural provisions: the defendant, deadlines for the initiation of the procedure, *cautio iudicatum solvii*, interim measures, rights of all shareholders to participate in the process as joining parties etc.

[5] Art. 335 of the Law on Companies of FBIH.

[6] Art. 293-296 of the Law on Companies of RS.

What makes the provisions of the Law on Companies in both entities of Bosnia and Herzegovina arbitration friendly on a general level is the lack of a request for an exclusive civil court jurisdiction in matters of annulment procedures. The starting point is in favour of the arbitrability.

3 Arbitration vs. Bosnian Civil Courts

The civil court system in Bosnia and Herzegovina is of a kind that is specific to the countries of European civil law, but still with some general differences between two entities. The Federation of Bosnia and Herzegovina has only one type of civil courts vertically structured through the system of Municipal Courts, Cantonal Courts and Supreme Court of the FBIH. There are no special commercial courts with jurisdiction for commercial disputes.

In the Republic of Srpska, the judicial system is a little different. While retaining a similar structure as in FBIH (for civil law matters), it has a two-level structure of commercial courts. Whereas district commercial courts are the first instance courts, the Higher Commercial Court is the second instance court. The Supreme Court of the Republic of Srpska is the court of final, third instance in both pure civil laws matters and commercial disputes.

Everything that is usually singled out as an argument for submitting disputes to the arbitration,[7] with of course certain specifics, applies for arbitration of this type of disputes. Neutrality of the forum could be an important aspect, especially in cases where foreign investors are directly or indirectly involved. Whenever foreign and domestic investors are engaged in business, it is a reasonable expectation by foreign investors that dispute will be resolved in a more neutral manner if it is submitted before the international arbitral tribunal and not the local court sharing the same nationality as the domestic investor.[8]

Flexibility of the arbitration is one of its advantages over formal civil court procedures. Arbitrators are flexible[9] to the extents necessary to handle one arbitrator as a tailor-made procedure most suitable to the needs of the parties and complexity of the case before them. Flexibility of the proceeding shall allow at least a reasonable opportunity to the parties to present its case. Arbitrators in close cooperation with the

[7]Trifković and Omanović (2001), p. 509.

[8]Stanivuković (2014), p. 29.

[9]O'Malley (2009), par. 1.16 "Thus, arbitral tribunals today may look to such principles for guidance as to what is considered a fair and equitable manner of administering an evidentiary procedure in international arbitration. These and principles like them are the generally recognized "rules of evidence", but seen in the context of due process, they are simply guidelines for what is considered to be fair. That being said, because of the necessity for flexibility in international arbitration, their application by an arbitral tribunal may be amended in some instances and set aside in favor of other approaches, depending on what the needs of the case are."

parties, at the very beginning of the arbitration, try to find most suitable solutions in regard to procedure. Court simply lacks that flexibility.

The specific knowledge of the arbitrators, in particular their knowledge of the applicable law,[10] is also a factor determining the decision of the shareholders on whether to submit their disputes to arbitration. Shareholder disputes can be a highly complex dispute, which may override the capabilities of local courts.[11] It is reasonable to expect that such dispute will be resolved with a higher degree of quality if it is to be handled by experts with a specific knowledge in corporate and international business law. Experienced arbitrators shall enjoy the trust of the parties that are able to participate in constitution of the Arbitral tribunal. Unlike the arbitrators, who are usually specialised experts, judges of civil courts, even those in special commercial departments, are not specialised in this matter. They tend to work on different types of court cases, which prevents them from developing expertise in corporate and business law.

Confidentiality of the proceedings is of remarkable value[12] in the world of business. Shareholders often prefer to keep their internal business confidential without any exposure to the general public. Contrary to usual practice in arbitration, court proceedings are usually wide open to the general public; court hearings are also open to the public, making it impossible for their business information to be protected. Therefore, arbitration is a logical choice if one wants to keep confidential information or general business information hidden behind the doors of the arbitral tribunal. The approaches of arbitral institutions in regard to this matter are different, but a general remark is that arbitration is conceptually friendlier towards the protection of important business information. However, there are always exceptions.[13]

Based on the experience of the author of this article, shareholder disputes share a common fate to all other disputes handed over to the hands of the civil courts in Bosnia and Herzegovina. In order to obtain a final and enforceable judgment before the Municipal and District Court in Sarajevo, a diligent claimant needs to spend anywhere between three and five years litigating. Having in mind that Municipal Court in Sarajevo holds register of the companies with highest amount of registered companies in Bosnia and Herzegovina, situation with duration of the proceedings is quite clear. By choosing civil courts as your forum, you will lose both time and money. Without resorting to economic analysis of the law, we must mention that the

[10]Fry et al. (2012), pp. 156–158. The ICC takes into account different factors for appointment of the arbitrators including, but not limited to: nationality, residence, other relations with the countries involved, availability, ability, expertise, experience, qualification, knowledge of international arbitration, legal qualifications, language skill.

[11]Not only shareholders disputes. Construction disputes are of a kind where expertise of the arbitrators if advantage of the arbitration before the civil courts. Brekoulakis and Thomas (2017), pp. 1–2.

[12]Croft et al. (2013), p. 193.

[13]UNCITRAL 2012 Digest of Case Law on the Model Law on International Commercial Arbitration (2012), p. 170.

cost issue in the arbitration is not always best pro-arbitration argument. A modern international arbitration can be quite costly as well.[14]

In case the matter in dispute is the legality of an important corporate decision (e.g. the appointment of the members of the supervisory board of a company), the pace, or better yet the tardiness, of the civil courts is much of a burden on the shoulders of shareholders. Five years of waiting for a final decision in a dispute can result to other adverse effects in between. Just looking at the given examples can be hair raising. If the decision regarding the appointment of the supervisory board is proclaimed null and void after five years of litigation, questions of the effects on all later decisions are obviously raised. This is something that the shareholders simply cannot afford if they wish well for the company and themselves.

On the opposite side remains arbitration as the most logical choice. While the experience of the author regarding the duration of civil proceedings is devastating, the author's experience with regard to arbitration is a different type of music. Arbitration proceedings under the rules of the Foreign Trade Chamber of Bosnia take less time, usually anywhere between 6 months for a simple case until 18 months for a highly complicated matter.

The choice is obvious. Arbitration is the preferred option in all aspects. This of course leads us to the central question of whether it is allowed under the Bosnian law to submit this kind of dispute to arbitration.

4 Issue of Arbitrability in Bosnian Law

Unlike most issues in Bosnian law, the issue of arbitrability is defined clearly and exactly the same way throughout the country. While there is no law on arbitration in any of the entities of Bosnia and Herzegovina, rules covering arbitration are exactly the same.

Arbitration is regulated only by the rules of the Civil Procedure Codes[15] of the Federation and of the Republic of Srpska,[16] Luckily enough, the rules of both Civil Procedure Codes (CPC) are exactly the same. Arbitration is regulated by the rules contained in Articles 434–454 of the CPC. The Civil Procedure Codes, while being uniform, cover only certain issues on arbitration. Unlike the rules in the region, Bosnian rules regarding arbitration are not extensive, meaning that they cover only basic issues. This does not mean anything bad, but it is a fact that one should bear in mind while assessing the issue of arbitration and arbitrability in Bosnia and Herzegovina.

---

[14]Julian et al. (1987), p. 10.

[15]Official Gazette of FBIH No. 53/03, 73/05, 19/06, 98/15.

[16]Official Gazette of RS No. 58/03, 85/03, 74/05, 63/07, 61/13.

On the issue of arbitrability, the CPC is not silent. It does not explicitly regulate which disputes are arbitrable but instructs that parties are generally allowed to submit their dispute to arbitration, unless the matter in dispute is not within the scope of their autonomy in light of Article 3 of the CPC. The Code of Civil Procedure, in its Article 3, limits the autonomy of the parties, stating that the court shall not accept any disposition of the parties that is against imperative rules (*ius strictum*). This approach sets boundaries to arbitrability in Bosnian law in the very same way as contractual freedom is subject to limitations.

That being said, it is important to state that boundaries of contractual freedom are clearly set within the Law on Obligations. The Law on Obligations sets boundaries on contractual freedom in several of its provisions. First, it states in Article 10 that contracting parties are generally free to contract, but such contracting cannot be against the Constitution, the imperative rules or the rules of morality. Second, the legislator defines a clear sanction for a breach of the set boundaries. Under Article 103 of the Law on Obligations, a contract that is against the Constitution, the imperative rules or the rules of morality is null and void *ex lege*. Third, the subject matter of the contract is forbidden if it goes against the Constitution, the imperative rules or morality. Fourth, *causa* of the contract is forbidden if it falls under the same scope. These several provisions of the Law on Obligations are general limitations on contractual freedom in Bosnian law.

Based on the above provisions of the law, we come to the conclusion that dispositions of the parties that would be against the imperative rules in case of the cases where exclusive civil court jurisdiction is established by the rules of law. The CPC bestows exclusive jurisdiction on the civil courts over different matters. The approach of the CPCs in Bosnia and Herzegovina is quite straightforward. Exclusive civil court jurisdiction is defined in a clear wording, not leaving any open space for a different interpretation. Cases where the civil courts have an exclusive jurisdiction are *expressis verbis* defined by the law, forming a numerus clausus of the matters with exclusive civil courts jurisdiction.

Disputes regarding ownership or other disputes related real estates must be resolved only by the civil courts. Therefore, the rule *forum rei sitae* shall be applied, and the competent civil court of the place where the real estate is located shall resolve the dispute.[17] Law determined exclusive jurisdiction of the courts of the register of the plan or ship, for disputes regarding ownership and other property rights on airplanes and ships.[18] Ali disputes arising out or in connection with execution procedure as well as bankruptcy procedure shall be settled exclusively by the court in accordance with the seat of those proceedings.[19] In this type of disputes the parties are not allowed to agree on jurisdiction of any other court. Therefore, parties' right to

[17] Art. 42 CPC.

[18] Art. 42 CPC.

[19] Art. 45 CPC.

entrust resolution of these disputes to arbitration is excluded on the basis of the exclusive jurisdiction of civil courts.

However, the law in Bosnia and Herzegovina did not define the exclusive jurisdiction of the civil courts in shareholder disputes regarding the legality of the decisions of the general assembly of shareholders in ltd or stock companies. Namely, when the Laws on Companies in the Federation[20] and in the Republic of Srpska[21] provide for the right of the shareholders to initiate a procedure for annulment by a claim before a competent court, they do not explicitly or implicitly state that any court shall have exclusive jurisdiction. Just for comparison, the Croatian Law on Companies refers to court with exclusive[22] jurisdiction.[23] Such reference is not included in the provisions of the Law on Companies in Bosnia and Herzegovina. Reference to exclusive jurisdiction of any court is missing.

5 Law on Companies: Ius strictum or Ius dispositivum?

If we carefully observe the provision of Article 338 of the Law on Companies of FBIH, we shall be able to identify only one part of the provision to be of imperative nature, which would normally limit the autonomy of the parties in respect of the matter at hand. Part of the provision giving right to the shareholder to initiate a proceeding for the annulment of the decision of the general assembly is *ius strictum* without any doubt. This provision entitles a shareholder to request from the court to review the legality of the decision against which it voted. In the absence of a provision of this kind, the majority shareholder or group of shareholders could use their voting powers in order to ensure that the decisions of the general assembly are protective of their interest only, irrespective of the legality of such decision. Since it is an essential right of the shareholders to pursue and to protect their legal rights, it would incompatible with such right to exclude the right of the shareholders to initiate a proceeding in order to protect their interests. *Ubi ius, ibi remedium.* However, another part of the very same provision, one that defines that procedure must be initiated by the claim before the competent court, in our view does not have imperative scope or meaning. The legislator did not use any term that would determine that a competent court is also "exclusively competent" to evaluate the legality of the decisions of the shareholder/s after the action of the shareholder/s who voted against it.

[20]Art. 338 Law on Companies of FBIH.

[21]Art. 293-296 Law on Companies of RS.

[22]Uzelac (2002), p. 6.

[23]Art. 363(1) Law on Companies of Croatia: "Claim can be initiated exclusively before the court referred to in Art. 40(1) of this law". Art. 40(1) of Law on Companies of Croatia determines, among other, that commercial court with seat in the seat of the company shall be competent for resolution of the disputes between shareholders and between shareholders and the company.

Imperative rules can be more or less precise, resulting in the classification of imperative rules into (a) perfect imperative rule (*perfecta*), (b) more than perfect imperative rule (*plus quam perfecta*), (c) non-perfect imperative rule (*minus quam perfecta*). This classification differentiation can be and is made on the basis of precision of the imperative rule in relation with the determination of sanction for the breach of the rule.[24] Imperative rule is a perfect one when nullity of the contract is a clear sanction for breach of norms dispositive part. Such norm not only has a dispositive part but also clearly defines a sanction for acting against the rule given by the norm. More than perfect imperative rule differs from a perfect norm by the fact that apart from nullity as an explicit sanction, it imposes additional sanction as well. Finally, imperfect imperative norm is a norm that does not define nullity as a civil sanction or does not define any other types of sanction. The terms used by the lawmakers in order to precisely define an imperative norm are distinctive, differentiated and might in some scenarios create interpretative problems in practice. There should be no dispute where the law strictly defines sanction in the form of nullity by using terms such as 'it is null and void'. Lawmakers often use different terms such as 'it must', 'it cannot', 'it is not allowed', 'it is forbidden' etc. If the lawmakers did not use a clear language, then we should firstly resort to interpretation of the goals the lawmaker had in mind with such norm.

Such an approach in the interpretation of Article 338 of the Law on Companies leads us to the conclusion that the lawmakers did not have the intention (implicit or explicit) to entrust the resolution of shareholder disputes only to civil courts. What legislative practice shows us clearly is that when the lawmakers want to reserve jurisdiction for the civil courts, they use linguistic simplicity in legislation with terms such as 'explicitly'. The use of this term or similar terms clearly solves any dilemma of encountering other several issues, most important of which is prorogation and arbitrability of dispute.

Ergo, part of the norm of Article 338 of the Law on Companies, which states that the procedure for the annulment of shareholders' decision can be initiated by a lawsuit before the competent court, is clearly of a dispositive nature with two most important consequences (among others), which stem from such nature. Firstly, the dispositive nature of this norm results in the freedom of the shareholders to agree that their dispute can be resolved by any civil court, not only by one that would have a general jurisdiction on the basis of the place of business of the company.[25] The shareholders could reach an agreement to resort to future dispute regarding the legality of the shareholders' decision not only before a court of general jurisdiction but also before another competent court. Secondly, it leads to the conclusion that this type of disputes could be entrusted to arbitration.

[24]Perović (1980), p. 36.

[25]Art. 52 of the CPC.

6 How to Negotiate Arbitration Clauses

There are several options for contracting the arbitration for shareholder disputes in the Bosnian law. First of all, arbitration could be contracted within the foundation act of the company.[26] The foundation act in Bosnian law is always signed by all the shareholders of the company. In regard to new shareholders, it is necessary to ensure their consent on arbitration clause from the foundation act. Arbitration could also be contracted by a later written agreement of the shareholders, outside of the scope of the foundation act, signed by all shareholders.[27] We find that there are no any legal obstacles for arbitration agreement to be part of the statute of the company, with same effect as such clause has as part of the Foundation act.

However, court practice was keen to open up the question of validity of such arbitration clauses. Arguments of the civil court went to different direction. The court argued that when a company is placed in the position of the defendant in an arbitration procedure, then the arbitration clause should also be signed by the company itself in order to establish the formal requirement of a written consent of all the parties, who are selecting arbitration as a forum for dispute resolution.[28] We find such approach as an example of pure formalism. It does not take into account several important aspects of the shareholder agreement and obligations of the company arising from it. Under the Bosnian law the shareholders agreement are never signed by the company. A dispute regarding the validity of the decision of the general assembly is not *per se* dispute between one shareholder and the company, but it is essentially a dispute between one shareholder (the claimant, who voted against the decision) against other shareholders (the respondents, who voted for the decision). But because of formal requirements and in order to ensure an effective procedure, the respondent always has to be the company, not one or more shareholders.

Having in mind the fact that the general assembly is actually one of the bodies of the company not having a separate legal capacity or having the ability to be a party in a proceeding, the only reasonable solution is the one actually accepted under the Bosnian law. The company always has to be in the position of the defending party (respondent), though it is clear that the decision in dispute is in fact the decision of the general assembly.

The company does not have any possibility to accept or to deny any resolution of the shareholders given in the foundation act. Company has to fully comply with all provisions of the foundation act. Just one obvious showcase. Provisions of the foundation act regarding seat of the company, its bodies, its activities—shall be

[26] Look for the similar problem in the USA: Lipton (2016).

[27] Art. 435(1) of the CPC.

[28] District Court of Sarajevo, 04.10.2017, 65 0 Ps 460889 15 Pž.

mandatory for the company event though the company did not sign the foundation act. If this is the case, and obviously it is, then we must ask rhetorical question why anything would be different with the arbitration clause equally not signed by the company, i.e. signed only by the shareholders.

7 Participation of Shareholders in Arbitration Proceeding

It is essential that court or arbitral decision regarding validity of the decision of the general assembly has a full effect against the company and all shareholders. In order to ensure such effect, it is necessary to ensure that (a) all shareholders are properly informed about initiation of the procedure; (b) all shareholder have an opportunity to participate in the procedure as a the joining parties on the side of the defendant or the respondent and (c) that all separate procedures are joined in one procedure in order to obtain identical decision.[29]

Right of all shareholders to be properly informed about the procedure can be easily protected. This could be achieved with the foundation act or statute of the company ensuring obligation of the board of the company to inform all the shareholders procedure initiated against the company. Though this is not a requirement arising from Article 338 of the Law on Companies, we consider it necessary in order to ensure the full effect of the decision of the arbitral tribunal upon all shareholders. This would also prevent initiation of annulment procedure against the arbitral award by those shareholders that did not have a chance to actively participate in the arbitration.

The right of the shareholders to participate in arbitration proceedings should not raise any conflict. It is undisputed that the CPC allows the inclusion of the shareholders in a civil litigation. The shareholders will be able to participate in the litigation through a joinder for a protection of its interest.[30] The decision made by the court with the participation of other shareholders shall have an effect on the joining shareholders as well.[31] Even without the participation of the other shareholders, the decision shall have a full effect on all other shareholders, though they did not participate in the proceeding. The Law on Companies in RS explicitly determines such effect on non-participating shareholders.[32]

Arbitration also enables the participation of third parties, provided that they have some legal interest in the outcome of the case. This right is usually enforced through a joinder in the arbitration. Autonomy of the will allows shareholders to include option of joinder for all shareholders even in the foundation act of the company. Even without such agreement in regard to joinder of shareholders, a joinder is not

[29] Barbić (2013), p. 499.

[30] Art. 369 of the CPC.

[31] Art. 371a of the CPC.

[32] Art. 297 of the Law on Companies RS.

unknown in modern arbitration law. Bearing in mind modern tendencies in international arbitration, joinder is an usual concept for securing shareholder's right to participate in the proceedings.

The vast number of rules of arbitration institutions allows joinder of third parties. The UNCITRAL Arbitration Rules (2013) includes the possibility of a third-party participation in arbitration.[33] This option is also defined by the ICC Rules of Arbitration (2017).[34] The Ljubljana Arbitration Rules (2014) allow the joinder of third parties, provided that they are bound by the arbitration agreement.[35] The Rules of Arbitration of the Permanent Arbitration Court at the Croatian Chamber of Economy (the Zagreb Rules) allows a person that has a legal interest to join any one of the parties in the dispute as an intervenor, subject to the agreement of both parties.[36] The Vienna Rules of Arbitration and Mediation (2018) allows for the participation of third parties in the arbitration in broader terms than the Zagreb Rules.[37]

In some sense, joinder could be compared with consolidation of two or more separate procedures involving shareholder disputes with the same merits and concerning the same general assembly decision. Such request is seen in the Law of Companies of RS, where mandatory consolidation is defined.[38] Modern arbitra-

[33] Art. 17.5 of the UNCITRAL Rules 2013: "The arbitral tribunal may, at the request of any party, allow one or more third persons to be joined in the arbitration as a party provided such person is a party to the arbitration agreement, unless the arbitral tribunal finds, after giving all parties, including the person or persons to be joined, the opportunity to be heard, that joinder should not be permitted because of prejudice to any of those parties. The arbitral tribunal may make a single award or several awards in respect of all parties so involved in the arbitration."

[34] Art. 7.1 of the ICC Rules 2017: "A party wishing to join an additional party to the arbitration shall submit its request for arbitration against the additional party (the "Request for Joinder") to the Secretariat. The date on which the Request for Joinder is received by the Secretariat shall, for all purposes, be deemed to be the date of the commencement of arbitration against the additional party. Any such joinder shall be subject to the provisions of Articles 6(3)–6(7) and 9. No additional party may be joined after the confirmation or appointment of any arbitrator, unless all parties, including the additional party, otherwise agree. The Secretariat may fix a time limit for the submission of a Request for Joinder."

[35] Art. 12 of the Ljubljana Rules.

[36] Art. 38 of the Zagreb Rules.

[37] Art. 14.1. of the Vienna Rules 2018: "The joinder of a third party in an arbitration, as well as the manner of such joinder, shall be decided by the arbitral tribunal upon the request of a party or a third party after hearing all parties and the third party to be joined as well as after considering all relevant circumstances."

[38] Art. 297 of the Law on Companies RS.

tion rules also includes the possibility of consolidation of two or more arbitration proceedings. This can be seen in ICC Rules,[39] as well as in the Ljubljana,[40] Zagreb[41] or Vienna Rules.[42]

8 Modern Tendencies

Different countries do have a different approach on a matter at hand. But what seems to be a general tendency is that pro-arbitrability of shareholder disputes is a modern trend. There are arguments that civil litigation is ineffective and produces high litigation costs for the shareholders.[43] It is also argued that negative effects of the civil litigation (publicity which resolves with potential misuse by the competitors) might be avoided by arbitration,[44] well known by its inclination to confidentially, though issue of the confidentiality has its own development in the world of arbitration. The Russian law and practice create risks on the issue of the arbitrability of intra-corporate disputes. However, one might argue that everything goes in pro-arbitration direction, even for type of disputes at hand.[45]

Minority oppression statutory claims in the USA are considered to be arbitrable.[46] The US Supreme Court also developed case law that might be read as pro-arbitration.[47] In the USA, a number of corporations turn to arbitration in order to minimise high litigation costs, including those of the shareholders.[48] The Supreme Court of the USA also observed arbitration clauses on an equal footing with other contracts.[49] The French law, with certain exceptions, accepts arbitrability for corporation-related issues.[50]

---

[39] Art. 10 of the ICC Rules 2017: "The Court may, at the request of a party, consolidate two or more arbitrations pending under the Rules into a single arbitration, where: ... b) all of the claims in the arbitrations are made under the same arbitration agreement..."

[40] Art. 11.1 of the Ljubljana Rules.

[41] Art. 36 of the Zagreb Rules.

[42] Art. 15.1 of the Vienna Rules 2018: "Upon a party's request, two or more arbitral proceedings may be consolidated if 1.1 the parties agree to the consolidation; or 1.2 the same arbitrator(s) was/were nominated or appointed; and the place of arbitration in all of the arbitration agreements on which the claims are based is the same."

[43] Weitzel (2013), p. 118.

[44] Lee (2015).

[45] Strembelev and Kryvoi (2014), pp. 108–118.

[46] L Capital Jones Ltd v Maniach Pte Ltd [2017] SGCA 3.

[47] Mitsubishi Motors Corp. v. Soler Chrysler-Plymouth, Inc., 473 U.S. 614 (1985).

[48] Hartlieb (2014), p. 132.

[49] AT&T Mobility LLC v. Concepcion, 563 U.S. 333 (2011).

[50] Brabant et al. (2015).

German law also shows the extension of arbitrability in shareholder disputes. Evolution is quite interesting.[51] The starting point was the decision of the German Federal Court of Justice from 1996 (Arbitrability I), which denied arbitrability for this type of dispute in the case of limited liability companies. However, a later decision from the same court in 2009[52] (Arbitrability II) allowed submitting to arbitration this kind of dispute under certain conditions: all shareholders must accept the arbitration clause, the clause has to include an obligation to inform all shareholders about the initiation of the arbitration with the right to be included in the arbitration, all shareholders have to have a right to participate in the selection of the arbitrators and it is necessary that all disputes regarding one decision must be resolved by the same arbitral tribunal.[53] The decision Arbitrability III confirms the standards laid down by Arbitrability II while extending arbitrability to a limited partnership.[54]

9 Conclusion

We find that there are no obstacles in negotiating arbitration clauses for the resolution of shareholder disputes in Bosnian law. The parties freedom to contract,[55] being one of the principles for internal relations of the shareholders, allows this legal issue of grave importance to be resorted to the hands of the Arbitral tribunals. All the benefits of arbitration compared with the disadvantages of court judicial systems should be the main reason for the acceptance of this model of resolution of intracorporate shareholder disputes. By using arbitration as a forum, we can easily lift the burden from the shoulders of the judicial system and allow investors to submit their disputes to arbitration and arbitrators with experience, expertise and availability for the resolution of highly complex disputes. Shareholder disputes naturally belong to arbitration, saving both time and money for the parties while ensuring dispute resolution by experts in the corporate industry.

References

Barbić J (2013) Tužba za pobijanje odluke glavne skupštine dioničkog društva – neka odabrana pitanja. Zbornik Pravnog fakulteta u Zagrebu 63(3–4)
Bikić E, Gagula A (2019) Pravo privrednih društava

[51]Hertel and Covi (2018).
[52]BGH, 6 April 2009, no. II ZR 255/08.
[53]Markert (2015), pp. 29–60.
[54]BGH, 6 April 2017, no. I ZB 23/16.
[55]Fulham Football Club (1987) Ltd v Richards [2011] EWCA Civ 855 (21 July 2011).

Brabant TA, Desplats M, Salem S (2015) Arbitration and company law in France. Eur Company Law 12(3)
Brekoulakis S, Thomas DB (2017) The guide to construction arbitration
Croft C, Kee C, Waincymer J (2013) A guide to the UNCITRAL arbitration rules
Fry J, Greenberg S, Mazza F (2012) The secretariat's guide to ICC arbitration
Hartlieb GD (2014) Enforceability of mandatory arbitration clauses for shareholder-corporation disputes. Mich Bus Entrep Law Rev 4(1)
Hertel T, Covi A (2018) 'Arbitrability of Shareholder Disputes in Germany', Kluwer Arbitration Blog
Julian L et al (1987) Contemporary problems in international arbitration
Lee J (2015) Intra-corporate dispute arbitration and minority shareholder protection: a corporate governance perspective. Available at SSRN: https://ssrn.com/abstract=2736981
Lipton A (2016) Manufactured consent: the problem of arbitration clauses in corporate charters and bylaws. Georgetown Law J 104:583
Markert LA (2015) Arbitrating corporate disputes – German approaches and international solutions to reconcile conflicting principles. Contemp Asia Arbitr J 8(1):29–60. Available at SSRN: https://ssrn.com/abstract=2612404
O'Malley N (2009) Rules of evidence in international arbitration: an annotated guide
Perović S (1980) Komentar Zakona o obligacionim odnosima
Stanivuković M (2014) Međunarodna arbitraža
Strembelev SV, Kryvoi Y (2014) Arbitrability of corporate disputes in Russia: to be or not to be. CIS Arbitration Forum Working Paper 1/2014; Journal "Zakon", April 2013, No. 4, pp 108–118. Available at SSRN: https://ssrn.com/abstract=2383736 or https://doi.org/10.2139/ssrn.2383736
Trifković M, Omanović S (2001) Međunarodno poslovno pravo i arbitraže. Sarajevo
UNCITRAL 2012 Digest of Case Law on the Model Law on International Commercial Arbitration (2012)
Uzelac A (2002) Nove granice arbitrabilnosti prema Zakonu o arbitraži. Pravo u gospodarstvu 41:2
Weitzel P (2013) The end of shareholder litigation? Allowing shareholders to customize enforcement trough arbitration provisions in charters and bylaws. BYU Law Rev (1)

Intra-EU Arbitral Awards After *Achmea*: Recognition and Enforcement Within the European Union Under the New York Convention

Aliz Káposznyák

Contents

1 Introduction

On March 6, 2018, the Grand Chamber of the Court of Justice of the European Union (CJEU) rendered its long-awaited judgment in the *Achmea case*,[1] in which the CJEU held that the investment arbitration clause contained in the Dutch-Czech-Slovakian Intra-EU Bilateral Investment Treaty (BIT) had an adverse effect on the autonomy of the European Union (EU) legal order and was, therefore, incompatible with EU law. The *Achmea* decision can be considered a landmark decision regarding the relationship between EU law and intra-EU investment arbitration and, as such,

[1]Case C-284/16, *Slovak Republic v Achmea B.V.*, EU:C:2018:158 (CJEU, March 6, 2018).

A. Káposznyák (✉)
Eötvös Loránd University, Faculty of Law, Department of Civil Procedure, Budapest, Hungary
e-mail: kaposznyak.aliz@provaris.hu

Z. Meškić et al. (eds.), *Balkan Yearbook of European and International Law 2019*,
Balkan Yearbook of European and International Law (2020) 2019: 69–90,
https://doi.org/10.1007/16247_2019_5, Published online: 24 December 2019

raises several additional questions that might significantly affect the currently pending[2] and future[3] intra-EU investor-state arbitration proceedings.

The *Achmea* case was initiated by a Dutch insurance company against Slovakia under the UNCITRAL Arbitration Rules, in 2008, pursuant to Article 8 of the Dutch-Czech-Slovakian intra-EU BIT of 1991. After having established its own jurisdiction in 2010,[4] the arbitral tribunal seated in Frankfurt am Main (Germany) ordered Slovakia to pay damages in 2012.[5] Slovakia initiated a setting aside procedure before the German courts, stating that the arbitration clause in the BIT in question was incompatible with Articles 18, 267, and 344 of the Treaty on the Functioning of the European Union (TFEU), and therefore the arbitral tribunal lacked jurisdiction. The German Federal Court of Justice, as an appellate court, referred questions to the CJEU for a preliminary ruling regarding the interpretation of these provisions of the TFEU.[6] Although in September 2017 Advocate General Wathelet gave his arbitration-friendly opinion, arguing that the intra-EU BITs were generally compatible with EU law,[7] the CJEU came to a different conclusion and held that an arbitration clause concluded between Member States, such as Article 8 of the BIT in question, was incompatible with Articles 267 and 344 TFEU. With reference to the preliminary ruling given by the CJEU, the German Federal Court of Justice set aside the final award on October 31, 2018, stating that there was no valid arbitration agreement between the parties.[8]

After 10 years, the *Achmea* case has now come to an end. However, according to the majority of views,[9] the overall implications of the *Achmea* case and, most importantly, those of the CJEU's ruling have not yet ended. Indeed, the future of intra-EU investment treaty arbitration is still hotly debated within the arbitration

---

[2]By July 31, 2018, the overall number of known intra-EU cases was 174 which constituted 20% of the 904 known investment arbitration cases globally. UNCTAD (2018), p. 1.

[3]As far as future intra-EU arbitration proceedings are concerned, a decreasing trend emerges after the *Achmea* decision since only three cases were initiated until July 31, 2018 which represents less than 10% of the 37 known cases submitted in the first seven months of 2018. These three known intra-EU arbitration cases were based on the Energy Charter Treaty (ECT). After July 31, 2018, two more intra-EU ICSID cases have been initiated, both based on intra-EU BITs. UNCTAD (2018), pp. 2–3.

[4]*Achmea B.V. (formerly Eureko B.V.) v. The Slovak Republic,* PCA Case No. 2008-13, Award on Jurisdiction, Arbitrability and Suspension (October 26, 2010).

[5]*Achmea B.V. (formerly Eureko B.V.) v. The Slovak Republic,* PCA Case No. 2008-13, Final award (December 7, 2012).

[6]German Federal Court of Justice (*Bundesgerichtshof*), Case I ZB 2/15, Decision (March 3, 2016).

[7]Case C-284/16, *Slovak Republic v Achmea B.V.*, Opinion of Advocate General Wathelet, EU: C:2017:699 (September 19, 2017).

[8]German Federal Court of Justice (*Bundesgerichtshof*), Case I ZB 2/15, Decision (October 31, 2018).

[9]Lavranos (2018), Nikitin (2018), Ponomarov (2018) and Newing et al. (2018).

community, and there are no clear and conclusive answers yet to the questions[10] raised by the *Achmea* ruling. One of these questions is whether the findings of the CJEU in *Achmea* can equally be applied to the investor-state dispute settlement (ISDS) provisions contained in other intra-EU BITs or the *Achmea* judgment is specific to the BIT in question, and therefore general conclusions cannot be drawn with respect to an arbitration clause provided for in other intra-EU BITs. This question is of paramount importance because if it can be answered in the affirmative, this would mean that the CJEU has put an end to intra-EU arbitration within the EU. In other words, from a recognition and enforcement perspective, if the *Achmea* ruling is applicable in a general manner to investment treaty arbitration based on other intra-EU BITs, an intra-EU arbitral award is highly unlikely to be enforceable within the EU.

With this in mind, this article seeks to address the main consequences of the *Achmea* ruling on the recognition and enforcement of non-ICSID[11] intra-EU arbitral awards within the EU. First, we give an overview of the increasing interplay between the intra-EU BITs and the EU legal order (Sect. 2) by briefly describing the history of the intra-EU BITs (Sect. 2.1) and the most relevant investment arbitration cases involving the question of compatibility of intra-EU BITs with EU law before *Achmea* (Sect. 2.2). Subsequently, we answer the question as to whether the *Achmea* ruling can really affect other intra-EU arbitral awards (Sect. 3). In this context, we follow the CJEU's line of argumentation by discussing, first, the applicable law clause contained in the BIT (Sect. 3.1), then the rules on preliminary reference procedure under Article 267 TFEU (Sect. 3.2), and the scope of the judicial review of an intra-EU arbitral award (Sect. 3.3). Following this, we address the recognition and enforcement issues after *Achmea* (Sect. 4), focusing on two grounds for refusal: validity of the arbitration agreement (Sect. 4.1) and violation of public policy (Sect. 4.2). Finally, we close this article with our conclusion (Sect. 5).

---

[10]There are more questions which have been left unresolved by the CJEU in its decision, such as the consequences of the ruling for pending and future intra-EU ICSID arbitration proceedings or for arbitration under the ECT. However, these questions are not subject to this article.

[11]Non-ICSID arbitration includes ad hoc arbitration conducted mostly under the UNCITRAL Arbitration Rules and institutional arbitration conducted under the ICSID Additional Facility Rules or the rules of other arbitral institutions (e.g. International Chamber of Commerce International Court of Arbitration, Arbitration Institute of the Stockholm Chamber of Commerce, London Court of International Arbitration).

2 Increasing Interplay Between the Intra-EU BITs and the EU Legal Order

2.1 Brief History of the Intra-EU BITs

The EU Member States, like other countries across the globe, started to enter into BITs with third countries as of the second half of the twentieth century[12] in order to stimulate cross-border investment activities and thereby facilitate economic growth. These international investment agreements were usually concluded between a developed country, such as the old Member States of the EU, and a developing country, including the post-communist Central and Eastern European countries in the 1990s. The Contracting States usually had different motivation by entering into a BIT because while the developed countries sought to protect their investors in the territory of the other Contracting State, the main goal of the developing countries was to attract foreign investment.[13]

From the early 1990s, after the fall of communism in the Eastern Bloc, the post-communist countries started their transition to the market economy, and as result of this process, they have concluded a number of BITs with the original Member States. Until the accession of the ten new Central and Eastern European countries to the EU in 2004, no particular attention has been given to these international investment agreements since they were concluded with a non-EU country.[14] Nevertheless, as of 2004, the situation has significantly changed because these BITs have acquired the intra-EU status, and a heated debate started about the relationship between intra-EU BITs and EU law.[15]

The European Commission has been objecting to the compatibility of intra-EU BITs with EU law from the very beginning, alleging that these two systems of international law have overlapping scope of application that cannot apply simultaneously. In November 2006, the European Commission's Directorate General responsible for the Internal Market and Services was of the position that "most of the provisions of such BITs have been replaced by provisions of Community law" and that "their legal character after accession is not entirely clear."[16] The Economic and Financial Committee (EFC), consisting of senior officials from national administrations and central banks of the Member States, as well as the European Central

[12]The first BIT ever was concluded between Germany and Pakistan in 1959; however, it did not yet include a direct investor-state dispute settlement clause.

[13]Fecak (2016), p. 14.

[14]Fecak (2016), p. 2; Eilmansberger (2009), p. 387.

[15]Although there were two intra-EU BITs in force concluded separately by Germany with Greece (1961) and Portugal (1980) before the 2004 enlargement, no arbitration cases arose under these intra-EU BITs, and therefore arbitration based on intra-EU BITs was not a real issue until the 2000s.

[16]The Free Movement of Capital, Note for the Economic and Financial Committee, prepared by the European Commission, Internal Market and Services DG, 26-27, cited by Wehland (2009), p. 298.

Bank and the Commission, confirmed the DG's concerns in its 2006 annual report and invited the Member States to "review the need for such BITs agreements; and inform the Commission about the actions taken in this context so that progress can be reviewed by the EFC by the end of 2007."[17]

In its later communication, the Commission clearly expressed its concerns about the intra-EU BITs, stating that "investors could try to practice forum shopping by submitting claims to BIT arbitration instead of—or additionally to—national courts. This could lead to BIT arbitration taking place without relevant questions of EC law being submitted to the ECJ, with unequal treatment of investors among Member States a possible outcome."[18]

Despite the Commission's numerous efforts to make the Member States terminate their existing intra-EU BITs, the majority of Member States preferred to maintain the existing investment regime[19] and have not taken any actions to terminate their intra-EU-BITs.[20] Hence, in this vivid legal environment, it was the task of the arbitral tribunals to consider the legality of an arbitration clause contained in a specific BIT and to decide on their own jurisdiction. As discussed below in more detail, the arbitral tribunals, not surprisingly, regarded themselves as competent to rule on a claim arising out of an intra-EU BIT without violating the EU legal order.

2.2 *Investment Arbitration Cases Involving the Question of Compatibility of Intra-EU BITs with EU Law Before* Achmea

After their accession to the EU, the newly acceded post-communist Member States, as respondents in the intra-EU arbitration cases, have argued that an intra-EU investment agreement could no longer be invoked by an EU investor and no arbitration procedure could be initiated under the arbitration clause contained in an intra-EU BIT because it was superseded by EU law and the ISDS mechanism was incompatible with the EU legal order.[21] The first cases in which this "intra-EU jurisdictional objection" had been raised were the *Eastern Sugar v. Czech Republic*[22] and *Binder v. Czech Republic*.[23]

---

[17] Economic and Financial Committee (2006), para. 16.

[18] Vis-Dunbar (2009).

[19] Wenhua and Sheng (2010), p. 1055.

[20] Nevertheless, there are certain EU Member States, for instance Ireland or Italy, who have ended all their intra-EU BITs prior to the *Achmea* decision.

[21] Söderlung (2007), p. 456; Kriebaum (2015), p. 28; Reinisch (2012), p. 159.

[22] *Eastern Sugar B.V. v. The Czech Republic*, SCC Case No. 088/2004, Partial Award (March 27, 2007).

[23] *Rupert Joseph Binder v. The Czech Republic*, UNCITRAL, Award on Jurisdiction (June 6, 2007).

In these two arbitration cases, the argument of the respondent Member State on the inapplicability of the intra-EU BITs was primarily based on Article 59(1) of the Vienna Convention on the Law of Treaties (VCLT), which regulates the implicit termination of an earlier treaty in the case of a conclusion of a later treaty between the same parties. In order for this provision to be applicable, the earlier and the later treaties must relate to the same subject matter, and the parties must either have intended the matter to be governed by the later treaty or the later treaty must be so incompatible with the earlier one that the two treaties cannot be applied at the same time.

Despite the Czech Republic's argument, the arbitral tribunal in the *Eastern Sugar* case came to the conclusion that the intra-EU BIT in question and EU law did "not cover the same precise subject-matter"[24] because the substantive guarantees included in the BIT were broader than those under EU law and the ISDS mechanism provided for in the BIT was also absent from EU law.[25] Moreover, as highlighted in the legal literature,[26] while EU law primarily intends to liberalize trade and investment between Member States and, therefore, seeks to facilitate access to other Member State markets by regulating the pre-establishment phase of an investment, investment law provides substantive guarantees in the post-establishment phase after the investment has already been made. Consequently, this also shows that even if there is some partial overlap, EU law and the applicable BITs do not address the same subject matter.

Similarly, the *Binder* tribunal has considered both the substantive protection and the specific procedural protection in the form of arbitration compatible with EU law and has not found any basis for holding that the provisions of the intra-EU BIT "have become automatically inoperative in application of the principle of the priority of EC law."[27]

Although the first line of argument put forward by the Czech Republic was the implied termination of the earlier BIT under Article 59 VCLT, in the *Eastern Sugar* case the respondent also invoked Article 30(3) VCLT. This provision leads to the inapplicability of certain provisions of the earlier treaty that are incompatible with those of the later treaty relating to the same subject matter.[28] As pointed out above, the tribunal in the *Eastern Sugar* case has found that the intra-EU BITs and EU law did not relate to the same subject matter and, therefore, refused respondent's alternative argument and concluded that Article 30 VCLT could not deprive the tribunal of jurisdiction.

[24] *Eastern Sugar B.V. v. The Czech Republic*, para. 160.

[25] *Ibid.*, paras 159–165, 180.

[26] Reinisch (2012), p. 167; Kriebaum (2015), p. 30.

[27] *Rupert Joseph Binder v. Czech Republic*, paras 63–66.

[28] Reinisch (2012), p. 174; Kriebaum (2015), p. 31.

After some other intra-EU arbitration cases,[29] an UNCITRAL tribunal in the *Achmea* case had the chance to answer the question of compatibility of intra-EU BITs with EU law. The Commission as *amicus curiae* was also intervened in this arbitration procedure and challenged, *inter alia*, the investor-state arbitration clause set forth in the BIT based on the principle of exclusive jurisdiction of the CJEU over EU-law-related matters.[30] Yet despite the lengthy submissions of the Commission and those of the Slovak Republic, the arbitral tribunal has not found any room for the application of Articles 59(1) and 30(3) VCLT and established its own jurisdiction.

In conclusion, the problem of intra-EU BITs from an EU law perspective emerged after the 2004 enlargement and culminated after the accession of Bulgaria and Romania in 2007, as well as the accession of Croatia in 2013. Although the Commission has many times called on the Member States to take action to terminate their intra-EU BITs, most of these investment agreements have been in force until now. Thus, it remained the task of the arbitral tribunals and, ultimately, the state courts with the assistance of the CJEU to consider these investment agreements' compatibility with EU law.

3 Does the *Achmea* Ruling Really Affect Other Intra-EU Arbitral Awards?

On July 19, 2018, the Commission published its communication to the European Parliament and the Council on the Protection of intra-EU investment in which the Commission clearly established that based on the *Achmea* judgment of the CJEU "all investor-State arbitration clauses in intra-EU BITs are inapplicable and that any arbitration tribunal established on the basis of such clauses lacks jurisdiction due to the absence of a valid arbitration agreement. As a consequence, national courts are under the obligation to annul any arbitral award rendered on that basis and to refuse to enforce it."[31]

Despite the Commission's firm statement, after a closer look at the *Achmea* ruling, the conclusion can be drawn that the findings of the CJEU do not necessarily relate to all arbitration clauses contained in other intra-EU BITs. While it is true that the operative part of the judgment is formulated in a rather general manner, suggesting that its findings are also applicable to other intra-EU arbitration cases, its reasoning can be considered specific to the intra-EU BIT in question in certain

[29]See, e.g., *Saluka Investments B.V. v. The Czech Republic*, UNCITRAL, Partial Award (March 17, 2006); *Ioan Micula, Viorel Micula, S.C. European Food S.A, S.C. Starmill S.R.L. and S.C. Multipack S.R.L. v. Romania*, ICSID Case No. ARB/05/20, Decision on Jurisdiction and Admissibility (September 24, 2008).

[30]European Commission Observations (July 7, 2010), quoted in *Achmea B.V. (formerly Eureko B. V.) v. The Slovak Republic*, PCA Case No. 2008-13, Award on Jurisdiction, Arbitrability and Suspension (26 October 2010) para. 193.

[31]Commission (2018), p. 3.

aspects. Hence, the question arises whether the *Achmea* ruling really affects other intra-EU arbitral awards. This question is of paramount importance regarding the pending intra-EU arbitration procedures because if the *Achmea* judgment has a general reach, it is highly likely that future intra-EU arbitral awards will not be enforceable within the EU under the New York Convention.[32] Therefore, in the following subsections, we will review as to how general the scope of the *Achmea* ruling is, as well as whether and to what extent its findings can be applied to other investor-state arbitration clauses set forth in intra-EU BITs.

3.1 The Possible Interpretation or Application of EU Law by the Arbitral Tribunal

The reasoning of the *Achmea* ruling is based on three interrelated arguments, which led the CJEU to the conclusion that an arbitration clause, such as Article 8 of the BIT, had an adverse effect on the autonomy of the EU legal order and was, therefore, incompatible with EU law.

The starting point of the CJEU's reasoning was the applicable law clause provided for in Article 8(6) of the BIT, according to which the arbitral tribunal had to take into account, among others, the law in force of the Contracting Party concerned and other relevant agreements between the Contracting Parties. With regard to the fact that EU law forms part of the law in force in every Member State, which derives from an international agreement between the EU Member States, the CJEU held that the arbitral tribunal established under Article 8 of the BIT "may be called on to interpret or indeed to apply EU law, particularly the provisions concerning the fundamental freedoms, including freedom of establishment and free movement of capital."[33] In other words, the entire argumentation of the CJEU about the incompatibility of the intra-EU BIT with EU law was primarily based on the choice of law clause of the BIT, namely that the arbitral tribunal was obliged to interpret or even apply EU law.

Nevertheless, it is important to underline that the different intra-EU BITs have different applicable law clauses, and therefore it cannot be ruled out that certain intra-EU BITs do not contain a similar provision on applicable law. Indeed, there are several intra-EU BITs that only stipulate the provisions of the BIT and/or the principles of international law as the law applicable to the merits of the case but do not refer to the applicability of any domestic laws.[34] Therefore, the question may

---

[32]Convention on the Recognition and Enforcement of Foreign Arbitral Awards, 330 U.N.T.S. 38.

[33]*Slovak Republic v Achmea B.V.*, paras 41–42.

[34]See for instance Article 9(4) of the Agreement between the Government of the Hellenic Republic and the Government of the Republic of Estonia on the Promotion and Reciprocal Protection of Investments of 1997; Article 7(1) of the Agreement between the Government of the Kingdom of

be asked: would the findings of the CJEU have been the same if the provisions of the relevant BIT relating to the applicable law had been different?

In our view, it is safe to assume that in the absence of an applicable law clause referring directly to the domestic law of the Member States, the CJEU would not have been in the situation to establish the adverse effect of the dispute settlement clause on the autonomy of EU law because it would have been hard to argue that an investor-state arbitration procedure undermines the autonomy of the EU legal order if EU law is not expressly touched upon during the procedure.

Notwithstanding the above, one may argue that EU law may arise in an investor-state arbitration procedure not only as part of the domestic legal order but also as part of the international legal order[35] or as a matter of fact.[36] Consequently, it is of no relevance that there is no direct reference to domestic laws in certain intra-EU BITs because EU law always arises in an intra-EU investment dispute, and the Member States cannot derogate from EU law by simply concluding an international investment agreement without any reference to EU law.[37] This means that the findings of the *Achmea* judgment can generally apply to all intra-EU arbitration cases, irrespective of whether the applicable BIT expressly refers to EU law or not.

Although such an interpretation of the *Achmea* ruling cannot be excluded, it is worth emphasizing that the starting point on which the CJEU based its decision is that EU law was applicable due to the explicit provision of the relevant intra-EU BIT, saying that the law in force of the Contracting Party concerned shall apply.[38] This means that the CJEU in the *Achmea* case based its conclusions on a specific provision of an international investment agreement, and the decision itself does not contain any further indication as to whether these conclusions can simply apply to other intra-EU arbitration cases if the applicable BIT does not have an equivalent provision. Or to put it differently, it cannot be concluded from the decision that in the absence of a specific reference to the domestic law of the Member States, an arbitral tribunal would be called on to interpret or apply EU law to such an extent that would reach the threshold that justifies the incompatibility of investor-state arbitration with EU law.

To sum up, the first central issue on the assessment of the compatibility of the intra-EU BIT was the examination of the applicable law clause.[39] The CJEU's argument on Article 8(6) of the BIT in question was specific to the case at hand, and therefore it can be concluded that its findings have limited reach in this respect.

Sweden and the Government of the Republic of Estonia on the Promotion and Reciprocal Protection of Investments of 1992.

[35]*Electrabel S.A. v. Republic of Hungary*, ICSID Case No. ARB/07/19, Decision on Jurisdiction, Applicable Law and Liability (November 30, 2012), para 4.122.

[36]*Ioan Micula, Viorel Micula, S.C. European Food S.A, S.C. Starmill S.R.L. and S.C. Multipack S.R.L. v. Romania*, ICSID Case No. ARB/05/20, Final Award (December 11, 2013), paras 327–329.

[37]Hess (2018), p. 10.

[38]Stefan (2018).

[39]Decleve (2018).

The ruling may have impact on other intra-EU arbitration cases and, more importantly, on the recognition and enforcement of other intra-EU arbitral awards only if the applicable BITs refer to the applicability of the Member States' domestic laws and EU law is directly affected in this way.

3.2 Authority to Make Preliminary References to the CJEU Under Article 267 TFEU

Since the first question on the applicability of EU law was answered positively by the CJEU, the second issue that the CJEU addressed was whether an arbitral tribunal such as that constituted under Article 8 of the BIT could be regarded as a court or tribunal of a Member State within the meaning of Article 267 TFEU.

Under the established case law of the CJEU, in determining whether a body can be considered a court or tribunal of a Member State for the purposes of Article 267 TFEU, a number of factors must be taken into account, "such as whether the body is established by law, whether it is permanent, whether its jurisdiction is compulsory, whether its procedure is *inter partes*, whether it applies rules of law and whether it is independent."[40]

Although the CJEU represented a firm position in this regard from the very beginning, stating that arbitral tribunals do not meet the above requirements, and thus they are unable to make preliminary references,[41] most recently, the CJEU seemed to depart from its previous case law by allowing arbitral tribunals under certain conditions to submit references for preliminary rulings.[42] Based on the *Merck Canada* order[43] and the *Ascendi* judgment,[44] several authors started to argue that investment tribunals should be permitted to refer questions to the CJEU under Article 267 TFEU,[45] and this line of argument appeared also in the Opinion of Advocate General Wathelet.[46]

However, the CJEU has not followed the Opinion and generally confirmed its well-known settled case law that arbitral tribunals, even if seated within the EU, lack

[40]Case C-54/96, *Dorsch Consult Ingenieurgesellschaft mbH v Bundesbaugesellschaft Berlin mbH*, EU:C:1997:413 (CJEU, September 17, 1997), para. 23.

[41]Case 102/81, *Nordsee Deutsche Hochseefischerei GmbH v Reederei Mond Hochseefischerei Nordstern AG & Co. KG and Reederei Friedrich Busse Hochseefischerei Nordstern AG & Co. KG.*, EU:C:1982:107 (CJEU, March 23, 1982), paras 7 et seq.

[42]For more details see Paschalidis (2016), Basedow (2015) and von Papp (2013).

[43]C-555/13, *Merck Canada Inc. v Accord Healthcare Ltd and Others*, EU:C:2014:92 (CJEU, February 13, 2014).

[44]C-377/13, *Ascendi Beiras Litoral e Alta, Auto Estradas das Beiras Litoral e Alta SA v Autoridade Tributária e Aduaneira*, EU:C:2014:1754 (CJEU, June 12, 2014).

[45]Paschalidis (2016), Basedow (2015) and von Papp (2013).

[46]*Slovak Republic v Achmea B.V.*, Opinion of Advocate General Wathelet, paras 84–131.

standing to refer questions to the CJEU for a preliminary ruling. The CJEU pointed out that the investment tribunal could not be considered part of the judicial system of any of the two EU Member States concerned but it was of exceptional nature, which generally means that there can be no direct dialogue between an investment tribunal and the CJEU under Article 267 TFEU.

3.3 *Judicial Review of Intra-EU Arbitral Awards by a Court of a Member State*

Having reviewed the first two questions, the CJEU drew the conclusion that if an intra-EU investment dispute was adjudicated by an arbitral tribunal constituted under Article 8 of the BIT, the CJEU could not ensure that in the interpretation and application of EU law, the law would be observed[47] since the investment tribunal was not sufficiently integrated in any of the Member States' judicial system.[48] Therefore, the next and final issue that the CJEU examined was whether an intra-EU arbitral award could be subject to judicial review by a court of a Member State, thereby ensuring that questions of EU law will reach the CJEU by means of a reference for a preliminary ruling.

The CJEU concluded that even though questions of EU law were referred for a preliminary ruling from the German Federal Court of Justice in the *Achmea* case, it was possible only because of the decision of the arbitrators who had chosen Frankfurt am Main (Germany) as the seat of arbitration. In other words, it was the decision of the arbitral tribunal that "made German law applicable to the procedure governing judicial review of the validity of the arbitral award" and that "enabled the Slovak Republic, as a party to the dispute, to seek judicial review of the arbitral award."[49]

The CJEU took the view that the judicial review under the German domestic law was not sufficient since its scope was limited only to certain errors of law, such as the validity of the arbitration agreement, and it was not guaranteed either in the BIT that the investment arbitration would take place in an EU Member State whose state courts have the authority to make preliminary references to the CJEU under Article 267 TFEU.[50] Although the grounds on which an award may be set aside is a matter governed by the law of the seat of arbitration, it is affirmed in the legal literature[51] that "an annulment court does not review the arbitral tribunal's decision in the nature

[47]Article 19(1) of the Treaty on European Union (TEU).

[48]Hess (2018), p. 11.

[49]*Slovak Republic v Achmea B.V.*, para. 52.

[50]Hess (2018), p. 11; *Slovak Republic v Achmea B.V.*, paras 50–53.

[51]Born (2014), p. 3185; Bjorklund and Vanhonnaeker (2015), p. 44.

of an appellate proceeding, but instead considers only whether one of a specified number of defined statutory grounds for annulment is present."[52] This means that the CJEU's concern on the limited scope of the judicial review during the annulment procedure can be regarded as a general one, which arises in all intra-EU arbitration cases.

In addition, the CJEU made a clear distinction between commercial and investment arbitration in this respect, generally concluding that while a judicial review procedure being limited in scope is acceptable in the case of commercial arbitration, in the case of investment arbitration it is not so. According to the CJEU, the annulment procedure, contrary to commercial arbitration, does not mean sufficient control over the intra-EU dispute settlement mechanism provided for in a BIT, and therefore the efficient application of EU law cannot be assured in the present form of intra-EU investor-state arbitration. Consequently, an arbitration clause set forth in a BIT, such as the Dutch-Czech-Slovakian intra-EU BIT, is contrary to Articles 267 and 344 TFEU because it is not capable of ensuring that the specific characteristics and the autonomy of EU law are preserved.

In light of the above, it can validly be argued that the findings given by the CJEU in the *Achmea* case can only have consequences for those intra-EU arbitration cases where the applicable BIT refers to the applicability of the Member States' domestic laws. These arbitral awards, however, will be affected by the *Achmea* ruling because the two other elements of the reasoning can generally apply to all intra-EU investment cases. Therefore, in the subsequent section, we will discuss the future of these intra-EU arbitral awards within the EU with special regard to their recognition and enforcement under the New York Convention.

4 Recognition and Enforcement of Intra-EU Arbitral Awards After *Achmea*

Although the *Achmea* decision forms part of EU law, and thus binds the national courts of the Member States by virtue of Article 267 TFEU, the arbitral tribunals are not bound by the decision, and therefore they are not required to decline jurisdiction even if the arbitration takes place within the EU. However, it is also worth keeping in mind that one of the main tasks of the arbitrators is to render a recognizable and enforceable award, and therefore the arbitrators cannot simply ignore the changed legal situation after *Achmea*.[53]

Whereas prior to the *Achmea* decision the arbitral tribunals dismissed the jurisdictional objections of the respondent host states, stating that the prerequisites of Articles 59(1) and 30(3) VCLT were not met, after *Achmea* the arbitral tribunals may reach a different conclusion, particularly in the case of non-ICSID arbitration.

[52] Born (2014), p. 3185.

[53] Hess (2018), p. 14.

Considering the fact that a non-ICSID intra-EU arbitral award may be challenged both in a setting aside procedure and in a recognition and enforcement procedure, it is likely that the arbitrators will also take into account the possible outcome of an annulment/enforcement procedure when they decide on their own jurisdiction.

In any case, if a non-ICSID arbitral tribunal disregards the *Achmea* decision and renders an award based on an intra-EU BIT, the question of enforcement before the national courts of the EU Member States seems likely to arise. This question can be answered under domestic laws and applicable treaties that usually provide for a limited judicial review of the awards.[54]

The most important treaty in this context is the New York Convention, which can be regarded as a worldwide instrument with its 161 Contracting States. The importance of the New York Convention cannot be denied because it "sets a 'ceiling', or the maximum level of control, which national courts of the Contracting States may exert over the recognition and enforcement of arbitral awards."[55] This means that the New York Convention determines an exhaustive list based on which recognition and enforcement of an arbitral award may be refused by the competent national authorities of the Contracting States where recognition and enforcement is sought.

Given that all Member States are parties to the New York Convention, if the enforcement of an intra-EU arbitral award is sought within the EU, the provisions of the New York Convention will be applicable.[56] Under Article III of the Convention, each Member State is obliged to recognize an arbitral award as binding and enforce it unless there is a ground listed in Article V of the Convention on which recognition and enforcement of the award may be refused. Within the EU, the *Achmea* ruling enters into the picture at this point, to the extent that it has general reach, because it can serve as a basis for refusal of recognition and enforcement of a future intra-EU arbitral award, particularly on two grounds: invalidity of the arbitration agreement and violation of public policy. These grounds will be addressed in more detail below.

4.1 Invalidity of the Arbitration Agreement

With regard to the fact that the CJEU held in *Achmea* that an arbitration clause, such as that provided for in Article 8 of the Dutch-Czech-Slovakian intra-EU BIT, was incompatible with EU law, the first defense to the recognition and enforcement of an intra-EU arbitral award under the New York Convention can be that the arbitration agreement is invalid under the law to which the parties have subjected it or, failing such agreement, under the law of the country where the award was made.

[54]Schreuer et al. (2009), p. 1118.

[55]Gaillard and Bermann (2016), p. 190.

[56]Provided that the arbitral award was made in the territory of another Contracting State in case the enforcing State had made a reservation set forth in Article I(3) of the New York Convention.

It is important to stress in connection with this ground set forth in Article V(1)(a) of the Convention that there is a significant difference between commercial and investment arbitration as to how the disputing parties can give their consent to arbitrate. Although Article II of the New York Convention requires the arbitration agreement to be in writing, it is well accepted both in theory and practice that, contrary to commercial arbitration, in the case of investment arbitration, there is no need for a direct contractual link between the host state and the foreign investor.[57] Based on the concept of *arbitration without privity*,[58] the requirement for "arbitration agreement in writing" for the purposes of Articles II and V(1)(a) of the New York Convention is satisfied when, by submitting a request for arbitration, the investor accepts the host state's standing offer to arbitrate included in the respective international investment agreement or in its domestic law. This means that the host state's consent to arbitrate is given in an intra-EU BIT, which, under certain conditions, is considered incompatible with EU law.

Consequently, based on this provision, at the request of the respondent host state, the national courts of the EU Member States may deny enforcement, holding that after the applicable BIT acquired the intra-EU status, the BIT itself, including the dispute settlement clause set forth therein, was superseded by EU law by virtue of the doctrine of supremacy, and therefore there is no longer a valid consent of the host state to arbitrate.

This implication of the *Achmea* decision is also confirmed by the relevant case law of the CJEU. Although there is no specific provision in EU law regulating the status of pre-existing inter-Member-State treaties, unlike the pre-accession treaties concluded with third countries,[59] the CJEU's jurisprudence addresses this issue.[60] According to this, the *inter se* international agreements of the Member States can no longer apply after these states have acceded to the EU if their agreements are found to be contrary to EU law.[61] Since the CJEU in the *Achmea* case held the ISDS mechanism provided for in an intra-EU BIT incompatible with EU law, it can be concluded that the consent to arbitration embodied in these international agreements can no longer be considered valid after the new Member States joined the EU. This means that, based on *Achmea*, the recognition and enforcement of an intra-EU award may be refused under Article V(1)(a) of the New York Convention, saying that as of the date of accession of the new Member State, there has been no valid state offer for the foreign investor to accept. Nevertheless, there is an additional condition that must be met in order for Article V(1)(a) of the Convention to be applicable.

---

[57] Audit and Forteau (2012), p. 581; Reinisch (2016), p. 784.

[58] Paulsson (1995).

[59] Article 351 TFEU.

[60] Nagy (2018), pp. 1002–1003.

[61] Case 10/61, *Commission of the European Economic Community v Italian Republic*, EU:C:1962:2 (CJEU, February 27, 1962); Case 235/87 *Annunziata Matteucci v Communauté française of Belgium and Commissariat général aux relations internationales of the Communauté française of Belgium*, EU:C:1988:460 (CJEU, September 27, 1988); C-3/91, *Exportur SA v LOR SA and Confiserie du Tech SA*, EU:C:1992:420 (CJEU, November 10, 1992).

Although, at first glance, this provision of the Convention seems to be an appropriate legal basis that the party opposing the recognition and enforcement of an intra-EU award may rely on, it must be kept in mind that this provision may be invoked only if the arbitration agreement is not valid under the law applicable to it. The law governing the validity of the arbitration clause can be determined in two ways under this provision.

First, the disputing parties are free to agree on the law applicable to the arbitration agreement, and second, in the absence of the parties' choice, the subsidiary rule will come into play. According to this latter rule, the validity of the arbitration agreement is to be assessed under "the law of the country where the award was made." Although the New York Convention does not provide any guidance as to how to determine where the award was made, based on the established arbitral practice, decisions of the courts, as well as the arbitration laws and rules, this place is the country of the seat of arbitration.[62]

Considering the fact that in the vast majority of investment arbitration cases there is no direct contractual link between the disputing parties and, thus, the parties do not agree on a choice of law rule, in determining whether the enforcement of an intra-EU award may be refused under Article V(1)(a) of the Convention, the real question is where the seat of arbitration was located.

Taking into account that EU law, including the CJEU's decisions, must be observed throughout the entire territory of the EU, in case the arbitration took place in an EU Member State, EU law forms an integral part of the *lex arbitri*. Hence, it is likely that the national court of another EU Member State will deny enforcement in the light of *Achmea*, holding that, under the *lex arbitri,* there was no longer a standing offer of the host state that could have been accepted by the foreign investor by initiating arbitration procedure.[63]

In contrast, the outcome of the enforcement procedure seems to be the opposite if the seat of arbitration is outside the EU. In this case, the *Achmea* ruling does not form part of the law governing the validity of the arbitration clause, and therefore the enforcement of the award may not be refused on the ground that the arbitration clause is incompatible with EU law. This means that if there is no other reason under the law of the non-EU Member State to declare the invalidity of the arbitration agreement, the recognition and enforcement of an intra-EU award may not be denied under Article V(1)(a) of the New York Convention even if the enforcement is sought within the EU.[64]

---

[62]Gaillard and Bermann (2016), p. 143; See, e.g., Article 32(3) of the ICC Rules (2017); Article 31 (3) of the UNCITRAL Model Law; Section 53 of the English Arbitration Act 1996; *Dallah Real Estate and Tourism Holding Company v. Ministry of Religious Affairs, Government of Pakistan*, High Court of Justice, England and Wales, August 1, 2008, [2008] EWHC 190.

[63]This is also the reasoning that the German Federal Court of Justice gave in its decision dated 31 October 2018 under the German Arbitration Law in which the final award has been set aside with reference to the CJEU's ruling.

[64]Singla (2018).

In conclusion, whereas the *Achmea* ruling can serve as a basis for the refusal of the recognition and enforcement of an intra-EU arbitral award under Article V(1)(a) of the Convention in case the arbitration took place within the EU, it is unlikely that the respondent state can successfully rely on this provision to prevent recognition and enforcement if the seat of arbitration was located in a non-EU Member State. Thus, the question arises whether there is a ground under the New York Convention on which the recognition and enforcement of an intra-EU arbitral award may be refused in all EU Member States, irrespective of the seat of arbitration. The answer to this question is the public policy exception provided for in Article V(2)(b) of the Convention.

4.2 Violation of Public Policy

The public policy exception set forth in Article V of the Convention is the only ground that allows the enforcing courts to review the merits of an award during the enforcement procedure, but only to the extent that the compatibility of the award with the most fundamental values of the enforcing state is assured. In other words, "invoking the public policy exception is a safety valve to be used in those exceptional circumstances when it would be impossible for a legal system to recognize an award and enforce it without abandoning the very fundaments on which it is based."[65]

Based on Article V(2)(b) of the Convention, the recognition and enforcement of an arbitral award may be refused if the award would be contrary to the public policy of the enforcing state. This means that, unlike Article V(1)(a) of the Convention, in relation to the assessment of the violation of public policy, the relevant law that must be taken into account by the national court is its own system. In addition, while a court may only refuse to enforce an award under Article V(1)(a) of the Convention at the request of the party opposing enforcement, the ground for refusal under Article V(2)(b) of the Convention may be raised by a national court *ex officio*.

Even though the New York Convention does not define public policy, and therefore there is room for different interpretation by the national courts, which may also change over time,[66] it is widely accepted across different jurisdictions that enforcement may be denied on public policy grounds "where enforcement would violate the forum state's most basic notions of morality and justice."[67] Consequently, the public policy exception cannot be given a broad scope of application,

[65] Gaillard and Bermann (2016), p. 240.

[66] Moses (2018).

[67] *Parsons & Whittemore Overseas v. Société Générale de L'Industrie du Papier (RAKTA)*, Court of Appeals, Second Circuit, United States of America, 508 F.2d 969, 974 (1974).

but it should be limited to the protection of the most fundamental principles of the enforcing state's legal order.[68]

While it is self-evident that EU law forms part of the national legal order of the Member States, it was not entirely clear until the late 1990s whether and, if so, what rules of the EU legal order may be part of the Member States' public policy and, thus, serve as a ground for annulment or for the refusal of recognition and enforcement. The answer was provided in the CJEU's 1999 judgment in *Eco Swiss*.[69]

In this case, the CJEU regarded the prohibition of restrictive agreements contained in Article 101 TFEU as a fundamental provision of the EU legal order, "which is essential for the accomplishment of the tasks entrusted to the Community and, in particular, for the functioning of the internal market."[70] In other words, the CJEU qualified EU competition law as a matter of public policy and, applying the principle of equivalence,[71] stated that in case the domestic rules of procedure require the national court of a Member State to annul an arbitral award for violation of national public policy, the national court must also annul an arbitral award for violation of EU public policy.[72] Then the CJEU went on to say that the provisions of Article 101 TFEU "may be regarded as a matter of public policy within the meaning of the New York Convention."[73]

Although one may come to the conclusion, based on the wording of the Eco Swiss judgment, that the national courts of the Member States have the discretion to refuse the enforcement of an award violating EU competition law, the CJEU made clear in its subsequent case law that "EU competition law is a matter of public policy which must be automatically applied by national courts."[74] This means that even if the enforcing EU Member States' courts are allowed to ignore the violation of national public policy in accordance with the spirit and the pro-enforcement bias of the New York Convention, they cannot do so in the context of EU public policy.[75] Indeed, if the national courts of the Member States establish that one of the provisions of EU law, which can be considered "essential for the accomplishment of the tasks entrusted to the Community" was not respected in the arbitration procedure, they are not only allowed but also required to refuse enforcement *ex officio*.

---

[68]Maurer (2012), p. 63.

[69]Case C-126/97, *Eco Swiss China Time Ltd v Benetton International NV*, EU:C:1999:269 (CJEU, June 1, 1999).

[70]*Ibid.*, para. 36.

[71]For more details about the principle of equivalence, see Bermann (2012).

[72]*Eco Swiss China Time Ltd v Benetton International NV*, para. 37.

[73]*Ibid.*, para. 39.

[74]C-295-298/04, *Vincenzo Manfredi v Lloyd Adriatico Assicurazioni SpA* (joined cases), EU: C:2006:461 (July 13, 2006), para. 31.

[75]von Papp (2013), p. 1056; Singla (2018).

While the *Eco Swiss* judgment laid down the framework of the concept of EU public policy, there were some uncertainties left in its application.[76] It remained an open question as to which norms of EU law would constitute EU public policy, the violation of which requires the national courts of the Member States to refuse to enforce an arbitral award. The only institution that has competence to identify the relevant EU law provisions having mandatory nature, and thus forming part of the EU public policy exception, is the CJEU. Accordingly, the CJEU determined in *Mostaza Claro*[77] that the EU consumer protection law is so fundamental that it triggers the application of the EU public policy exception. In addition, in this case, the CJEU has indicated its readiness to give a field-by-field assessment about the most fundamental provisions of EU law that satisfy the judicial standard laid down in *Eco Swiss* and, thereby, must prevail in all circumstances.[78]

With these considerations in mind, it can be concluded that, in the *Achmea* ruling, the CJEU has treated Article 344 TFEU and the autonomy of the EU and its legal order as fundamental and mandatory norms of EU law that are "essential for the accomplishment of the tasks" entrusted to the EU. Consequently, Article 344 TFEU can be considered part of the EU public policy exception.

By reinforcing *MOX Plant*,[79] the CJEU made clear in its ruling that, under Article 344 TFEU, the Member States are not allowed to agree on any dispute settlement mechanism outside the EU regime, as long as the dispute concerns the interpretation or application of EU law. The rationale behind this concept is that the consistency, uniformity and full effectiveness of EU law may be ensured only within the EU judicial system, consisting of the national courts of the Member States and the CJEU, which is the sole body entitled to provide authoritative decisions on EU law under the preliminary reference procedure.

However, by concluding intra-EU BITs, the Member States submit their investment disputes involving EU law for resolution to arbitral tribunals where the full application of EU law cannot be ensured since the arbitral tribunals cannot make a reference to the CJEU for a preliminary ruling. Thus, the CJEU reached the conclusion that investor-state arbitration, such as that provided for in the Dutch-Czech-Slovakian intra-EU BIT, had an adverse effect on the autonomy of EU law and was, therefore, incompatible with EU law.

Again, Article 344 TFEU, as one of the main bastions of the autonomy of the EU legal order, has acquired EU public policy status after *Achmea*. Assuming that the *Achmea* ruling has a general reach and the findings of the decision are applicable to other intra-EU BITs as well, this means that a future arbitral award rendered under an intra-EU BIT is highly likely to be unenforceable within the EU with regard to the

---

[76]Basedow (2015), p. 373.

[77]Case C-168/05, *Elisa María Mostaza Claro v Centro Móvil Milenium SL.*, EU:C:2006:675 (October 26, 2006).

[78]Bermann (2011), p. 1207.

[79]Case C-459/03, *Commission of the European Communities v Ireland*, EU:C:2006:345 (May 30, 2006).

fact that the national courts of the EU Member States will be obliged to deny enforcement due to the EU public policy exception. Consequently, the public policy defense set forth in Article V(2)(b) of the New York Convention seems to be the strongest argument to prevent the recognition and enforcement of an intra-EU arbitral award within the EU post *Achmea*.

5 Conclusion

The message sent by the CJEU to the arbitration world through the *Achmea* judgment is that the EU legal system does not tolerate a dispute settlement mechanism other than those provided for in the EU law itself unless the necessary safeguards are implemented that ensure the protection of the autonomy of the EU and its legal order. Considering the fact that the intra-EU investor-state arbitration does not provide these safeguards required by the CJEU, as long as EU law is applicable to an intra-EU investment dispute, arbitration can no longer be a viable alternative to the national courts of the EU Member States.

This consequence of the *Achmea* judgment is reflected in the recognition and enforcement of future intra-EU arbitral awards as well. As discussed above, the national courts are expected to refuse to enforce a non-ICSID intra-EU award within the EU, either due to the invalidity of the arbitration agreement or on public policy grounds.

It can be argued that the implications of the *Achmea* ruling cannot apply generally to all intra-EU BITs because the CJEU's reasoning relies on the specific provisions of the BIT in question, and therefore intra-EU arbitration can still have a future within the EU. Nevertheless, we cannot ignore the fact that, according to the overwhelming majority of views, the *Achmea* decision affects all intra-EU BITs in force. This understanding of the *Achmea* ruling is confirmed by the declaration issued by the governments of the Member States on January 15 and 16, 2019, in which all the 28 Member States undertook to terminate their intra-EU BITs by December 6, 2019.[80] In addition, as the latest development, the Commission announced on October 24, 2019 that the EU Member States agreed on a plurilateral treaty to terminate their existing intra-EU BITs.[81] Thus, the *Achmea* decision seems to have put an end to intra-EU arbitration within the EU, which means that, in the future, an EU investor may only enforce its rights before the (sometimes not sufficiently independent) national administration and courts of another Member State.

---

[80]Representative of the Government of Hungary (2019); Representatives of the Governments of the Member States (2019a, b); The sole disagreement among the Member States is whether the *Achmea* judgment applies equally to intra-EU investor-State arbitration under the ECT.

[81]Commission (2019).

References

Audit M, Forteau M (2012) Investment arbitration without BIT: toward a foreign investment customary based arbitration? J Int Arbitr 29:581–604

Basedow J (2015) EU law in international arbitration: referrals to the European Court of Justice. J Int Arbitr 32:367–386

Bermann GA (2011) Reconciling European Union law demands with the demands of international arbitration. Fordham Int Law J 34:1193–1216

Bermann GA (2012) Navigating EU law and the law of international arbitration. Arbitr Int 28:397–446

Bjorklund AK, Vanhonnaeker L (2015) Stays of enforcement pending annulment and set-aside proceedings in investment arbitration. In: Fouret J (ed) Enforcement of investment treaty arbitration awards: a global guide. Globe Law and Business, pp 43–66

Born GB (ed) (2014) International commercial arbitration. Kluwer Law International

Commission (2018) Communication from the Commission to the European Parliament and the Council on Protection of intra-EU investment. Brussels, COM(2018) 547 final. https://eur-lex.europa.eu/legal-content/EN/TXT/PDF/?uri=CELEX:52018DC0547&rid=8. Accessed 7 Dec 2019

Commission (2019) Statement - EU Member States agree on a plurilateral treaty to terminate bilateral investment treaties. https://ec.europa.eu/info/sites/info/files/business_economy_euro/banking_and_finance/documents/191024-bilateral-investment-treaties_en.pdf. Accessed 7 Dec 2019

Decleve Q (2018) Does Achmea invalidate all intra-EU BITs? Not necessarily! International Litigation Blog. http://international-litigation-blog.com/does-achmea-invalidates-all-intra-eu-bits-not-necessarily/. Accessed 7 Dec 2019

Economic and Financial Committee (2006) EFC Report to the Commission and the Council on the Movement of Capital and the Freedom of Payments. http://register.consilium.europa.eu/doc/srv?l=EN&f=ST%205044%202007%20INIT. Accessed 7 Dec 2019

Eilmansberger T (2009) Bilateral investment treaties and EU law. CML Rev 46:383–429

Fecak T (2016) International investment agreements and EU law. Kluwer Law International

Gaillard E, Bermann GA (eds) (2016) UNCITRAL Secretariat Guide on the Convention on the Recognition and Enforcement of Foreign Arbitral Awards (New York, 1958). United Nations, Vienna. http://newyorkconvention1958.org/pdf/guide/2016_Guide_on_the_NY_Convention.pdf. Accessed 7 Dec 2019

Hess B (2018) The fate of investment dispute resolution after the Achmea decision of the European Court of Justice. MPILux Research Paper Series 2018(3). https://papers.ssrn.com/sol3/papers.cfm?abstract_id=3152972. Accessed 7 Dec 2019

Kriebaum U (2015) The fate of intra-EU BITs from an investment law and public international law perspective. ELTE Law J 2015(1):27–35

Lavranos N (2018) After Achmea: the need for an EU investment protection regulation. Kluwer Arbitration Blog. http://arbitrationblog.kluwerarbitration.com/2018/03/17/achmea-need-eu-investment-protection-regulation/. Accessed 7 Dec 2019

Maurer AG (2012) The public policy exception under the New York Convention history, interpretation and application. JurisNet, Huntington

Moses M (2018) Public policy: national, international and transnational. Kluwer Arbitration Blog. http://arbitrationblog.kluwerarbitration.com/2018/11/12/public-policy-national-international-and-transnational/. Accessed 7 Dec 2019

Nagy CI (2018) Intra-EU bilateral investment treaties and EU law after *Achmea*: "know well what leads you forward and what holds you back". German Law J 19:981–1016

Newing N, Alexander L, Meredith L (2018) What next for intra-EU investment arbitration? Thoughts on the Achmea decision. Kluwer Arbitration Blog. http://arbitrationblog.kluwerarbitration.com/2018/04/21/what-next-for-intra-eu-investment-arbitration-thoughts-on-the-achmea-decision/. Accessed 7 Dec 2019

Nikitin P (2018) The CJEU's Achmea judgment: getting through the five stages of grief. Kluwer Arbitration Blog. http://arbitrationblog.kluwerarbitration.com/2018/04/10/cjeus-achmea-judgment-getting-five-stages-grief/. Accessed 7 Dec 2019

Paschalidis P (2016) Arbitral tribunals and preliminary references to the EU Court of Justice. J Int Arbitr:1–23

Paulsson J (1995) Arbitration without privity. ICSID Rev – FJLJ 10:232–257

Ponomarov V (2018) CJEU does not buy Wathelet's opinion in Achmea – what is left unanswered? Kluwer Arbitration Blog. http://arbitrationblog.kluwerarbitration.com/2018/04/14/cjeu-not-buy-wathelets-opinion-achmea-left-unanswered/. Accessed 7 Dec 2019

Reinisch A (2012) Articles 30 and 59 of the Vienna Convention on the Law of Treaties in action: the decisions on jurisdiction in the Eastern Sugar and Eureko Investment Arbitrations. Leg Issues Econ Integrat 39:157–178

Reinisch A (2016) Will the EU's proposal concerning an investment court system for CETA and TTIP lead to enforceable awards? – The limits of modifying the ICSID Convention and the nature of investment arbitration. J Int Econ Law 19:761–786

Representative of the Government of Hungary (2019) Declaration on the Legal Consequences of the Judgment of the Court of Justice in *Achmea* and on Investment Protection in the European Union. http://www.kormany.hu/download/5/1b/81000/Hungarys%20Declaration%20on%20Achmea.pdf. Accessed 7 Dec 2019

Representatives of the Governments of the Member States (2019a) Declaration on the Enforcement of the Judgment of the Court of Justice in *Achmea* and on Investment Protection in the European Union. https://www.regeringen.se/48ee19/contentassets/d759689c0c804a9ea7af6b2de7320128/achmea-declaration.pdf. Accessed 7 Dec 2019

Representatives of the Governments of the Member States (2019b) Declaration on the Legal Consequences of the Judgment of the Court of Justice in *Achmea* and on Investment Protection in the European Union. https://ec.europa.eu/info/sites/info/files/business_economy_euro/banking_and_finance/documents/190117-bilateral-investment-treaties_en.pdf. Accessed 7 Dec 2019

Schreuer CH et al (2009) The ICSID Convention: A Commentary Art. 54. Cambridge

Singla T (2018) Achmea: the fate and future of intra-EU investment treaty awards under the New York Convention. EJIL: Talk! https://www.ejiltalk.org/achmea-the-fate-and-future-of-intra-eu-investment-treaty-awards-under-the-new-york-convention/. Accessed 7 Dec 2019

Söderlung C (2007) Intra-EU BIT investment protection and the EC treaty. J Int Arbitr 24:455–468

Stefan F (2018) Brace for impact? Examining the reach of Achmea v Slovakia. Kluwer Arbitration Blog. http://arbitrationblog.kluwerarbitration.com/2018/06/24/brace-for-impact-examining-the-reach-of-achmea-v-slovakia/?print=print. Accessed 7 Dec 2019

UNCTAD (2018) Fact sheet on intra-European Union investor-State arbitration cases IIA Issues Note. https://unctad.org/en/PublicationsLibrary/diaepcb2018d7_en.pdf. Accessed 7 Dec 2019

Vis-Dunbar D (2009) EU Member States reject the call to terminate intra-EU bilateral investment treaties. Investment Treaty News. https://www.iisd.org/itn/2009/02/10/eu-member-states-reject-the-call-to-terminate-intra-eu-bilateral-investment-treaties/. Accessed 7 Dec 2019

von Papp K (2013) Clash of "autonomous legal orders": can EU Member State courts bridge the jurisdictional divide between investment tribunals and the ECJ? A plea for direct referral from investment tribunals to the ECJ. CML Rev 50:1039–1082

Wehland H (2009) Intra-EU investment agreements and arbitration: is European Community law an obstacle? ICLQ 58:297–320

Wenhua S, Sheng Z (2010) The Treaty of Lisbon: half way toward a common investment policy. EJIL 21:1049–1073

Granting and Enforcing Interim Measures in International Commercial Arbitration in Bosnia and Herzegovina

Ilma Kasumagić

Contents

1 Introduction

Interim measures are an important remedy and tool in international arbitration. Because of the time gap between commencement of the proceedings and the grant of final relief, a relief sought in a principal action is often insufficient to protect the rights and/or interests of a requesting party. Namely, by the time arbitral award is issued, an opposing party may already cause irreparable and non-compensatory harm to the requesting party, and thus, in situations like these, effective protection of requesting party's position can be only achieved by appropriate interim measures. Interim measures take various forms and they are understood and applied differently

I. Kasumagić (✉)
Attorney at Law in Cooperation with Wolf Theiss, Sarajevo, Bosnia and Herzegovina
e-mail: ilma.kasumagic@lawoffice-kasumagic.com

Z. Meškić et al. (eds.), *Balkan Yearbook of European and International Law 2019*, Balkan Yearbook of European and International Law (2020) 2019: 91–108, https://doi.org/10.1007/16247_2019_6, Published online: 17 January 2020

in different legal systems. Generally, they are sought in the situation where there is an imminent risk that the opposing party will jeopardise the position of the requesting party by disposing of its assets or otherwise preventing the satisfaction of its claim in case it succeeds in the arbitral proceedings. Thus, adequate legal protection can be achieved provided that these measures, if ordered by an arbitral tribunal, are enforced by the competent state courts or, in case such interim measures cannot be obtained from an arbitral tribunal, both ordered and enforced by the competent state courts in support of arbitration. This paper investigates whether and to what extent this is currently possible in Bosnia and Herzegovina. The second chapter provides an overview of the reasons and forms of the interim measures in international commercial arbitration. The third chapter focuses on enforcement before the state courts of interim measures ordered by arbitrators or arbitral tribunals, while the following chapter discusses the jurisdiction of the courts to grant interim measures in support of arbitration.

2 Reasons and Forms of Interim Measures in International Commercial Arbitration

The power of arbitral tribunal to order interim relief depends on the agreement reached between the parties in this respect, which is either made explicitly in the arbitration agreement or done by the choice of the *lex arbitri* and/or the arbitration rules that allow arbitrators to order such relief. The power to order interim relief is considered implied in many arbitration laws and most leading international arbitration rules contain provisions for the granting of interim measures by the arbitral tribunal. In such instances, the parties are nevertheless free to agree otherwise.

Interim measures take various forms and they are understood and applied differently in different legal systems. In general, the arbitrators' authority in relation to the type of interim measures is limited as interim measures must be "in respect of the subject matter of the dispute", while protective measures not dealing directly with the subject matter are not covered.[1] In addition, the arbitral tribunal derives its powers from the arbitration agreement and thus, it cannot order acts to be done or omitted by third parties who are not parties to the arbitration agreement. While such measures may be available before the state courts, they cannot be granted by an arbitration tribunal. Finally, the arbitral tribunals' power to grant interim relief effectively arises with constituting the tribunal. Very often, measures are needed before that time and it is impossible or at least impractical to wait until the tribunal has been constituted.[2]

In response, many leading arbitral institutions have introduced emergency arbitrator procedures that seek to fill that gap by allowing parties to obtain urgent arbitral

[1]Lew et al. (2003), p. 592.

[2]Lew et al. (2003), p. 594.

relief before the tribunal is formed (e.g., International Centre for Dispute Resolution (ICDR) in 2006, the Stockholm Chamber of Commerce (SCC) and the Singapore International Arbitration Centre (SIAC) in 2010, the International Chamber of Commerce (ICC) in 2012, the Hong Kong International Arbitration Centre (HKIAC) in 2013, the London Court of International Arbitration (LCIA) in 2014). Under the emergency arbitrator procedures, a sole arbitrator is appointed by the arbitral institution on an expedited basis to decide on the applications for interim relief that cannot wait for the substantive tribunal to be set up. Generally, the relevant arbitral rules provide that decisions by an emergency arbitrator are interim binding as they can be subsequently varied or suspended by the substantive tribunal once formed. In some instances, such interim measures may expire by default after a certain period has elapsed.[3]

Depending on the applicable arbitral rules and/or law, an emergency arbitrator (and/or arbitral tribunal) may grant interim relief in a number of ways: in the form of a preliminary order, a procedural order, a direction, or an interim or partial award. The ICC, for example, requires that the emergency arbitrator's decisions take the form of an order, thus avoiding the ICC's "scrutiny" process for awards, which would delay the issuance of the emergency decision. By contrast, the SCC and ICDR rules permit a decision in the form of either an order or an award.[4] Regardless of the form of interim measure, because of lack of coercive power of emergency arbitrators and arbitral tribunals, the intervention of state courts will usually be necessary for the enforcement of the measure (see Sect. 3).

3 Enforcement of Interim Measures Ordered by the Arbitral Tribunal

3.1 General Overview

Arbitrators and arbitral tribunals in general lack the power to enforce orders over the parties or their assets, which is imminent to the state authorities. Moreover, penalties for non-compliance are only possible if the parties have either agreed to that effect or the applicable law specifically provides for it. Thus, the lack of coercive powers is at least partially compensated by the persuasive powers of the arbitral tribunal. Namely, it can draw negative inferences from non-compliance with its orders or consider that when deciding on the costs of arbitration.[5]

However, if parties do not comply with the measures ordered by the arbitral tribunal voluntarily, because of lack of coercive powers of the tribunal, intervention of state courts will be necessary for the enforcement of such measures. In the past,

[3]Valasek and de Jong (2018).

[4]Ibid.

[5]Lew et al. (2003), p. 610.

problems of enforcement have been one of the major arguments against interim measures ordered by arbitration tribunals. Provisions related to enforcement contained in national laws were usually interpreted to apply only to final awards. The provisional character disqualified any interim measure from enforcement under national laws. To deal with this problem, some modern arbitration laws contain special provisions regulating the enforcement of interim measures ordered by arbitral tribunals (e.g., see German CCP, Swiss PILA, English Arbitration Act and Austrian CCP).

In international commercial arbitration, the key enforcement mechanisms are the 1958 United Nations Convention on the Recognition and Enforcement of Foreign Arbitral Awards (New York Convention) and the applicable domestic arbitration laws, many of which are based on the UNCITRAL Model Law.

The New York Convention is silent on the question of interim measures ordered by arbitral tribunals. It applies only to "awards" and although there is no definition of "award", finality is considered an essential characteristic of awards in many jurisdictions.[6] In addition, in line with the Convention, a party may resist the enforcement of an award because it is not yet "binding", which is considered as a prevailing argument against the enforceability of interim orders and awards as only interim-binding, issued only for the duration of the arbitration proceedings and that can be reopened at any time during the proceedings.[7] This was illustrated by the Supreme Court of Queensland in *Resort Condominiums v Bolwell* where the court denied enforcement of an interim award issued by arbitral tribunal and held that:

> It does not appear that the relevant Arbitration Act or the New York Convention contemplates any type of "award" or "order" of an arbitrator, other than an award which determines at least all or some of the matters referred to the arbitrator for the decision [...] an interlocutory order which may be rescinded, suspended, varied or reopened by the tribunal which pronounced it, is not final and binding on the parties.[8]

On the other hand, the updated version of the UNICITRAL Model Law from 2006 covers the enforcement of interim measures under Article 17H pursuant to which an interim measure issued by an arbitral tribunal shall be recognised as binding and, unless otherwise provided by the arbitral tribunal, enforced upon application to the competent court, irrespective of the country in which it was issued, subject to the provisions of Article 17I (Grounds for refusing recognition or enforcement). However, it is unclear if the respective provision also applies to an emergency arbitrator interim relief.

In addition, it is worth mentioning that less than half of the signatories of the UNICITRAL Model Law adopted amendments from 2006. Moreover, a number of domestic arbitration laws, including those in some of the leading seats of arbitration

---

[6]Valasek and de Jong (2018).

[7]ICCA'S Guide to the Interpretation of the 1958 New York Convention: A Handbook for Judges (2011), p 18.

[8]*Resort Condominiums International, Inc v Ray Bolwell and others*, XX YBCA 628 (1995) (Supreme Court of Queensland, 29 October 1993).

(e.g., England, France and US), are not based on the UNCITRAL Model Law at all and only few domestic arbitration laws address the enforceability of emergency arbitrator relief.[9]

The approach taken by the state courts has varied across jurisdictions, whereas there is a visible tendency of growth of the pro-enforcement approach. In fact, some national legal systems are seeking to assist arbitration by enforcing interim measures either with express provisions or through the court practice. Courts have thus found that where interim measures rendered in arbitration finally dispose of certain issues, they are enforceable as awards. In the United States, for example, in *Island Creek Coal Sales Company v City of Gainesville Florida* (1985), the Court held that:

> Arbitrator interim measures are enforceable as an award provided the ruling containing the interim measure finally and definitely disposes of a self-contained issue.[10]

As noted, very often by the time arbitral award is issued, an opposing party may already cause irreparable and non-compensatory harm to the requesting party, and thus, in situations like these, effective protection of requesting party's position can be only achieved by appropriate interim measures. Accordingly, non-possibility to enforce such measures by state courts results in non-possibility to achieve adequate protection of requesting party's rights and interests and could lead in deterring parties from deciding to arbitrate their disputes. Thus, it seems that pro-enforcement approach in national legal systems is not only preferred but also necessary in international arbitration nowadays.

3.2 Enforcement of Interim Measures in Slovenia, Serbia and Croatia

The arbitration laws in Slovenia, Croatia and Serbia, which are chosen as a reference system because of the similarities with the legal system and legal traditions of the BiH, grant the arbitral tribunals the power to issue interim measures. However, enforcement of interim measures ordered by domestic arbitration still seems to be an issue in some of the countries in the region (e.g., Serbia). On the other hand, in Slovenia a comprehensive set of rules regulates enforcement of interim measures ordered by arbitral tribunals.

The Slovenian Arbitration Act[11] permits an arbitral tribunal to order interim measures. However, to be enforced in Slovenia, the interim measure must be recognised by the state court under a special procedure set out in the Article 43 of the Arbitration Act. In line with the Article 43 Slovenian Arbitration Act:

---

[9]Valasek and de Jong (2018).

[10]Ibid.

[11]Official Gazette of the Republic of Slovenia, no. 45/2008 of 9 May 2008.

> The recognition of an interim measure issued by a domestic arbitration shall be decided by the court having jurisdiction pursuant to the rules governing the enforcement and securing of claims.

Under the Slovenian Arbitration Act, interim measures issued by a domestic and foreign arbitration are treated equally; therefore, interim measures issued by a foreign arbitral tribunal are enforceable too. However, they also must be recognised by the state court before their enforcement. The court shall permit the enforcement of an interim measure ordered by an arbitral tribunal, unless a request for the issuance of the same interim measure has already been made before the court and/or grounds for refusal of declaration of enforceability of a domestic arbitral award exist (i.e., subject matter of the dispute is not capable of settlement by arbitration, or the award is in conflict with the public policy of the Republic of Slovenia) or grounds for refusal of recognition of a foreign arbitral award exist. The request for enforcement of interim measures may also be refused if the party against whom the enforcement has been sought establishes that the arbitral tribunal's decision with respect to the provision of security in connection with the interim measure has not been complied with or that the arbitral tribunal modified, suspended or terminated the interim measure.

In Croatia, under Article 16(2) of the Croatian Arbitration Act,[12] a party is entitled to request the enforcement of the interim measure ordered by an arbitral tribunal if the other party does not voluntarily comply with such a measure. However, in legal theory it is disputable as to what extent the state court is obliged to enforce the interim measures ordered by the arbitral tribunal if they do not meet the mandatory requirements set out in Croatian law (e.g., in relation to the probability of the claim and subjective risk that such claim would be jeopardised).[13] Another problem related to the lack of any requirements in the provision, which has been identified in the commentaries, is whether the court may refuse enforcement on the grounds of public policy. On the enforcement of the interim measures rendered by the arbitral tribunal seated abroad, the Croatian legal theory seems to have ununiformed standing. Because of non-existence of the official updated database of the relevant case law, it is not possible to say if there is any court practice in this respect, and what is the position of the acting judges, if any. Namely, under one standing the legal basis for the enforcement of the interim measures rendered by the arbitral tribunal seated abroad is in the Enforcement Act.[14] Under Article 19 of the Croatian Enforcement Act, a decision rendered by a foreign court may be enforced in the Republic of Croatia if such decision meets the preconditions for enforcement. Together with Article 24 of the Enforcement Act, where the "court decisions" is defined as "judgments, rulings, payment orders and other decisions rendered in a procedure before the court or the arbitration court", and Article 23 which among the "enforceable decisions" lists also the "enforceable arbitral award", the basis is

---

[12] Official Gazettes of Republic of Croatia, no. 88/2001.

[13] Triva and Uzelac (2007), p. 18.

[14] Official Gazettes of Republic of Croatia, nos. 112/12, 25/13, 93/14, 55/16, 73/17.

created for the enforcement in Croatia of the interim measures rendered by foreign arbitral tribunals.[15] However, according to other authors (i.e., A. Uzelac and T. Nagy), the right to turn to state court for enforcement of arbitral interim measures applies only to arbitral tribunals seated in Republic of Croatia even if the foreign interim measures are issued in the form of arbitral award. Namely, under Article 2 (1) paragraph 8) of the Croatian Arbitration Act the term "award" relates only to the decisions on the merits. Any decision on interim measures issued by a foreign arbitral tribunal would be considered as a procedural order, and its false denomination as an award would not make it enforceable under New York Convention or Croatian national laws. These authors conclude that parties can however submit a copy of the interim measure issued by arbitrators in the proceedings before Croatian state courts. Albeit not binding, this decision, in their opinion, could provide proof of the necessity of the measure, as well as provide usable guidance to the judge who decides on application.[16]

On the other hand, under the existing legal framework in Serbian law it remains unclear if interim measures issued by the arbitral tribunal in general can be enforced before the state courts. The Serbian Arbitration Act[17] was adopted in line with the UNCITRAL Model Law on International Commercial Arbitration[18] (UNCITRAL Model Law); however, amendments to the UNCITRAL Model Law adopted in 2006 are not incorporated therein. Consequently, the Act neither recognises the difference between interim measures and preliminary orders, nor regulates the enforcement of interim measures ordered by an arbitral tribunal. In general, the granting and enforcement of interim measures is regulated under the Enforcement and Security Act,[19] which contains explicit provisions in relation to measures ordered by the competent state court. The type of interim measures and conditions under which they can be granted differs from those provided under the Arbitration Law. Accordingly, it is the prevailing opinion that such provisions do not apply to the enforcement of interim measures ordered by the arbitral tribunal in line with the Arbitration Law.[20] On the enforcement of the interim measures rendered by the arbitral tribunal seated abroad, the Serbian legal theory seems to have a firm position that interim measures cannot be recognised and enforced before state courts.[21]

Although it can be seen that Slovenia, Croatian and Serbia did make significant step towards creating pro-arbitration friendly legal environment in relation to granting and (to certain extent) enforcing interim measures, it seems that any lack of explicit and clear provisions under national laws that enable court to recognise

[15]Butorac (2017), p. 244.

[16]Morek (2007), p. 88.

[17]Official Gazette of the Republic of Serbia, no. 46/2006.

[18]UNCITRAL Model Law on International Commercial Arbitration, UNCITRAL Yearbook, vol. XVI: 1985 (United Nations publication, Sales No. E.87.V.4).

[19]Official Gazette of the Republic of Serbia, no. 106/2015, 106/2016 and 113/2017.

[20]Knežević and Pavić (2015), p. 22.

[21]Varadi et al. (2012), p. 539.

and/or enforce interim measures ordered by the arbitration still results in narrow interpretation of existing legal framework. Accordingly, it can be concluded that amendments of relevant laws in Croatia and Serbia are needed to enable adequate protection of requesting party's position when such protection can be only achieved by interim measures enforced in these countries.

3.3 *Enforcement of Interim Measures in Bosnia and Herzegovina*

Before discussing the issue of interim measures in Bosnia and Herzegovina (BiH), it is necessary to point to the state's internal structure and competences. The state of BiH consists of two entities—the Federation of Bosnia and Herzegovina (FBiH) and the Republika Srpska (RS), and a special autonomous district under the direct sovereignty of the state—the Brčko District (BD). Litigation proceedings and arbitration, including interim measures ordered to secure the main claim, are regulated under the laws on civil proceedings adopted by each entity and BD.[22] Provisions on interim measures rendered in arbitration proceedings are fully harmonised under the Civil Proceedings Acts of both entities and accordingly, the below analysis applies to both entities, unless indicated otherwise.

In line with the entities' Civil Proceedings Acts, enforcement of interim measures ordered by the competent court in BiH is conducted before the court that has jurisdiction to enforce a final and binding court decision on the merits (secured with the relevant interim measure). Decision on interim measure has effect of decision on enforcement (*rješenje o izvršenju*)[23] while competent (enforcement) court only undertakes relevant activities in relation to enforcement of such decision (e.g., seizure of the assets). Accordingly, decision on interim measure has to contain all relevant elements/information needed for enforcement of such measure, i.e., type of interim measure, means and object of the enforcement (*sredstva i predmet izvršenja*), as required under the relevant enforcement law.[24] The jurisdiction for enforcement is established in line with the law governing the enforcement proceedings, in particular general rules on jurisdiction (based on the seat of the opposing party) or specific rules on jurisdiction (e.g., based on the location of the assets affected by such interim measure).

---

[22]FBiH Civil Proceedings Act (Official Gazettes of FBiH, nos. 53/03; 19/06, 98/15), RS Civil Proceedings Act (Officia Gazettes of RS, nos. 58/03, 85/03, 74/05, 63/07, 49/09, 61/13), BD Civil Proceedings Act (Official Gazettes of BD, no. 28/18).

[23]See Article 279 (3) of the Civil Proceedings Act.

[24]FBiH Enforcement Act (Official Gazettes of FBiH, nos.32/03, 33/06, 39/06, 39/09, 35/12, 46/16), RS Enforcement Act (Official Gazettes of RS, nos. 59/03, 85/03, 64/05, 118/07, 29/10, 57/12, 67/13, 98/14, 5/17, 66/18), BD Enforcement Act (Official Gazettes of BD, nos. 39/13, 47/17).

However, the Civil Proceedings Acts are silent on whether arbitral tribunals seated in BiH have the power to order interim measure and whether interim measures ordered by an arbitral tribunal can be enforced by the state courts in BiH. Namely, from procedural point of view, even if one argues that arbitral tribunals seated in BiH have the power to order interim measure because of lack of mandatory provisions stating otherwise, it is disputable if such measure can be enforced by the state courts in BiH.

As noted, in line with the Civil Proceedings Acts, interim measures ordered by the state courts in BiH have effect of a decision on enforcement and such interim measures are ex officio executed *(prinudno izvršene)* by competent (enforcement) courts. In any other case when enforcement is needed, relevant enforcement proceedings is commenced before the competent court, upon request of a party (motion for enforcement) based on an enforcement title document, such as an enforceable court decision or any other document defined as enforceable under special law. In that respect, a "court decision" has been defined as a judgment (*presuda*), a decree (*rješenje*) and any other decision issued in the course of the court or arbitral proceedings. In line with the relevant law, only binding (*pravosnažna*) court decision is "enforceable" and accordingly, deemed as an enforcement title document. Thus, it is disputable whether a decision on interim measures made by an arbitral tribunal would meet the requirements to be considered an enforcement title document.

However, even if it can be argued that interim measure issued by arbitral tribunal is enforceable title under the Enforcement Act, it remains unclear if competent (enforcement) court would be entitled to review such decision (and to which extent) and if it would be entitled to refuse enforcement of the relevant interim measure in case of non-compliance with the mandatory laws (e.g., in respect to conditions for granting interim measure, type of interim measure, etc.) and to which extent. Based on the information available to the author under the publicly available data and information provided by the courts in BiH, it was not possible to determine if there is any court practice established in this respect so far.

On the issue of enforcement of awards rendered by the foreign-seated arbitral tribunals, it should be noted that BiH is also a signatory country to the New York Convention. However, BiH has made three reservations concerning its application: (i) the Convention applies to the recognition and enforcement of awards made in the territory of another contracting state; (ii) the Convention applies only to disputes arising out of legal relationships, whether contractual or not, that are considered commercial under the national law; and (iii) the Convention does not apply retroactively pursuant to the reservation made by BiH. Based on the publicly available databases of the relevant court practice, there is no practice in BiH in relation to the interpretation and implementation of the New York Convention on the recognition of interim measures issued by foreign-seated arbitrations. Therefore, it is not possible to say whether the conservative approach to its interpretation will prevail as in some other jurisdictions mentioned above.

On the other hand, the recognition of foreign arbitral awards in BiH is also subject to the rules of recognition and enforcement under the Resolution of Conflicts with

Legislation of Other Countries in Certain Relations Act (PIL Act).[25] However, based on the majority view, interim measures are not final and binding awards, and thus they are not considered as awards within the meaning of the PIL that can be recognised and enforced before state courts.[26]

4 Granting Interim Measures by State Courts in Support of Arbitration

4.1 General Overview

In international arbitration, interim measures are generally sought in the situations where there is an imminent risk that the opposing party will jeopardise the position of the requesting party by disposing of its assets or otherwise preventing it from satisfying its claim in case it succeeds in the arbitration proceedings. Thus, effective protection of one's rights and interests in these situations can be achieved only if interim measures are ordered and enforced in urgent proceedings before the competent state court. This will, in particular, be the case if the tribunal is not yet composed and/or when assets affected by the relevant interim measure are located outside the country of the seat of arbitration. It is almost a universally accepted rule that state courts may order interim measures and that such an action is not an exercise of excessive jurisdiction by the court or a negation of the arbitration clause.

Under Article VI(4) of the European Convention on International Commercial Arbitration[27]:

> A request for interim measures or measures of conservation addressed to a judicial authority shall not be deemed incompatible with the arbitration agreement or regarded as a submission of the substance of the case to the court.

Similar provisions can be found in a number of arbitration laws adopted in line with the UNCITRAL Model Law that explicitly provides that:

> It is not incompatible with an arbitration agreement for a party to request, before or during arbitral proceedings, from a court an interim measure of protection and for a court to grant such measure.

As it can be seen from the wording of the respective provisions, the Model law permits such authorisation of state courts regardless of the seat of arbitration. However, some arbitration laws, even if based on the UNCITRAL Model Law,

[25] Official Gazettes of Socialist Federal Republic of Yugoslavia, nos. 43/082, 72/82, Official Gazettes of Republic of Bosnia and Herzegovina, nos. 2/92, 13/94.

[26] Varadi et al. (2012), p. 539.

[27] European Convention on International Commercial Arbitration of 1961 Done at Geneva, April 21, 1961 United Nations, Treaty Series, vol. 484, p. 364 No. 7041 (1963–1964).

differ in this respect by limiting such power of the courts only in relation to domestic arbitrations (e.g., India).[28]

Whether and to what extent a party is entitled to request interim measures from a state court, is usually provided under the arbitration agreement, either by clearly stipulating the agreement reached between the parties in this respect under the arbitration agreement or by referring to the application of particular rules and legal mechanisms provided therein. In that sense, a right to submit a request of interim measures to the state court(s) may be general (i.e., at any time during the arbitration proceedings) or limited to the time before the tribunal is constituted.

While UNCITRAL Arbitration Rules provide for only a general rule, under rules of many institutional arbitrations, different standards apply if measures are requested before the file has been transferred to the arbitral tribunal and for those requested thereafter. Under most of these rules, the right to refer to a court after the tribunal has been constituted may be restricted. For example, in line with Article 23(3) of the ICC Rules:

> Before the file is transmitted to the Arbitral Tribunal, and *in appropriate circumstances* even thereafter, the parties may apply to any competent judicial authority for interim or conservatory measures.[29]

Similar provisions are seen in the LCIA Rules as well. They limit the right to apply to a state court after the formation of the tribunal to *exceptional cases*. What are considered "appropriate circumstances" or "exceptional cases" is determined on case-by-case basis and depends on the particularities of the case at hand.

Finally, parties can agree to preclude a state court from granting interim measures. Based on the majority view, such intent of the parties would have to be explicitly stated under the agreement and a mere general reference often found in arbitration clauses that disputes shall be decided by arbitration to the exclusion of all court proceedings should not amount to exclusion of the court jurisdiction to grant interim measures.[30]

4.2 Interim Measures in Slovenia, Serbia and Croatia

There is a possibility to request interim measures before competent courts in Serbia, Slovenia and Croatia in aid to domestic arbitration; however, it remains unclear if it is possible to request interim measures before competent courts in aid to foreign-seated arbitration in some jurisdictions (e.g., in Croatia).

Under the Slovenian Arbitration Act, it is provided that:

---

[28] Lew et al. (2003), p. 618.

[29] Emphasis added.

[30] Lew et al. (2003), p. 614.

> It is not incompatible with an arbitration agreement for a court to grant, at the request of a party, before or during arbitral proceedings an interim measure of protection relating to the subject matter of the arbitration. This applies also in the case of arbitral proceedings abroad.

Under Article 15 of the Serbian Arbitration Law, each party is entitled, before the commencement of the arbitral proceedings or during the course of such proceedings, to request interim measures from the court and the court is further empowered to grant the requested measure. This provision applies even in case of foreign-seated arbitration. As the Serbian Arbitration Law is quiet on the form and content of the interim measures that may be issued by courts, the power of the courts shall be constrained by general provisions of the Enforcement and Security Act regulating the matter of interim measures, while the courts would be entitled to order the requested interim measures only if they find that the conditions prescribed in that law have been met.[31] Considering that the Enforcement and Security Act provides a non-exhaustive list of possible interim measures, directed at protecting a monetary claim and a non-monetary claim, the courts possess a wide range of discretion and may grant any type of interim measure they find appropriate.[32] The territorial competence to decide on such requests has been established under the Enforcement and Security Act pursuant to which the request for interim measures filed before or during arbitration proceedings shall be decided upon by a court, which is territorially competent to decide on the motion for enforcement.[33] This further implies that the respective rules on jurisdiction for enforcement should be followed, in particular general rules on jurisdiction (based on the seat of the opposing party) or specific rules on jurisdiction (based on the location of the assets affected by such interim measure).

In line with Article 44 of the Croatian Arbitration Act, it is not incompatible with an arbitration agreement for a party to request, before or during arbitral proceedings, a court to issue an interim measure and for it to grant one. This has been confirmed under the decision of the Croatian Supreme Court pursuant to which a court is authorised to grant interim measure, upon party's request, before or during arbitral proceedings, all in line with the Article 44 of the Croatian Arbitration Act, whereas in such case a court shall decide on interim measures under the relevant provisions of the Enforcement Act.[34] However, because of the scope of application of the Croatian Arbitration Act (to domestic-seated arbitration only), it remains unclear if the same would be applicable in the case of foreign-seated arbitrations. It could be argued that the provision of Article 44 of the Arbitration Act should be interpreted in a way that it provides for a jurisdiction of the Croatian courts to decide on the motion for interim measure in support of foreign-seated arbitration as long as the jurisdiction can be established in line with the rules of the Enforcement Act (e.g., based on the location of the assets affected by such interim measure). However, because of lack

[31]Bojović and Milačević (2016), p. 238.

[32]Stanivuković (2008), p. 18.

[33]See Article 448 (2) of the Enforcement and Security Act.

[34]Decision of the Croatian Supreme Court, no. Rev-671/17-2 dated 20 September 2017.

on publicly available case law database, it is not possible to confirm if there is any court practice established in this respect and what is current standing of the competent courts in Croatia.

4.3 Interim Measures in Bosnia and Herzegovina

4.3.1 General Overview

Under BiH law, interim measures are instruments of legal protection of the main claim when there is (a) a probability of its claim or rights and (b) a jeopardy that the opposing party could prevent or substantially complicate the realisation of the claim or rights of the party seeking interim measures by the disposal of its assets or otherwise adversely affect rights and interests of the party seeking the interim measure.

Provisions related to interim measures are contained in the Civil Proceedings Acts of the entities and BD (see Sect. 3.3). Under these laws, a request for interim measure is submitted to *the court that has a jurisdiction to decide on a main claim*. The request can be submitted before or after the lawsuit has been filed. If an interim measure is granted before the commencement of the litigation proceedings, the party seeking the interim measure will be obliged to commence the respective proceedings within 30 days from the date of the decision on the interim measure. As it will be further elaborated herein, the law remains silent on whether the jurisdiction of the state court can be established in the situations where the parties agreed that the main claim shall be subject to arbitral proceedings (see Sect. 3.3).

A request for interim measure has to be submitted in written form and has to contain the claim, type of the interim measure (defined in line with the law), statement of the facts and the evidence that supports the claim and respective request. The law recognises various types of the interim measures depending on the purpose of the interim measure in the case at hand. For example, to secure a monetary claim, there is a possibility to seek, *inter alia*, that the court issues the prohibition to the opposing party to dispose of its assets in the amount needed to secure the claim, or prohibition to the debtor of the opposing party to settle its debt towards its creditor/opposing party in the case at hand. To secure rights or maintain the *status quo,* the party seeking the injunction is entitled to ask for prohibition to the opposing party to undertake certain actions or an order to undertake certain actions to maintain the *status quo* or to prevent the damages that might be incurred by the party seeking the injunction.[35]

In case of urgency, a party seeking interim measures is also entitled to request preliminary interim relief (together with the request for the interim measure), where it has to prove that the request for an interim measure is a *prima facie* grounded and

[35]See Articles 271–273 of the Civil Proceedings Act.

that the preliminary interim relief is urgent, i.e., that any subsequently granted interim measure would lose its purpose if the requested preliminary interim relief is not granted. Such preliminary relief is issued in *ex-parte* proceedings and only the court decision on preliminary interim relief shall be served to the opposing party.[36]

Once the interim measure (or preliminary interim relief) is granted, it shall be enforced in line with the rules of the enforcement (see Sect. 3.3). If the court that ordered the interim measure does not have the jurisdiction to conduct the enforcement proceedings, it shall, *ex officio*, transfer the file to the competent (enforcement) court.

4.3.2 Jurisdiction of the State Courts to Order Interim Measures in Support of Arbitration

BiH does not have a single legislation providing for a detailed regulation of arbitration. Statutory provisions on arbitration are provided under the Civil Proceedings Act, in particular under nineteen articles set forth in Chap. 30 thereof. These provisions cover the formal validity of an arbitration agreement, the composition of an arbitral tribunal, the procedure for challenging the arbitrators, court involvement in the arbitral procedure, limited procedural aspects, and rendering and setting aside of the arbitral award. However, the Civil Proceedings Act does not explicitly provide for the possibility to apply its other provisions (those not contained under the respective chapter) to arbitration proceedings as a gap-filling mechanism. Therefore, it is unclear if and to what extent other provisions, including the provisions on interim measures, contained under the Civil Proceedings Act are applicable if parties agree to submit their dispute to arbitration in BiH. The jurisdiction to decide on the motion for interim measures is regulated under Article 268 of the Civil Proceedings Act, which states:

> Deciding on motion for interim measures, including interim measures over the property of the opposing party located outside of BiH, filed prior to or in the course of the litigation proceedings, falls under the competence of the court that has jurisdiction to decide on the main claim in relation to which the interim measure is requested.

Because the Act remains silent on whether the jurisdiction of a state court can be invoked when the parties have agreed that disputes arising out or in connection with their relationship shall be settled in arbitration, the question remains on whether it is possible to protect the interest of the requesting party by ordering interim measures before courts in BiH if parties agreed on a foreign-seated arbitration. It is questionable whether the jurisdiction of the state court could be established in support of arbitration by interpreting the provision in question using linguistic, systematic, historical and/or teleological methods. Where the wording is unclear, the adequate interpretation of a provision of law requires interpretation of its wording in light of the historical development, context in which the provisions is paced in the system

---

[36]See Article 278 of the Civil Proceedings Act.

and the underling aim of the provision(s).[37] As regards interim measures, that means that adequate interpretation of the Article 268 of the Civil Proceedings Act requires one to consider the underlying purpose of this legal mechanism (securing the rights and interests of the requesting party when mandatory conditions are met) and to determine, if under the systematic and/or teleological method of interpretation of the respective provision, there is a possibility to invoke a court's jurisdiction in support of arbitration.

Based on the drafting history of the provision of Article 268 of the Civil Proceedings Act, the main aim of the rule was to prevent the practice, present at the time, of concurrent jurisdiction between court that had jurisdiction for main claim, and court that had a territorial competence to order and enforce interim measures (see Sect. 3.3). The underlying rationale lies in a fact that such practice is contrary to the main principles of the litigation proceedings, which require that all requests raised by the parties be settled in most efficient way with least costs for the parties.[38] At the same time, it could not have been justified by protection of any greater interest which could not have been effectively protected otherwise.

On the other hand, it should be considered that in certain cases relief sought in a principal action is insufficient to protect the rights and/or interests of a requesting party, and accordingly granting and enforcing interim measure is a precondition to achieve effective protection of party's position. Since arbitration does not have coercive powers, a rationale behind current wording of the Article 268 of the Civil Proceedings Act, as defined in preceding paragraph, is not fully applicable in case parties agree on arbitration (i.e., prevention of concurrent jurisdiction between court that had jurisdiction for main claim, and court that had a territorial competence to order and enforce interim measures which could not have been justified by protection of any greater interest). At the same time, there are no statutory limitations under BiH law in respect to power of the state courts to decide on interim measure in support of arbitration if such jurisdiction could be established for the merits of the case in the absence of the arbitration agreement as long as it is in line with parties' intent expressed under the relevant agreement.

However, under the court case law the wording of Article 268 of the Civil Proceedings Act leaves very limited possibility for any interpretation that would differ from what is deemed by the courts a very clear wording of the provision explicitly stating that the jurisdiction to decide on interim measures lies with the court that has the jurisdiction to decide on the main claim. This analysis is based on the information available to the author under the publicly available data and official information provided by the competent courts in BiH, which is very limited in regard to this issue. Recent final and binding decisions issued by two second-instance courts (in Sarajevo[39] and Banja Luka[40]) ruled that state courts do not have the jurisdiction

[37]Harašić (2011), p. 57–72.

[38]See Article 10 of the Civil Proceedings Act.

[39]Decision of the Canton Court in Sarajevo, no. 65 0 Ps 706568 18 Mož, dated 19 September 2018.

[40]Decision of the Dictrict Court in Banja Luka, no. 71 0 P 265454 18 Mož, dated 3 October 2019.

to decide on interim measures when parties agreed on arbitration. In both cases, parties agreed that disputes arising out of or in connection with their contractual relationship shall be settled by and abroad seated arbitration. Since the respondents in the said cases were BiH companies, the claimants filed for interim measures before the competent courts in BiH that would have the jurisdiction to decide on the main claim in the respective cases if there was no arbitration agreement.

The Court in Sarajevo held that by agreeing to arbitration, the parties excluded the jurisdiction of state courts to decide on any issues related to such matters, including interim measures. Accordingly, it was concluded that the relevant undertakings of the requesting party are contrary to the arbitration agreement concluded between the parties. However, the Court failed to determine that the arbitration agreement explicitly provided that any dispute arising out of or in connection with the relevant relationship shall be settled in line with ICC Rules, which entails the applicability of all legal mechanisms provided under these rules, including Article 23(3). Under this provision, the parties may apply to any competent judicial authority for interim or conservatory measures before the file is transmitted to the arbitral tribunal and in appropriate circumstances even thereafter.

In its decision, the District Court in Banja Luka went a step further by reasoning that because of the mere existence of the arbitration agreement, the relevant dispute does not fall within the competence of the court, and thus the court is obliged to *ex officio* decline jurisdiction at any time in the course of the proceedings, until the decision on merits is final and binding. This reasoning could prove to be very problematic since it indicates that there is still a lack of understanding of arbitration in general, which results in a narrow and, to certain extent, erroneous interpretation of the mandatory laws. Under the applicable national law, court jurisdiction is declined because of the existence of the arbitration agreement based only on the respondent's timely objection to the court jurisdiction (which must be raised in the response to the lawsuit at the latest).[41] Accordingly, the existence of an agreement to arbitrate may not be raised at any time in the course of the proceedings, but only before or at the time of submitting the response to the lawsuit. In addition, this is not the issue to be determined by the court *ex officio*, as erroneously concluded by the District Court in Banja Luka.

It follows from the above that jurisdiction of the courts in BiH cannot be established if the parties agreed on the jurisdiction of an arbitral tribunal by entering into an arbitration agreement. Consequently, there is no ground to establish jurisdiction to decide on motion for interim measure by any state court in BiH.

[41] See Article 438 of the Civil Proceedings Act.

5 Conclusion

Based on the analysis of existing legal framework in BiH on interim measures issued and/or enforced by national courts in BiH in support of arbitration, we note that the current practice provides neither for legal certainty nor for an effective protection of rights and interests of the claimant. There is still an evident lack of understanding of the general principles of the arbitration law by some judges, which leads to narrow interpretation of the law. At the same time, it is evident that there is a need for a new legal framework that would provide a more detailed regulation of interim measures in arbitration. This could be achieved either by adopting a new law (on an entity or state level) or amending the respective Civil Proceedings Act.

What message does this carry for foreign investors in BiH? While there are various arguments why parties should refer disputes to arbitration (domestic-seated or foreign-seated), parties may be concerned about specific issues related to securing a claim before or in the course of the arbitral proceedings. Because BiH is lacking explicit provisions supporting arbitration and there is legal uncertainty about effective protection under available legal mechanisms, parties may generally be deterred from deciding to arbitrate their disputes in BiH. This being said, parties might be directed to explore other options. For the time being, investors should consider not relying on interim measures but rather secure their interests by other means, such as, for example, by security instruments that could be directly enforceable under BiH law.

References

Bojović M, Milačević J (2016) International arbitration. Global Legal Group, London

Butorac V (2017) Interpretation and application of the New York Convention in Croatia. In: Bermann GA (ed) Recognition and enforcement of foreign arbitral awards: the interpretation and application of the New York Convention by National Courts. Springer, Cham

Harašić Ž (2011) Viskovićeva teorija tumačenja u pravu, Zbornik radova Pravnog fakulteta u Splitu, Split

ICCA'S Guide to the Interpretation of the 1958 New York Convention: a Handbook for Judges (2011) Published by the International Council for Commercial Arbitration

Knežević G, Pavić V (2015) Arbitraža i ADR, Belgrade

Lew J, Mistelis L, Kröll SM (2003) Comparative international commercial arbitration. Kluwer Law International, The Hague

Morek R (2007) Interim measures in arbitration law and practice in Central and Eastern Europe: the need for further harmonization. Maklu Publishers and Association for International Arbitration

Stanivuković M (2008) Serbian arbitration law. Oxford University Press

Triva S, Uzelac A (2007) Hrvatsko arbitražno pravo, Zagreb

Valasek MJ, de Jong JA (2018) Enforceability of interim measures and emergency arbitrator decisions. https://www.nortonrosefulbright.com/en/knowledge/publications/6651d077/enforceability-of-interim-measures-and-emergency-arbitrator-decisions. Accessed 2 Mar 2019

Varadi T, Bordaš B, Knežević G, Pavić V (2012) Međunarodno privatno pravo, Belgrade

EU Directive on Unfair Trading Practices in Business-to-Business Relationships in the Agricultural and Food Supply Chain: Dipping a Toe in the Regulatory Waters?

Anna Piszcz

Contents

1 Introduction

This paper aims to critically review the provisions of the newly adopted Directive (EU) 2019/633 of the European Parliament and of the Council of 17 April 2019 on unfair trading practices in business-to-business (hereinafter, B2B) relationships in the agricultural and food supply chain (hereinafter, the UTP Directive).[1]

The following questions emerge as essential to achieve the research aim: What are the peculiarities that characterise the new provisions, also compared to the preceding proposal of a directive from the EU Commission? What are their pros and cons? What suggestions for further development of the legal framework, if any, can be formulated? What recommendations for national legislatures can be made?

First, the paper sheds light into the history of the EU developments in the field of regulating unfair trading practices (UTPs). Second, it analyses the scope *ratione personae* of the new legal framework. Third, it shows the scope *rationae materiae* of

[1]OJ L 111, 25.04.2019, p. 59.

A. Piszcz (✉)
Faculty of Law, University of Białystok, Białystok, Poland
e-mail: piszcz@uwb.edu.pl

Z. Meškić et al. (eds.), *Balkan Yearbook of European and International Law 2019*,
Balkan Yearbook of European and International Law (2020) 2019: 109–128,
https://doi.org/10.1007/16247_2019_7, Published online: 11 December 2019

the UTP Directive. In the last part, before the conclusion, the topic required a spot of further thought on public enforcement institutions and proceedings.

The point of the analysis is both normative and descriptive. The comparative method is employed to some extent, as the topic may benefit from being examined in the light of comparative evidence drawn from various Member States (mainly EU Central and Eastern European ones).

2 Background

First, one needs to distinguish competition law and laws aimed at preventing unfair trading practices. Competition law may capture certain UTPs in B2B relations, but, frequently, because of different objectives of competition law, UTPs fall within its scope neither at the EU level nor at Member State level. The EU competition law itself recognises this in the preamble to Regulation 1/2003 as follows: "Member States may under this Regulation implement on their territory national legislation that prohibits or imposes sanctions on acts of unfair trading practice, be they unilateral or contractual. Such legislation pursues a specific objective, irrespective of the actual or presumed effects of such acts on competition on the market".[2]

Moreover, the concept of unfair trading practices may seem normatively and contextually embedded within the unfair competition law and/or the contract law frame. At the EU level, UTPs are not, however, addressed directly within the frame of the Unfair Commercial Practices Directive, which stipulates in its preamble that: "This Directive directly protects consumer economic interests from unfair business-to-consumer commercial practices. Thereby, it also indirectly protects legitimate businesses from their competitors who do not play by the rules in this Directive and thus guarantees fair competition in fields coordinated by it. It is understood that there are other commercial practices which, although not harming consumers, may hurt competitors and business customers. The Commission should carefully examine the need for Community action in the field of unfair competition beyond the remit of this Directive and, if necessary, make a legislative proposal to cover these other aspects of unfair competition".[3]

On the other hand, a cross-sectoral EU instrument aiming at addressing certain unfair practices in trading relationships is Directive 2006/114/EC of the European

---

[2]Recital 9, Council Regulation (EC) No 1/2003 of 16 December 2002 on the implementation of the rules on competition laid down in Articles 81 and 82 of the Treaty, OJ L 1, 4.01.2003, p. 1.

[3]Recital 8, Directive 2005/29/EC of the European Parliament and of the Council of 11 May 2005 concerning unfair business-to-consumer commercial practices in the internal market and amending Council Directive 84/450/EEC, Directives 97/7/EC, 98/27/EC and 2002/65/EC of the European Parliament and of the Council and Regulation (EC) No 2006/2004 of the European Parliament and of the Council, OJ L 149, 11.06.2005, p. 22. Similarly, only consumers are protected against unfair terms in contracts by Council Directive 93/13/EEC of 5 April 1993 on unfair terms in consumer contracts, OJ L 95, 21.04.1993, p. 29.

Parliament and of the Council of 12 December 2006 concerning misleading and comparative advertising.[4] Its purpose is to protect traders against misleading advertising and the unfair consequences thereof.

Additionally, the specific issue of payment terms is dealt with by Directive 2011/7/EU of the European Parliament and of the Council of 16 February 2011 on combating late payment in commercial transactions.[5] It obliges Member States to provide that a contractual term or a practice relating to the date or period for payment, the rate of interest for late payment or the compensation for recovery costs is either unenforceable or gives rise to a claim for damages if it is grossly unfair to the creditor.

The UTP Directive seems to bridge the gaps between a "patchwork" of three areas of law used so far, to the possible extent, for counteracting UTPs: contract law, unfair competition law and competition law. These three parts of this "enforcement mosaic" are, however, beyond the frontiers of this paper. This background may shape the question whether the EU Commission have spent years developing expertise in the field of regulating unfair trading practices. In fact, the idea of regulating unfair trading practices was addressed by the EU Commission only recently in 2009,[6] when it published its first sectoral communication on the subject titled "A better functioning food supply chain in Europe".[7] In 2011, the EU Commission-led High Level Forum for a Better Functioning Food Supply Chain endorsed a set of principles of good practice in vertical relations in the food supply chain, which was agreed by organisations representing a majority of the operators in the food supply chain; those principles became the basis for the Supply Chain Initiative launched in 2013.[8] However, very soon the Supply Chain Initiative was considered unlikely to develop into a comprehensive governance framework. It was spotted quickly that because of its voluntary nature, it has not covered all operators in the food supply chain.

On 31 January 2013, the Commission published its Green Paper on unfair trading practices in the business-to-business (B2B) food and non-food supply chain.[9] Then, this non-sectoral initiative entered its public consultation stage. Next, in July 2014, the Commission released a communication titled "Tackling unfair practices in the B2B food supply chain"[10] encouraging Member States to look for ways to improve protection of small food producers and retailers against the unfair trading practices of

---

[4]Directive 2006/114/EC of the European Parliament and of the Council of 12 December 2006 concerning misleading and comparative advertising, OJ L 376, 27.12.2006, p. 21.

[5]Directive 2011/7/EU of the European Parliament and of the Council of 16 February 2011 on combating late payment in commercial transactions, OJ L 48, 23.02.2011, p. 1.

[6]For more on the Commission's works see Di Marcantonio and Ciaian (2017) and Renda et al. (2014).

[7]COM (2009) 591.

[8]See at https://www.supplychaininitiative.eu (accessed 7.04.2019).

[9]COM (2013) 37 final.

[10]COM (2014) 472 final.

their sometimes much stronger trading partners. Thus, it can be seen clearly that, in the meantime, the field of the Commission's works was narrowed again to only one sector. Since then, only sectoral initiative has been gaining momentum.

In the next document, "Report from the Commission to the European Parliament and the Council on unfair business-to-business trading practices in the food supply chain" of 29 January 2016,[11] the Commission concluded that at this stage there was no need for EU legislative measures in the field of unfair trading practices. The Commission took this view based on the idea that operators in the supply chains should participate in voluntary schemes designed to reduce unfair trading practices, and Member States should provide effective and independent enforcement at national level. Thus, regulatory initiatives in the discussed field were left by the Commission to Member States that through trial and error have gained a knowledge underpinning legislation, have worked out their ways to respond to UTPs and even have amended them rendering the original legal provisions more effective.

The U-turn by the Commission came after overwhelming opposition from the European Economic and Social Committee,[12] European Parliament (EP)[13] and the Council.[14] Within one year from the publication of the Commission's report, they "rallied" around the cause and called for actions to be taken at the EU level. The lack of action could have been damaging, particularly for some market participants, but also for the regulator's reputation.[15] This opposition resulted to the revision of the previous plans and the preparation of the Commission of its proposal against unfair trading practices in business-to-business food supply chains, which was preceded by an open public consultation that had taken place from August to November 2017.[16] The draft Directive of the European Parliament and of the Council on unfair trading practices in business-to-business relationships in the food supply chain (hereinafter, the draft Directive) was published on 12 April 2018.[17] The Commission admitted that it is difficult to give a precise quantitative estimate of how operators will benefit from a proposed directive because of its adoption and implementation; however, it emphasised that each of the targeted UTPs has a clear negative impact on their bottom line through the undue transfer of risk and generation of uncertainty.[18]

[11]COM (2016) 32 final.

[12]Opinion of 30 September 2016 on report from the Commission to the European Parliament and the Council on unfair business-to-business trading practices in the food supply chain, No. NAT/680.

[13]Resolution of 7 June 2016 on unfair trading practices in the food supply chain, No. P8_TA (2016) 0250.

[14]Conclusions of 12 December 2016 on strengthening the position of farmers in the food supply chain and tackling unfair trading practices, No. 15508/16.

[15]Daskalova (2018), p. 29.

[16]See https://ec.europa.eu/info/consultations/food-supply-chain_en (accessed 14.04.2019).

[17]COM (2018) 173 final, 2018/0082 (COD). See Piszcz (2018).

[18]Explanatory Memorandum, p. 10.

Some Member States' perception of the draft Directive was that it was much more liberal than domestic provisions; it received a negative reaction from them.[19] There were also some doubts in relation to whether "the mere existence of divergent legislation and its effects provide sufficient reasons for EU intervention".[20]

In October 2018, the EP's Committee on Agriculture and Rural Development evaluated the draft Directive. The Committee agreed that within the agricultural and food supply chain, imbalances in bargaining power between suppliers and buyers of agricultural and food products exist and are likely to generate and amplify significant negative social and environmental impacts in most countries producing agricultural products, both inside and outside the Union; that is a high price to pay for those imbalances in bargaining power. The Committee, however, recommended material amendments to the draft Directive.[21]

Negotiations commenced and in December 2018 the agreement on the directive was reached. The Council's Special Committee on Agriculture followed by the EP's Committee on Agriculture and Rural Development approved the agreed text allowing its submission for debate and plenary vote on, respectively, 11 and 12 March 2019.[22]

On 17 April 2019, Directive (EU) 2019/633 of the European Parliament and of the Council on unfair trading practices in business-to-business relationships in the agricultural and food supply chain was eventually adopted. A comparison of the UTP Directive with the EU Commission's proposal for a directive (draft Directive) enables us to arrive at a conclusion that explicitly confirmed interests protected by the UTP Directive are narrowly focused on those of agricultural producers and enterprises with an annual turnover of up to EUR 350,000,000 (including SMEs)[23] and on the living standards of the agricultural community,[24] whereas the EU Commission's proposal was loaded up with values scattered around its text such as food safety, SMEs' interests, fair standard of living, enhancing income, environment, deeper and fairer internal market, viable food production, maintaining market stability and improving agricultural competitiveness.[25]

Article 1(1) of the UTP Directive lays down the principle of the prospective harmonisation of national legislation, i.e., the minimum harmonisation ("this

---

[19]Pecotić Kaufman and Patrlj (2019), p. 83; Papp (2019), p. 152; Blažo et al. (2019), p. 258.

[20]Schebesta et al. (2018), pp. 8–9.

[21]Report of 10 October 2018 on the proposal for a directive of the European Parliament and of the Council on unfair trading practices in business-to-business relationships in the food supply chain, A8-0309/2018.

[22]See at http://www.europarl.europa.eu/legislative-train/theme-deeper-and-fairer-internal-market-with-a-strengthened-industrial-base-products/file-unfair-trading-practices-in-the-food-supply-chain (accessed 7.04.2019) and https://oeil.secure.europarl.europa.eu/oeil/popups/ficheprocedure.do?reference=2018/0082(COD)&l=en (accessed 8.04.2019).

[23]See, e.g., Recital 9.

[24]Recital 7.

[25]They can be found in the draft Directive, Explanatory Memorandum, Legislative Financial Statement. More see Piszcz (2018), pp. 150–152.

Directive establishes a minimum list of prohibited unfair trading practices in relations between buyers and suppliers in the agricultural and food supply chain and lays down minimum rules concerning the enforcement of those prohibitions and arrangements for coordination between enforcement authorities"). Article 9(1)–(2) is even much clearer than that, allowing both to maintain or introduce rules stricter than those laid down by the UTP Directive, and maintain or introduce rules aimed at combating unfair trading practices that are not within the scope of the UTP Directive. There are, however: one condition under Article 9—such rules need to be compatible with the rules on the functioning of the internal market—and additional, obvious condition laid down in the preamble to the UTP Directive—such rules need to be proportionate.[26]

A vast majority of Member States already have been adopting national (albeit diverging) rules on unfair trading practices in the food supply chain, starting from Germany in the 1970s. Consequently, in 2018, only 5 out of 28 Member States did not have specific regulations addressing UTPs.[27] The introduction of a minimum standard of protection under Union law is believed by the European Parliament and the Council to enable Member States to integrate the relevant rules into their national legal order in such a way as to enable cohesive regimes to be established.[28] However, it is rather full harmonisation, and not minimum harmonisation, that is a means of increasing cohesiveness. On the other hand, the minimum harmonisation better complies with the principles of subsidiarity and proportionality, respects the Member States' autonomy, allows to fully respect their legal traditions and gives them a freedom to propose more innovative and far-reaching solutions.[29]

3 Economic Agents Covered by the UTP Directive (*ratione personae*)

There are both differences and similarities between the scope *ratione personae* of the draft Directive and of the UTP Directive when we look a little closer. First, only suppliers are protected against unfair trading practices of buyers. Admittedly, a "one-sided" protection is preferred by the UTP Directive, as it was from the beginning of the draft Directive.[30] This means in turn that the rest of the relations between buyers and suppliers are out of the scope of the UTP Directive, possibly falling under contract law, unfair competition law and/or antitrust law. In some Member States, however, a "two-sided" protection (of both suppliers against buyers and buyers

[26]See also Recital 39, sentence 3 and Recital 40, sentence 1.

[27]Daskalova (2018), p. 2. Regarding Estonia see Pärn-Lee (2019), p. 130.

[28]Recital 39, sentence 2.

[29]Gac (2017), pp. 441 and 460.

[30]Piszcz (2018), pp. 152–153.

against suppliers) is available.[31] The principle of the minimum harmonisation described in the previous section of this paper should let them leave the previously built systems in this regard.[32]

A question open for debate is whether the protection of buyers of agricultural and food products in the supply chain—in addition to the protection of suppliers—in the future would be justified.[33] The review of the application of the UTP Directive under Article 12 should pay particular attention to this question. In practice, the use of unfair trading practices by suppliers occurs (although they are not as frequent as such practices of buyers). Leaving them outside the scope of the UTP Directive does not seem justified.

The UTP Directive defines "supplier" covering a broad range of entities in Article 2(4), where "any agricultural producer or any natural or legal person, irrespective of their place of establishment, who sells agricultural and food products", including "a group of such agricultural producers or a group of such natural and legal persons, such as producer organisations, organisations of suppliers and associations of such organisations", are encompassed.

The above definition considers unfair trading practices suffered downstream in the food supply chain, that is by intermediary suppliers of agricultural and food products (operators who are not farmers) whose weak bargaining position in the downstream chain makes them vulnerable to UTPs.[34] This, rightly, prevents unintended consequences for farmers due to trade being diverted to their investor-owned competitors—for example at the processing stage—which would not enjoy protection.

The term "buyer" means any natural or legal person, irrespective of that person's place of establishment, or any public authority in the Union, who buys agricultural and food products, including a group of such natural and legal persons.[35] Therefore, suppliers in the Union will be protected not only against unfair trading practices by buyers from the same Member State as the supplier or established in a different Member State than the supplier, but also against unfair trading practices by buyers established around the world.

Second, the category of small and medium-sized enterprises (SMEs) was a category around which the protection against unfair trading practices of non-SME buyers was constructed under the draft Directive, which was also accepted by the EP's Committee on Agriculture and Rural Development. The European Parliament and the Council took a bit different approach described in Recital 9 of the UTP Directive as a dynamic approach, considered a more relevant option for the

---

[31]E.g., in Bulgaria and Poland. For a deeper look at this, see Dinev (2019), pp. 57–58; Piszcz (2018), p. 152.

[32]See also Recital 40, sentence 2 ("(...) national rules could go beyond this Directive, for example as regards the (...) protection of buyers (...)").

[33]Recital 43, sentence 3.

[34]Recital 9, sentence 7.

[35]Article 2(2).

protection against unfair trading practices for those operators who need it most. It is based on the relative size, or rather relative bargaining power, of the supplier and the buyer, but in terms of annual turnover. The annual turnover is considered a suitable approximation for relative bargaining power.[36] Although Recital 9 of the UTP Directive recognises unfair trading practices in the agricultural and food supply chain as particularly harmful for SMEs, it assumes that the cascading effect on agricultural producers appears to be particularly significant for enterprises with an annual turnover of up to EUR 350,000,000. On the categories of suppliers protected under the UTP Directive, it is noteworthy that a significant proportion of farmer-constituted cooperatives are enterprises larger than SMEs but with an annual turnover not exceeding EUR 350,000,000.[37]

Under Article 1(2), the UTP Directive applies to certain unfair trading practices that occur in relation to sales of agricultural and food products by:

(a) suppliers which have an annual turnover not exceeding EUR 2,000,000 to buyers which have an annual turnover of more than EUR 2,000,000;
(b) suppliers which have an annual turnover of more than EUR 2,000,000 and not exceeding EUR 10,000,000 to buyers which have an annual turnover of more than EUR 10,000,000;
(c) suppliers which have an annual turnover of more than EUR 10,000,000 and not exceeding EUR 50,000,000 to buyers which have an annual turnover of more than EUR 50,000,000;
(d) suppliers which have an annual turnover of more than EUR 50,000,000 and not exceeding EUR 150,000,000 to buyers which have an annual turnover of more than EUR 150,000,000;
(e) suppliers which have an annual turnover of more than EUR 150,000,000 and not exceeding EUR 350,000,000 to buyers which have an annual turnover of more than EUR 350,000,000.

In other words, suppliers which have an annual turnover required for: (a) microenterprises are protected against buyers which have an annual turnover required for non-microenterprises, (b) small enterprises—against buyers which have an annual turnover required for medium and bigger (non-SME) enterprises; (c) medium enterprises—against buyers which have an annual turnover required for bigger (non-SME) enterprises. For the two additional categories (points (d)–(e)), the SME criteria are not central.

By way of derogation from the above, the second subparagraph of Article 1 (2) lays down the principle according to which the UTP Directive applies in relation to sales of agricultural and food products by suppliers which have an annual turnover not exceeding EUR 350,000,000 to all buyers which are public authorities. Public authorities are defined as national, regional or local authorities, bodies governed by public law or associations formed by one or more such authorities or one or more

[36] Recital 14, sentence 2.

[37] Recital 10, sentence 4.

such bodies governed by public law.[38] Unsurprisingly, all public authorities, when buying agricultural and food products, should be held to the same standards as enterprises.[39] Therefore, quite rightly, the adopted scheme includes a kind of presumption of strong bargaining power of buying public authorities, although this presumption cannot be rebutted with evidence to the contrary, based on, e.g., the frequency and/or size of orders.

As a category central to the scope *ratione personae* of the prohibition, the annual turnover—admittedly—gives operators predictability concerning their rights and obligations under the UTP Directive,[40] greater than in the case of the draft Directive that utilised a full range of criteria that must be met for a supplier to be considered SME and for a buyer to be considered non-SME enterprise. Moreover, the comparison allows to arrive at a conclusion that the protection under the draft Directive and based on the division between non-SME infringers and protected SME suppliers appeared to be narrower in scope than that under the UTP Directive.

The new provisions will not necessarily leave their imprint on national legal framework of Member States that provide for the protection of a broader scope, since the principle of the minimum harmonisation described in the previous section of this paper results in that the transformation of existing rules is not required.[41] However, the *de minimis* rules based on a turnover criterion would be challenged (e.g., Poland used to have such a rule before 11 December 2018).[42]

4 Scope *rationae materiae* of the UTP Directive

First, as concerns *rationae materiae*, the possible dimensions of the prohibition of unfair trading practices may be broken down into two:

- sectoral: limited to food (and agricultural) supply chains,
- non-sectoral: covering trade in general.

Sectoral prohibitions are set throughout the range of Member States, including Croatia, Czech Republic, Hungary, Lithuania, Poland, Slovakia.[43] Similarly, the UTP Directive should be considered narrowly focused, since it relates only to the agricultural and food supply chains. The EU legislature stresses the need to address unfair trading practices in this sector (primarily), stating that while business risk is inherent in all economic activity, agricultural production is particularly fraught with

[38]Article 2(3).

[39]Recital 11, sentence 1.

[40]Recital 14, sentence 3.

[41]See also Recital 40, sentence 2 ("(...) national rules could go beyond this Directive, for example as regards the size of the buyers and suppliers (...)").

[42]Piszcz (2018), p. 157.

[43]Jasser and Piszcz (2019), p. 273.

uncertainty because of its reliance on biological processes and its exposure to weather conditions.[44] In other words, there are some complex circumstances in which producers in that field must operate. Agricultural and food products (agricultural products, including fishery and aquaculture products[45]) are precisely defined in the UTP Directive as products listed in Annex I to the Treaty on the functioning of the European Union, as well as products not listed in that Annex, but processed for use as food using products listed in that Annex.[46] However, national rules could go beyond this definition, as regards the scope of products (and/or the scope of services).[47] Therefore, developing national prohibitions, so that they become non-sectoral prohibitions (or maintaining them where they already exist), is within a margin of manoeuvre for Member States.

Second, there are different kinds of legal techniques that can be employed on the prohibition of unfair trading practices. One of them is that of establishing the open-ended prohibition based on the definition of "unfair trading practices" (or equivalent, such as "unfair abuse of bargaining power/contractual advantage") employing the general clause of "good morals" (or similar) and accompanied by exemplifications of prohibited practices. The substantial part of the UTP Directive does not define the notion of "unfair trading practices", but Recital 1 of the preamble alludes to it when it notes that "imbalances in bargaining power are likely to lead to unfair trading practices when larger and more powerful trading partners seek to impose certain practices or contractual arrangements which are to their advantage in relation to a sales transaction" and also exemplifies such practices ("Such practices may, for example: grossly deviate from good commercial conduct, be contrary to good faith and fair dealing and be unilaterally imposed by one trading partner on the other; impose an unjustified and disproportionate transfer of economic risk from one trading partner to another; or impose a significant imbalance of rights and obligations on one trading partner. (...)"). Placing this in the preamble of the UTP Directive does not result in that those Member States that do not have the above notions in their legal frameworks will need to introduce them when developing national legislation and oblige enforcement institutions to prove the lack of good commercial conduct, good faith or fair dealing in particular cases. However, Recital 1 can have potentially profound effects on the interpretation of the UTP Directive and, consequently, national legal provisions resulting from its implementation.

Some reflection is also needed on the fact that the UTP Directive uses a definition of neither bargaining power (strong/superior/excessive bargaining power or contractual advantage) nor its abuse. It is a result of "measuring" bargaining power by the UTP Directive with the afore-mentioned annual turnover thresholds. It must be admitted that this approach allows for avoiding difficulties in defining bargaining power of operators (however named in individual countries, e.g., superior bargaining

[44]Recital 6.

[45]See Recital 5, sentence 3.

[46]Article 2(1).

[47]Recital 40, sentence 2.

position,[48] significant market power,[49] contractual advantage[50]). It is clear from the previous practice of Member States that the difficulties can be connected to the relativeness of bargaining power. The Czech example is instructive here, as the original relative concept of significant market power was replaced by a second type of the concept of significant market power, i.e., the absolute one assessed through a combination of the market structure, barriers to entry and financial power.[51] What some Member States did to simplify the application of the adopted concepts is the introduction of presumptions of bargaining power.[52] However, depending on the construction of this type of presumptions, they may not be exactly as efficient as an annual turnover threshold being the point at which the UTP Directive provides for the protection for suppliers or the application of prohibitions to buyers.

The legal technique consisting in establishing the open-ended prohibition is a common thread for the Czech Republic, Bulgaria and Poland.[53] It means for enforcement institutions the need to deal with ambiguity but also provides them with a degree of flexibility.

The second technique is that of establishing the closed list of prohibited trading practices that almost certainly reduces legal uncertainty of operators.[54] This second, more static approach has been in the EU Commission's agenda long before the adoption of the UTP Directive. In Article 3(1)–(2) of the draft Directive, the Commission built out four-point "black" list and four-point "grey" list of unfair trading practices. There is a real sense of evolution from these short lists of UTPs to, respectively:

- nine-point "black" list of the buyer's practices (understood as prohibited *per se*) related to: making late payments (a) or requiring payments (d, e), cancelling orders of perishable products (b), unilateral changes of the terms of a supply agreement (c) or refusal to confirm them in writing (f), unlawful acquisition, usage or disclosure of the trade secrets of the supplier (g), threat to carry out, or carrying out, acts of commercial retaliation against the supplier (h), requiring compensation from the supplier for certain costs (i);
- six-point "grey" list of the buyer's practices ("prohibited, unless they have been previously agreed in clear and unambiguous terms in the supply agreement or in a

48In Bulgaria: Dinev (2019), pp. 54 *et seq.*

49In the Czech Republic: Bejček et al. (2019), pp. 89 *et seq.*, in Hungary: Papp (2019), pp. 148 *et seq.* and in Lithuania: Moisejevas et al. (2019), pp. 195 *et seq.*

50Namysłowska and Piszcz (2019), pp. 223 *et seq.*

51Quite paradoxically, in practice it is being slightly shifted now to a more individualised (subjective) concept by the enforcement authority, which is considered to be in accordance with the more economic approach to enforcement; see Bejček et al. (2019), p. 122.

52In the Czech Republic: Bejček et al. (2019), pp. 103–105 and in Lithuania: Moisejevas et al. (2019), p. 192. See also the example of Croatia: Pecotić Kaufman and Patrlj (2019), p. 70.

53Jasser and Piszcz (2019), p. 274.

54Croatia, Hungary, Lithuania and Slovakia have them; see Jasser and Piszcz (2019), p. 274.

subsequent agreement between the supplier and the buyer"[55]) related to: the return of unsold products (a), charging payment from the supplier as a condition for certain activities of the buyer (b) or charging the supplier for staff for fitting-out premises used for the sale of the supplier's products (f), requiring the supplier to bear all or part of the cost of discounts (c) or to pay for the advertising (d) or marketing (e) by the buyer of products.

It is important to recognise that the late payment provisions laid down in UTP Directive constitute specific rules for the agricultural and food sector in relation to the provisions on the payment periods set out in Directive 2011/7/EU on combating late payment in commercial transactions.[56] The prohibition referred to in Article 3(1) (a) of the UTP Directive shall:

- be without prejudice to the consequences of late payments and remedies as laid down in Directive 2011/7/EU, which shall apply, by way of derogation from the payment periods set out in that Directive, on the basis of the payment periods set out in the UTP Directive;
- not apply to payments made by public entities providing healthcare in the meaning of point (b) of Article 4(4) of Directive 2011/7/EU.[57]

The national law of Member States lays down the definitions of supply agreements[58] and their formative elements.

Moreover, in both paragraph (1) and paragraph (2) of Article 3 of the UTP Directive, the EU legislature uses the additional component, absent from the draft Directive, i.e., "at least", which captures two crucial ideas. First, in fact, it results in that the lists created in Article 3 of the UTP Directive are open for Member States to broaden their scope in the case of their implementation to national legal frameworks or maintain the broader lists that are already in place. Second, it confirms the principle of the minimum harmonisation under Articles 1(1) and 9 of the UTP Directive.

What is ahead of Member States is ensuring that the prohibitions laid down in paragraphs (1)–(2) constitute overriding mandatory provisions, which are applicable to any situation falling within the scope of those prohibitions, irrespective of the law that would otherwise be applicable to the supply agreement between the parties.[59] National legal frameworks should evolve, so that they contain at least the same lists under Article 3 of the UTP Directive. National rules could go beyond the number and type of prohibited unfair trading practices listed in the Directive.[60] Member States will need to make amendments to those legal frameworks where the

[55]The quoted wording is considered "obscure" (Wolski 2019, pp. 36–38).

[56]Recital 18, sentence 1.

[57]Article 3 paragraph 1.

[58]Recital 24, sentence 2.

[59]Article 3 paragraph 4.

[60]Recital 40, sentence 3.

prohibition of unfair trading practices is set using the first legal technique mentioned above. The detailed prohibitions modelled on the lists contained in the UTP Directive must not "intersect" with the test for the application of the previous open-ended prohibition using criteria of "good morals" or similar. Such overlap could lead to "tensions" contrary to Article 3 of the UTP Directive inasmuch as it could exempt, in individual cases, some practices specifically prohibited by the UTP Directive, and thus, "revise" this prohibition. However, Member States can be heading towards maintaining the previous open-ended prohibition but only as playing a subsidiary role (besides the lists), i.e., prohibiting practices that are not within the lists contained in the UTP Directive.

Those Member States that realise the prohibition of UTPs through the second technique may need to fine-tune their legal provisions or, if there is no such need, can use the opportunity to improve the existing legal frameworks.

5 Public Enforcement Institutions and Proceedings

The institutional ("technical") and procedural design of public law enforcement has also received due regard from the EU legislature whose approach is based on decentralisation (enforcement by Member States). Under Article 4(1) of the UTP Directive, each Member State is required to designate one or more authorities to enforce the prohibitions laid down in Article 3 at national level ("enforcement authority"). The UTP Directive does not include too many recommendations on the designated enforcement authorities. From Article 6(1), it is clear that to ensure the effective enforcement of the prohibition of unfair trading practices, the designated enforcement authorities should have the necessary resources and expertise to perform their duties. In my opinion, ideally, each designated enforcement authority should have sufficient resources in terms of human resources (qualified staff able to conduct proficient assessments), financial means, technical and technological expertise and equipment, to ensure they are able to perform their tasks effectively. In the requirement for the designated enforcement authorities to have the necessary resources and expertise, the UTP Directive is similar to Directive (EU) 2019/1 of the European Parliament and of the Council of 11 December 2018 to empower the competition authorities of the Member States to be more effective enforcers and to ensure the proper functioning of the internal market.[61] However, it does not propose a legal "transplant" from the latter to be used in the enforcement of the UTPs prohibition, consisting in the requirement to have the necessary guarantees of independence for designated national authorities.[62] Although this requirement would be reasonable in the case of the enforcement of the UTPs prohibition if we

[61]OJ L 11, 14.01.2019, p. 3.

[62]Sousa Ferro (2018), pp. 133–134.

consider that the UTP Directive applies to all public authorities acting as buyers and they are held to the same standards as enterprises.

The enforcement authority does not have to be a newly established one. Member States can expand the mandate of an existing authority to realise economies of scope. However, it is only the Explanatory Memorandum to the draft Directive that submitted the example of existing enforcement authorities in the area of competition law, i.e., national competition authorities (NCAs).[63] It should perhaps have been obvious that, in numerous Member States, competences of national institutions long-established as NCAs would be, sooner or later, starting to cover the enforcement of the prohibition of unfair trading practices, especially that the interaction of the latter with competition law might be considered confusing. The power to investigate cases, as well as to take enforcement decisions concerning UTPs, is entrusted to competition authorities in Bulgaria, Croatia, Czech Republic, Lithuania, Poland, and also France, Germany and Italy. Competition law can be enforced by NCAs in their "purest" form (only competition protection) or be part of a broader system of competences of an NCA, including consumer protection (e.g., Poland, Finland) or sector-specific regulation (Estonia, Spain) or both (the Netherlands). As if that was not enough, in some Member States the enforcement of the UTPs prohibition is NCAs' additional competence. In Polish legal literature, concern has been expressed that a new "consolidating" trend might have appeared consisting of entrusting the NCA with regulatory competences in markets not covered by the competences of any other specialised authority.[64] A little more far-reaching concern has also been drawn from the fact that the vast majority of Member States have national authorities enforcing the UTPs prohibition, usually NCAs, empowered to carry out all the activities as stated in Article 6 of the UTP Directive, i.e., that to this extent the UTP Directive does not bring any real change (and, moreover, will not make any real difference in combating UTPs in the agricultural and food supply chains).[65]

Examples of the institutional design from Member States where other agencies were selected are rarer, e.g., in Hungary—National Food Chain Safety Office supervised by the Ministry of Agriculture, in Slovakia—Ministry of Agriculture and Rural Development, in Lithuania—Agency for Development of Agricultural Business and Market and State Agency of Food and Veterinary in the area of sectoral prohibition of unfair activities of business entities buying-selling raw milk and trading in dairy products, in Portugal—the Agency for Food and Economic Security as the main body to oversee economic activities in the food and non-food sectors.[66]

The analysis of the literal reading of Article 6 of the UTP Directive may lead to the conclusion that each Member State should designate an enforcement authority that will investigate cases, as well as take enforcement decisions concerning them (rather than an enforcement authority that only carries out the investigations and then

[63]Explanatory Memorandum, p. 14.

[64]Krasnodębska-Tomkiel (2017), p. 690.

[65]Wolski (2019), p. 38.

[66]Wolski (2019), p. 32.

brings the cases before a court for a decision on substance and/or on a fine[67]). This pattern is similar to that of most Member States adopted for NCAs. Yet the powers of enforcement authorities are determined not by reference to rules prescribing NCA's powers but based on the detailed provisions of the UTP Directive, although the parallel between them is considerable (but not unlimited). The powers of enforcement authorities under Article 6(1) of the UTP Directive are those related to: investigations of prohibited trading practices (a), gathering all necessary information to conduct investigations (b), unannounced on-site inspections within the framework of investigations (c), decisions finding an infringement of the prohibitions and requiring the buyer to bring the prohibited trading practice to an end, as well as abstaining from taking any such decision for certain reasons (d), fines and other equally effective penalties and interim measures (e), the publication of decisions on a regular basis (f).

In the vanguard of those competences, there are deterrents including the powers related to fines and other equally effective penalties, as well as to the publication investigation results. They can change behaviours and encourage developing pre-litigation solutions between the parties. Parties may be influenced in particular by effective and dissuasive fines.[68]

One of the competences of enforcement authorities is the power to initiate and conduct investigations on its own initiative or based on a complaint.[69] Some Member States shall be pressured to react to this requirement, if they have legal frameworks focusing specifically on an *ex officio* basis of the initiation of proceedings, even when it does not exclude the possibility of informing the agency about infringements (Czech Republic, Poland). In this context, the UTP Directive vest suppliers,[70] producer organisations, other organisations of suppliers, associations of such organisations and independent non-profit-making legal persons that have a legitimate interest in representing suppliers,[71] with the right to submit a complaint to the enforcement authority of the Member State in which either the suppliers, or the buyers suspected to have engaged in a prohibited trading practice,[72] are established. Fear of commercial retaliation has been an increasingly important factor in legislative works leading to the introduction of provisions requiring enforcement authorities to take the necessary measures to protect the information submitted to the authority.[73] In Article 5(4)–(6) a key set of the responsibilities of enforcement authorities related to complaints is defined. Member States shall ensure that the enforcement authority, within a reasonable period of time:

[67]But see the interpretation of Article 6(1)(e) in Recital 34, sentence 1.

[68]See Recital 34.

[69]Article 6(1)(a).

[70]Article 5(1).

[71]Article 5(2).

[72]Article 5(1).

[73]Article 5(3). See also Recital 28, sentence 6.

- inform the complainant of how it intends to follow up on the complaint;
- inform the complainant of the reasons for insufficient grounds for acting on a complaint;
- initiate, conduct and conclude an investigation of the complaint, where an enforcement authority considers that there are sufficient grounds for acting on a complaint.

It is not clear from this framework whether acting by the enforcement authority "on the basis of a complaint" means only acting in terms of complaints submitted by the afore-mentioned complainants or also others. The preamble has made the issue in question much more complex mentioning, quite reasonably, also complaints by whistle-blowers and anonymous complaints.[74] It is hard to imagine a system in which the enforcement authority could not act based on these complaints; however, the preamble could mirror the substantial part of the UTP Directive in a more accurate way (and vice versa) and not only have implications for the interpretation of the latter affecting its results.

The UTP Directive does not leave its imprint on the rules on the burden of proof to be applied in proceedings before the national enforcement authorities. Therefore, the rules on the burden of proof are those laid down by the national law of Member States.[75] The UTP Directive does not mention the standard of proof at all. Thus, it is for the national law to determine not only the party on whom the burden of proof lies (including reverse burdens of proof and/or intricate statutory defences) but also the extent to which the party has to prove its case or its certain elements. The focus should be centred, however, on that those proceedings should be shaped subject to appropriate safeguards in respect of rights of defence, meeting the standards of the general principles of Union law and the Charter of Fundamental Rights of the European Union.[76] These standard and their challenges are shown in details in the case-law of the Court of Justice of the European Union.

6 Conclusion

The UTP Directive and the preceding works have been intended to lead to a departure from the low-key enforcement in business-to-business relationships in the agricultural supply chains and food supply chains alike. However, there have since been discussions on the adequacy of the UTP Directive to face the challenges that Member States' legal frameworks are confronted with. Once speaking of the criticism of the legislative proposal (draft Directive) as being too liberal, a word may be said on the fact that, compared to the proposal from the Commission, additions

[74] Recital 28, sentence 2.

[75] Recital 24.

[76] Article 6(2).

and changes have been made to the UTP Directive in both "black" and "grey" parts of the catalogue (list) of prohibited unfair trading practices. With its many positions, this casuistic catalogue is a minimum target model for Member States. The minimum harmonisation is in this case a means of considering Member States' different preferences and so to design an ever more effective way of the protection against UTPs under national laws. The UTP Directive does not base the prohibition of UTPs on any open-ended concept of bargaining power, its abuse or unfairness. All of them, if used, would give the enforcement authority greater flexibility embedded in them. Most importantly, however, the approach adopted by the UTP Directive results in less ambiguity and, consequently, more legal certainty. On the scope *ratione personae*, solutions adopted in the UTP Directive do not entirely follow the Commission's line and, in the case of protected entities, they extend this scope to more than only SMEs. Furthermore, now only annual turnover is used as a suitable approximation for relative bargaining power, giving operators greater predictability concerning their rights and obligations. It is also worth emphasising that neither the broad definition of supplier nor the broad definition of buyer is controversial in and of itself. Rightly, the concept of buyer contains all public authorities, when buying agricultural and food products.

What remains unknown at the time of writing is how this regulatory landscape will be further developed at the EU level. First, attention should be attracted to the need for a "two-sided" protection, i.e., the protection of both suppliers against buyers and buyers against suppliers, which is missing from the UTP Directive. Perhaps it would not be very well-supported in the context of the current overall objectives of the UTP Directive, but suppliers' unfair B2B practices function in practice and the tools for counteracting them are equally needed. Second, it should be reconsidered whether it would not be more appropriate for the EU legislature to broaden the scope of the prohibition of unfair trading practices, thus making it a non-sectoral prohibition to use its legal power to protect operators in other sectors too. Third, the institutional and procedural design of public enforcement of the UPTs prohibition, modelled to a considerable extent on NCAs and respective competition law toolboxes, could be considered uncontroversial in itself; however, it would be most advisable to equip the enforcement authority with the guarantees of independence that should typically be attached to NCAs.

Member States shall work on the transposition of the UTP Directive into the national laws. They surely will be allowed to maintain or introduce non-sectoral prohibitions, a "two-sided" protection and/or the broader scope *ratione personae* of the protection as regards the size (turnover) of the buyers and/or suppliers. Member States should introduce (unless they have them already) at least the same "black" and "grey" lists of prohibited practices (in every detail) under the UTP Directive. On the other hand, the main solutions to be deleted are, first, *de minimis* rules that, when excluding the smallest operators and/or transactions from the protection, do not comply with the UTP Directive. Perhaps most importantly, all tests for the application of the previous open-ended prohibition using criteria of "good morals" or similar will need to be either removed or transformed into merely an instrument playing a subsidiary role (besides the "black" and "grey" lists), i.e., prohibiting practices that are not within the list contained in the UTP Directive. The typical national institutional solution is to designate NCAs as competent also in the field of UTPs. Generally, however, this approach, while aimed to realise economies of scale (but still inevitably having resource and cost implications), should jeopardise neither the extent nor quality of the NCA's work, in particular, competition protection. Since there are Member States that do not have proceedings initiated based on a complaint, they need to accommodate the public enforcement system to the UTP Directive and complete it, so that this system fits right into the UTP Directive's procedural standards.

References

Bejček J, Petr M, Pipková P (2019) Czech Republic. In: Piszcz A, Jasser A (eds) Legislation covering business-to-business unfair trading practices in the food supply chain in Central and Eastern European Countries. University of Warsaw Faculty of Management Press, Warszawa

Blažo O, Kováčiková H, Patakyová MT (2019) Slovakia. In: Piszcz A, Jasser A (eds) Legislation covering business-to-business unfair trading practices in the food supply chain in Central and Eastern European Countries. University of Warsaw Faculty of Management Press, Warszawa

Daskalova V (2018) Counterproductive regulation? The EU's (mis)adventures in regulating unfair trading practices in the food supply chain. Tilburg Law and Economics Center, Discussion Paper 27, pp 1–42

Di Marcantonio F, Ciaian P (eds) (2017) Unfair trading practices in the food supply chain: a literature review on methodologies, impacts and regulatory aspects. Publications Office of the European Union, Luxembourg

Dinev A (2019) Bulgaria. In: Piszcz A, Jasser A (eds) Legislation covering business-to-business unfair trading practices in the food supply chain in Central and Eastern European Countries. University of Warsaw Faculty of Management Press, Warszawa

Gac M (2017) Group litigation as an instrument of competition law enforcement – analysis based on European, French and Polish experience. University of Warsaw Faculty of Management Press, Warszawa

Jasser A, Piszcz A (2019) Summary. In: Piszcz A, Jasser A (eds) Legislation covering business-to-business unfair trading practices in the food supply chain in Central and Eastern European Countries. University of Warsaw Faculty of Management Press, Warszawa

Krasnodębska-Tomkiel M (2017) Kilka uwag na temat ustawy o przeciwdziałaniu nieuczciwemu wykorzystywaniu przewagi kontraktowej w obrocie produktami rolnymi i spożywczymi. In: Bernatt M, Jurkowska-Gomułka A, Namysłowska M, Piszcz A (eds) Wyzwania dla ochrony konkurencji i regulacji rynku. C.H. Beck, Warszawa

Moisejevas R, Mikelėnas V, Zaščiurinskaitė R (2019) Lithuania. In: Piszcz A, Jasser A (eds) Legislation covering business-to-business unfair trading practices in the food supply chain in Central and Eastern European Countries. University of Warsaw Faculty of Management Press, Warszawa

Namysłowska M, Piszcz A (2019) Poland. In: Piszcz A, Jasser A (eds) Legislation covering business-to-business unfair trading practices in the food supply chain in Central and Eastern European Countries. University of Warsaw Faculty of Management Press, Warszawa

Papp M (2019) Hungary. In: Piszcz A, Jasser A (eds) Legislation covering business-to-business unfair trading practices in the food supply chain in Central and Eastern European Countries. University of Warsaw Faculty of Management Press, Warszawa

Pärn-Lee E (2019) Estonia. In: Piszcz A, Jasser A (eds) Legislation covering business-to-business unfair trading practices in the food supply chain in Central and Eastern European Countries. University of Warsaw Faculty of Management Press, Warszawa

Pecotić Kaufman J, Patrlj V (2019) Croatia. In: Piszcz A, Jasser A (eds) Legislation covering business-to-business unfair trading practices in the food supply chain in Central and Eastern European Countries. University of Warsaw Faculty of Management Press, Warszawa

Piszcz A (2018) The EU 2018 Draft Directive on UTPs in B2b food supply chains and the Polish 2016 Act on combating the unfair use of superior bargaining power in the trade in agricultural and food products. Yearb Antitrust Regul Stud 11(17):143–167

Renda A, Cafaggi F, Pelkmans J, Iamicelli P, Correia de Brito A, Mustilli F, Bebber L (2014) Study on the legal framework covering business-to-business unfair trading practices in the retail supply chain. Retrieved from http://ec.europa.eu/internal_market/retail/docs/140711-study-utp-legal-framework_en.pdf

Schebesta H, Purnhagen KP, Keirsbilck B, Verdonk T (2018) Unfair trading practices in the food chain: regulating right? Wageningen Working Paper Law and Governance 3, pp 1–20. Retrieved from https://www.researchgate.net/publication/328305407_Unfair_Trading_Practices_in_the_Food_Chain_Regulating_Right

Sousa Ferro M (2018) Institutional design of national competition authorities: EU requirements. Competition Law Rev 13(2):109–137

Wolski D (2019) Regulating unfair trading practices in selected West European EU member states – in search of equilibrium. In: Piszcz A, Jasser A (eds) Legislation covering business-to-business unfair trading practices in the food supply chain in Central and Eastern European Countries. University of Warsaw Faculty of Management Press, Warszawa

The Effectiveness of Judicial Enforcement of the EU Consumer Protection Law

Emilia Mišćenić

Contents

1 Introduction

The development of consumer protection law has been at the forefront of many jurisdictions worldwide. At the Union level, consumer protection requirements are to be considered in defining and implementing other Union policies and activities under Article 12 of the Treaty of the Functioning of the European Union (hereinafter: TFEU),[1] while a high level of consumer protection is to be ensured by Union policies under Article 38 of the EU Charter of Fundamental Rights.[2] Consequently, the European Union has introduced various consumer protection measures to ensure greater consumer protection throughout, but also within its Member States (hereinafter: MS). An illustrative example is the famous Directive 93/13/EEC on protection

[1]Consolidated version of the Treaty on the Functioning of the European Union, OJ C 202/1, 7 June 2016.

[2]Charter of Fundamental Rights of the European Union, OJ C 202/389, 7 June 2016.

E. Mišćenić (✉)
Faculty of Law, University of Rijeka, Rijeka, Croatia
e-mail: emiscenic@pravri.hr

Z. Meškić et al. (eds.), *Balkan Yearbook of European and International Law 2019*,
Balkan Yearbook of European and International Law (2020) 2019: 129–154,
https://doi.org/10.1007/16247_2019_8, Published online: 5 December 2019

of consumers from unfair contract terms (hereinafter: UCTD),[3] Directive 2005/29/EC on unfair business-to-consumer commercial practices (UCPD),[4] as well as Directive 2011/83/EU on consumer rights (CRD).[5] Once these EU Directives have been transposed into the MS' national laws, the protection of consumer rights guaranteed by them has to be *effective*. This quest for effectiveness of the EU Directives at the MS' national level was developed by the CJEU in its case law, and here it plays two important roles. On the one hand, it provides for an effective protection of consumer rights at the national level; on the other hand, it guarantees a uniform interpretation and application of EU law across the Union. Nonetheless, the same CJEU case law that sets high demands upon the protection of consumer rights contains numerous obstacles that ordinary MS courts are faced with when enforcing consumer protection law. The latter sometimes concern even the most basic questions, such as who is to qualify a person as "consumer" in a national civil law dispute, the court or the claimant himself/herself?[6] Additionally, is consumer protection law to be observed *ex officio* by MS national courts,[7] and so on.[8]

Moreover, another ongoing battle concerns the role of courts in fulfilling their guarantee of effective enforcement of consumer protection law. This is the battle between the courts themselves and existing mechanisms of alternative dispute resolution (ADR), which can be found worldwide. Because of the mentioned obstacles and many other flaws of court proceedings, such as the length and expensiveness of national civil law procedures, there is a growing attitude that the enforcement of consumer protection law can be guaranteed more effectively by ADR bodies that are faster, cheaper and therefore more convenient for consumers.[9] To evaluate the role of the courts in the enforcement of consumer protection law, this paper first defines what

[3]Council Directive 93/13/EEC of 5 April 1993 on unfair terms in consumer contracts, OJ 1993 L 95/29.

[4]Directive 2005/29/EC of the European Parliament and of the Council of 11 May 2005 concerning unfair business-to-consumer commercial practices in the internal market and amending Council Directive 84/450/EEC, Directives 97/7/EC, 98/27/EC and 2002/65/EC of the European Parliament and of the Council and Regulation (EC) No 2006/2004 of the European Parliament and of the Council, OJ 2005 L 149/22.

[5]Directive 2011/83/EU of the European Parliament and of the Council of 25 October 2011 on consumer rights, amending Directive 93/13/EEC and Directive 1999/44/EC and repealing Directive 85/577/EEC and Directive 97/7/EC, OJ 2011 L 304/64, 22 November 2011.

[6]This issue appeared in the case *Faber*, where the court *Rechtbank Arnhem* (District Court, Arnhem, Netherlands) considered that there is no need to examine whether Ms. Faber is acting in her capacity as a consumer. See judgment of 4 June 2015, C-497/13, *Faber*, EU:C:2015:357.

[7]See *infra*, title 4.1.

[8]Many of these questions are elaborated in the *European Commission Evaluation Study of the Impact of National Procedural Laws and Practices on the Free Circulation of Judgements and on the Equivalence and Effectiveness of the Procedural Protection of Consumers under EU law*, JUST/2014/RCON/PR/CIVI/0082, February 2018, available at: http://ec.europa.eu/newsroom/just/document.cfm?action=display&doc_id=49503. Prof. Dr. Tomljenovic, judge of the General Court of the CJEU and the author of this paper were engaged by the Max Planck Institute Luxemburg to contribute to the research as national reporters for Croatia.

[9]Critically Rühl (2015), pp. 431–456.

is to be understood under the guarantee of effective enforcement in general; it then compares the role of the ordinary courts regarding ADR mechanisms, and finally questions the most important instrument of effective protection of consumer rights, namely the *ex officio* control and application of consumer protection law.

2 Effective Enforcement of the EU Consumer Protection Law

It has been a while since the CJEU set "*the requirement of giving Community law its **full effect** within the framework of the judicial systems of the Member States*".[10] Over the years, within its case law the CJEU has developed and established various institutions and principles guaranteeing the effectiveness or the so-called "*full effect*" of the EU law.[11] The variety of these interrelated instruments includes, for example, the request on *effet utile* of EU directives, as well as the request on effective (judicial) protection. While the "*effet utile*" requires from the MS to which the EU directive is addressed "*to adopt, within the framework of its national legal system, all the measures necessary to ensure that the directive is fully effective, in accordance with the objective it pursues*",[12] the principle of effective (judicial) protection[13] demands effective protection of the rights guaranteed by the relevant EU Directive or other relevant source of EU law.

This principle was developed by the CJEU by relying upon the general principle of efficient judicial protection common to the constitutional traditions of the MS and as enshrined in the European Convention for the Protection of Human Rights and Fundamental Freedoms (ECHR).[14] It was back in 1986 that the CJEU stated in the case *Marguerite Johnston v Chief Constable of the Royal Ulster Constabulary* that by the virtue of the Directive's provision "*interpreted in the light of the general principle*

[10]Judgment of 16 January 1974, C-166/73, *Rheinmühlen-Düsseldorf v Einfuhr- und Vorratsstelle für Getreide und Futtermittel*, EU:C:1974:3, para. 2.

[11]In this respect, the legal doctrine is having trouble in the interpretation of the meaning and relation between the principle of effectiveness and "effet utile" as one of its manifestations. While *Heinze* encompasses all under the principle of effectiveness, other authors observe "effet utile" as a special principle of EU law developed by the CJEU case law. A further problem can be recognised in relation to the inconsistent use of the relevant terminology, where the "principle of effective (judicial) protection" is often named "principle of effectiveness", while its subprinciple is called "principle of effectiveness in narrow sense". See Heinze (2009), p. 337.

[12]Judgment of 7 May 2002, C-478/99, *Commission v Sweden*, EU:C:2002:281, para. 15, by invoking cases C-336/97, *Commission* v *Italy* [1999] ECR I-3771, para. 19, and C-97/00, *Commission* v *France* [2001] ECR I-2053, para. 9.

[13]The corresponding German term relates to effective *legal* protection: *Grundsatz des effektiven Rechtsschutzes*.

[14]Judgment of 15 May 1986, C-222/84, *Marguerite Johnston v Chief Constable of the Royal Ulster Constabulary*, EU:C:1986:206, para. 18: "*The requirement of judicial control (...) reflects a general principle of law which underlies the constitutional traditions common to the Member*

stated above, all persons have the right to obtain an effective remedy in a competent court (. . .) It is for the Member States to ensure effective judicial control as regards compliance with the applicable provisions of Community law and of national legislation intended to give effect to the rights for which the directive provides."[15] Today, the reflection of this principle is found in Article 19(1) of the Treaty of the European Union (TEU),[16] as well as in Article 47 of the EU Charter of Fundamental Rights (EUCFR). Under the second sentence of Article 19(1) TEU introduced by the amendments to the Lisbon Treaty,[17] the MS "*shall provide remedies sufficient to ensure effective legal protection in the fields covered by Union law*". The access to justice and the right to a fair trial and effective remedy are guaranteed by Article 47 (1) EUCFR regulating that "*[e]veryone whose rights and freedoms guaranteed by the law of the Union are violated has the right to an effective remedy before a tribunal in compliance with the conditions laid down in this Article*".[18]

There are two important conclusions that can be derived from the above presented provisions of EU primary law. The first one concerns the request regarding the effectiveness of the enforcement of EU law. To this purpose, CJEU's case law developed two special principles of *effectiveness* and *equivalence* setting criteria that national (enforcement) rules have to comply with to guarantee an efficient legal protection at the level of the Member States. As it shall be demonstrated within this paper, these two principles play a special role in the enforcement of consumer protection law.[19] The second one concerns the role of the courts regarding other enforcement bodies. The latter are not excluded by the above Treaty provision requesting remedies ensuring *effective legal protection* in the fields covered by Union law including consumer protection law. The EU consumer protection directives foresee various enforcement possibilities. For example, Article 7 UCTD or Articles 11 to 12 UCPD refer to the protection of consumers' interests before the courts or other competent administrative bodies[20] and Article 13 UCPD requires from MS to introduce penalties for unfair commercial practices, which must be effective, proportionate and dissuasive, i.e., contribute to the "effet utile" of the directive. When elaborating the principle of *effectiveness*, the CJEU case law acknowledges the possibility of consumer protection before the *various national*

States. That principle is also laid down in Articles 6 and 13 of the European Convention for the Protection of Human Rights and Fundamental Freedoms of 4 November 1950."

[15] *Ibid.*, para. 19.

[16] Consolidated version of the Treaty on European Union, OJ C 202/1, 7 June 2016.

[17] Treaty of Lisbon, OJ C 306, 17 December 2007.

[18] On the role of Article 47 EUCFR see van Duin (2017), pp. 190–198; see also Mak (2014), pp. 236–258.

[19] See *infra*, title 4.

[20] Under Art. 7(2) UCTD "*The means referred to in paragraph 1 shall include provisions whereby persons or organizations, having a legitimate interest under national law in protecting consumers, may take action according to the national law concerned before the courts or before competent administrative bodies (. . .) so that they can apply appropriate and effective means to prevent the continued use of such terms.*"

bodies.[21] However, not all of the enforcement bodies protecting consumers' interests represent a "*tribunal*" under Article 47(2) EUCFR. The provision guarantees a fair trial by "*an independent and impartial tribunal previously established by law*". The same concerns exist regarding Article 267 TFEU enabling the CJEU a preliminary ruling on the interpretation or validity of EU law *only when* national courts and tribunals initiated the procedure. The CJEU Recommendations regarding preliminary ruling proceedings of 2016 relate to the status of courts and tribunals "*as a self-standing concept of EU law, (where) the Court (is) taking account of a number of factors such as whether the body making the reference is* ***established by law****, whether it is* ***permanent****, whether its jurisdiction is* ***compulsory****, whether its procedure is* ***inter partes****, whether it applies* ***rules of law*** *and whether it is* ***independent***".[22] It confirms the acknowledged standing of the CJEU case law, reflected in cases such as *De Coster*, where the Advocate General *Ruiz-Jarabo Colomer* elaborated when arbitral tribunals are out of the picture in the context of Article 267 TFEU.[23] This seems to be a very important conclusion for the enforcement of consumer rights arising from EU Directives. As a unique authority for the interpretation of EU law, the CJEU is ruling on the interpretation of key notions arising from the EU consumer protection directives. In doing so, the CJEU regularly accentuates the role of courts for the effective enforcement of consumer rights and *effective* ***judicial*** *protection of consumer rights and interests*.[24]

3 Judicial Protection *vs*. Alternative Dispute Resolution (ADR)

Even so, over the last twenty years the focus of consumer protection redress and enforcement has unquestionably been put on the establishment of consensual dispute resolution mechanisms. In 1998, the Commission issued the Recommendation 98/257/EC on the principles applicable to the bodies responsible for out-of-court settlement of consumer disputes that was followed by Recommendation 2001/310/

---

[21]Judgment of 3 October 2013, C-32/12, *Duarte Hueros*, EU:C:2013:637, para. 34; judgment of 14 June 2012, C-618/10, *Banco Español de Crédito*, EU:C:2012:349, para. 49; judgment of 14 March 2013, C-415/11, *Aziz*, EU:C:2013:164, para. 53; judgment of 6 October 2009, C-40/08, *Asturcom Telecomunicaciones*, EU:C:2009:615, para. 39 etc. stating that "*every case in which the question arises as to whether a national procedural provision makes the application of European Union law impossible or excessively difficult must be analysed by reference to the role of that provision in the procedure, its progress and its special features, viewed as a whole, before the various national bodies*".

[22]Recommendations to national courts and tribunals, in relation to the initiation of preliminary ruling proceedings, OJ C 439, 25 November 2016, p. 2. Emphasis added by the author.

[23]Extensive interpretation of the meaning of the notion "*courts or tribunals*" from *ex* Art. 234 TEC (now: Art. 267 TFEU) was given by the Advocate General *Ruiz-Jarabo Colomer* in the Opinion delivered on 28 June 2001 in the case C-17/00, *De Coster*, EU:C:2001:366 where he elaborated when arbitration tribunals or administrative bodies are excluded.

[24]See *infra*, title 4.1.

EC on the principles for out-of-court bodies involved in the consensual resolution of consumer disputes.[25] In 2008, Directive 2008/52 covered certain aspects of mediation in civil and commercial matters/EC,[26] while in 2013 the Directive 2013/11/EU on alternative dispute resolution for consumer disputes (ADR Directive)[27] was adopted. The ADR Directive is closely connected and intertwined with the Regulation (EU) No 524/2013 on online dispute resolution for consumer disputes (ODR Regulation)[28] establishing an Online Dispute Resolution Platform (ODR Platform). The ODR Platform[29] that was established in February 2016 "(...) *offers consumers and traders a single point of entry for the out-of-court resolution of online disputes, through ADR entities which are linked to the platform and offer ADR through quality ADR procedures*".[30] The primary goal of this recently introduced ADR/ODR system is to contribute to the better functioning of the EU Digital Single Market.[31] By offering faster and cheaper solutions for B2C online disputes, the EU legislation is guaranteeing more legal certainty for the parties in "*online sales and services contracts*"[32] and therefore boosting their confidence in cross-border and online trade in the EU Digital Single Market.[33]

In reality, the introduction of the European ADR/ODR regulation has not *de facto* affected significantly the already existing enforcement mechanisms of consumer

[25]Commission Recommendation 98/257/EC of 30 March 1998 on the principles applicable to the bodies responsible for out-of-court settlement of consumer disputes, OJ L 115, 17 April 1998, pp. 31–34; Commission Recommendation 2001/311/EC of 4 April 2001 on the principles for out-of-court bodies involved in the consensual resolution of consumer disputes, OJ L 109, 19 April 2001, pp. 56–61.

[26]Directive 2008/52/EC of the European Parliament and of the Council of 21 May 2008 on certain aspects of mediation in civil and commercial matters, OJ L 136, 24 May 2008, pp. 3–8.

[27]Directive 2013/11/EU of the European Parliament and of the Council of 21 May 2013 on alternative dispute resolution for consumer disputes and amending Regulation (EC) No 2006/2004 and Directive 2009/22/EC (Directive on consumer ADR), OJ L 165, 18.6.2013, pp. 63–79.

[28]Regulation (EU) No 524/2013 of the European Parliament and of the Council of 21 May 2013 on online dispute resolution for consumer disputes and amending Regulation (EC) No 2006/2004 and Directive 2009/22/EC (Regulation on consumer ODR), OJ L 165, 18.6.2013, pp. 63–79.

[29]The ODR platform is a web-based platform of the European Commission available at: https://ec.europa.eu/consumers/odr/main/index.cfm?event=main.home.show&lng=EN (last visited: 25 July 2018).

[30]Recital 11 of the ADR Directive.

[31]The *Digital Single Market Strategy for Europe* from 2015 defines it as the "*one in which the free movement of goods, persons, services and capital is ensured and where individuals and businesses can seamlessly access and exercise online activities under conditions of fair competition, and a high level of consumer and personal data protection, irrespective of their nationality or place of residence*". See Communication from the Commission to the European Parliament, the Council, the European Economic and Social Committee and the Committee of the Regions, *A Digital Single Market Strategy for Europe*, COM(2015) 192 final, Brussels, 6.5.2015.

[32]Art. 4(1)(e) of the ODR Regulation defines them as "*sales or service contract where the trader, or the trader's intermediary, has offered goods or services on a website or by other electronic means and the consumer has ordered such goods or services on that website or by other electronic means*".

[33]An overview was given by Mišćenić (2018a), pp. 219–246.

rights across the Union. The ODR platform is functioning as a contact point for both consumers and traders and contains information on available ADR bodies in every MS. Upon their request, applicants are encouraged to contact the so-called national contact points (NCPs) to solve their dispute in an out-of-court procedure. Despite the notion of an "online" procedure, the whole procedure does not guarantee an "online" solution of the dispute because numerous of the enlisted ADR bodies require the presence of the parties or their representatives during the proceeding.[34] One could also raise the question whether the enlisted out-of-court bodies of various MS can really guarantee an *effective* protection of consumer rights. Not only is the ADR/ODR system functioning as a mechanism for the complaints of both traders and consumers,[35] but some of the ADR bodies are far from being *independent* and include, for example, even private companies registered as ADR bodies on the ODR platform.[36,37] However, the key barrier to an effective enforcement of consumer protection laws is the fact that there are more than 10 various ADR bodies in every single MS, which operate according to their own rules, procedures and criteria.[38]

[34]As an example one could mention Belgium Commission Conciliation Automoto - Verzoeningscommissie Automoto, Commission de Litiges Voyages - Geschillen Commissie reizen, Croatian Mediation Centre of the Croatian Chamber of Trades and Crafts, Mediation Centre at the Croatian Insurance Bureau, French Association des médiateurs européens, Association L.A. Médiation, Centre de la Médiation de la Consommation des Conciliateurs de Justice (CM2C), Hungarian Conciliatory Body of Hajdú-Bihar County and many other ADR bodies requiring the physical presence of the parties and/or their representatives in some cases.

[35]Article 2(2) ODR Regulation and recital 16 ADR Directive.

[36]For example, the list of out-of-court bodies available in Croatia includes a registered company with limited liability PROFI TEST d.o.o., Centar za mirenje "Medijator". Under the German Gesetz zur Umsetzung der Richtlinie über alternative Streitbeilegung in Verbraucherangelegenheiten und zur Durchführung der Verordnung über Online-Streitbeilegung in Verbraucherangelegenheiten, BGBl. Jahrgang 2016 Teil I Nr. 9 vom 19. Februar 2016, an ADR entity can also be a private body, see §1(1): "*Dieses Gesetz gilt für die außergerichtliche Beilegung von Streitigkeiten durch eine nach diesem Gesetz anerkannte private Verbraucherschlichtungsstelle* (. . .)".

[37]Critically about this issue: Eidenmüller and Fries (2016), pp. 87–114.

[38]For example, the list of out-of-court bodies available in Germany is quite long: Allgemeine Verbraucherschlichtungsstelle des Zentrums für Schlichtung e. V., Anwaltliche Verbraucherschlichtungsstelle NRW e. V., Kundenbeschwerdestelle beim Bundesverband der Deutschen Volksbanken und Raiffeisenbanken e. V., Ombudsmann der Privaten Banken, Ombudsmann Immobilien IVD/VPB - Grunderwerb und Verwaltung, Ombudsmann Private Kranken- und Pflegeversicherung, Ombudsstelle für Investmentfonds, Ombudsstelle für Sachwerte und Investmentvermögen, Schlichtungsstelle Bausparen, Schlichtungsstelle bei der Bundesanstalt für Finanzdienstleistungsaufsicht, Schlichtungsstelle bei der Deutschen Bundesbank, Schlichtungsstelle beim Deutschen Sparkassen- und Giroverband e. V., Schlichtungsstelle der Rechtsanwaltschaft, Schlichtungsstelle Energie e. V., Schlichtungsstelle für gewerbliche Versicherungs-, Anlage- und Kreditvermittlung, Schlichtungsstelle Luftverkehr beim Bundesamt für Justiz, Schlichtungsstelle Nahverkehr, Schlichtungsstelle Post der Bundesnetzagentur, SNUB - Die Nahverkehr-Schlichtungsstelle, söp_Schlichtungsstelle für den öffentlichen Personenverkehr e. V., Sparkassen-Schlichtungsstelle Baden-Württemberg, Verbraucherschlichtungsstelle beim Bundesverband Öffentlicher Banken Deutschlands e. V. (VÖB), Verbraucherschlichtungsstelle Telekommunikation der Bundesnetzagentur, Versicherungsombudsmann e. V., VuV-Ombudsstelle beim Verband unabhängiger Vermögensverwalter Deutschland e. V.

The ADR Directive acknowledges this issue and accentuates in its preamble that "*ADR has not been correctly established and is not running satisfactorily in all geographical areas or business sectors in the Union*".[39] To this purpose, the ADR Directive introduced common rules, criteria and principles applicable to all existing ADR mechanisms and procedures across the Union. For example, Article 8 ADR Directive establishes rules, which facilitate the access of consumers to ADR entities and procedures,[40] while Article 6 requires the *expertise*, *independence* and *impartiality* of the competent staff working in ADR bodies. The ADR Directive emphasises the need for the *transparency* and *efficiency* of ADR procedures,[41] and introduces criteria concerning their *fairness* and *legality*.[42] The new rules require from all traders established in the Union and engaged in online sales or services to provide on their official website and within the general terms of business the information on ADR bodies together with a link to the ODR platform.[43]

Despite its many advantages, the ADR/ODR system suffers from many disadvantages.[44] Under the ADR Directive, "*ensuring access to simple, efficient, fast and low-cost ways of resolving domestic and cross-border disputes which arise from sales or service contracts should benefit consumers and therefore boost their confidence in the market*".[45] However, the transposition of the ADR Directive into the laws of different MS revealed problems regarding its scope of application.[46] By mixing the ADR rules on the scope of application of the above-mentioned criteria with all domestic and cross-border disputes from Article 2, and those on the access to ADR bodies from Article 5 of the ADR Directive, numerous MS, such as the United Kingdom, Austria, Slovenia, Slovakia and Croatia significantly restricted the scope

---

[39]Recital 5 ADR Directive.

[40]An exception to this rule is Art. 5(4) ADR Directive allowing MS to permit to ADR entities to refuse solving the dispute in the therein enumerated cases, such as when the consumer omitted to contact the trader previously with the intention of solving the dispute, where the dispute is frivolous or vexatious etc.

[41]Arts. 7 to 8 ADR Directive.

[42]Arts. 9 and 11 ADR Directive.

[43]Under Art. 13 ADR Directive, such a duty exists also regarding online marketplaces, e.g., online platforms, where traders offer their products to consumers online. According to recital 30 of the ODR Regulation preamble, traders can use clickable web-banners available in the different EU languages to signpost the ODR platform.

[44]For critical remarks on the ADR system see Cauffmann (2016), pp. 155–160; Weber (2015), pp. 265–285; Inchausti (2014), pp. 197–208.

[45]Recital 4 ADR Directive.

[46]Under Art. 2 ADR Directive the above mentioned criteria are applicable to "*procedures for the out-of-court resolution of domestic and cross-border disputes concerning contractual obligations stemming from sales contracts or service contracts between a trader established in the Union and a consumer resident in the Union through the intervention of an ADR entity which proposes or imposes a solution or brings the parties together with the aim of facilitating an amicable solution*". Art. 2(1) of ADR Directive. Art. 2(2) enumerates the list of procedures to which these criteria are not applicable, such as procedures before consumer complaint-handling systems operated by the trader, disputes between traders, procedures initiated by a trader against a consumer etc.

of application of the ADR rules regarding "*cross-border disputes*". Although the rules of the ADR Directive should apply to the out-of-court resolution of *domestic*[47] and *cross-border*[48] disputes, the transposition acts of these countries limited their scope of application to domestic disputes and disputes involving only traders established on their own territories.[49] This is a direct consequence of the misunderstanding of the provision of Article 5(1) of the ADR Directive regulating that MS are about to facilitate access by the consumers to the ADR procedures and "*ensure that disputes covered by this Directive and which involve a trader established on their respective territories can be submitted to an ADR entity which complies with the requirements set out in this Directive*". Unfortunately for consumers, this misunderstanding left the mainstream of B2C cases in which domestic consumers are buying online from traders established abroad in another MS out of the picture.[50] By

[47]Under Art. 4(1)(e) ADR Directive "'*domestic dispute*' means a contractual dispute arising from a sales or service contract where, at the time the consumer orders the goods or services, the consumer is resident in the same Member State as that in which the trader is established".

[48]Under Art. 4(1)(f) ADR Directive "'*cross-border dispute*' means a contractual dispute arising from a sales or service contract where, at the time the consumer orders the goods or services, the consumer is resident in a Member State other than the Member State in which the trader is established".

[49]For example, the United Kingdom regulation from 2015, No. 1392, Consumer Protection, The Alternative Dispute Resolution for Consumer Disputes (Amendment) Regulations 2015 defines cross-border dispute as a "(...) dispute concerning contractual obligations arising from a sales contract or a service contract where, at the time the consumer orders the goods or services, the *trader is established in the United Kingdom* and the consumer is resident in another member State". Similar definitions can be found in §1(1) of the Austrian Bundesgesetz über alternative Streitbeilegung in Verbraucherangelegenheiten (Alternative-Streitbeilegung-Gesetz—AStG), BGBl. I Nr. 105/2015 last amended by BGBl. I Nr. 32/2018 referring to domestic and cross-border disputes between "(...) *einem in Österreich niedergelassenen Unternehmer* und einem in Österreich oder in einem sonstigen Vertragsstaat des Abkommens über den Europäischen Wirtschaftsraum wohnhaften Verbraucher", or Art. 4(4) of the Slovenian Zakon o izvensodnem reševanju potrošniških sporov, Ur. l. 81/2015 defining cross-border dispute as a dispute between the consumer resident in the MS and the trader established in Slovenia: "(...) spor, ki izvira iz pogodbenega razmerja med ponudnikom in potrošnikom, kadar ima potrošnik ob naročilu blaga ali storitev prebivališče v državi članici Evropske unije, ponudnik pa sedež v Republiki Sloveniji, *ponudnik pa sedež v Republiki Sloveniji*". Corresponding definitions can be found in §1(2) of the Slovakian ZÁKON z 12. novembra 2015 o alternatívnom riešení spotrebiteľských sporov a o zmene a doplnení niektorých zákonov, 391/2015 Z.z. and in Art. 1 on the scope of application of the Croatian Zakon o alternativnom rješavanju potrošačkih sporova, NN br. 121/16.

[50]However, this is not the case in all MS, such as Italy, Ireland, Malta or France, which transposed the definition from Art. 4(1)(f) ADR Directive correctly. For example, Art. 1(c) of the French Ordonnance n° 2015-1033 du 20 août 2015 relative au règlement extrajudiciaire des litiges de consommation NOR: EINC1512728R, JORF n°0192 du 21 août 2015, page 14721 texte n° 43 defines the cross-border dispute as: "(...) *un litige de nature contractuelle entre un consommateur et un professionnel portant sur l'exécution d'un contrat de vente ou de fourniture de services, lorsqu'au moment de sa conclusion le consommateur réside dans un Etat membre autre que celui du lieu d'établissement du professionnel.*" Corresponding definitions can be found in Art. 1(2)(f) of the Italian Decreto Legislativo, 6 agosto 2015, No. 130, Ireland S.I. No. 343/2015, European Union Alternative Dispute Resolution for Consumer Disputes Regulations 2015, and Malta Consumer Alternative Dispute Resolution (General) Regulations, 2015, Consumer Affairs Act (CAP. 378), Gov. gazette No. 19503 from 20 November 2015. There are also some excellent

restricting the definition of "*cross-border disputes*" only to those involving traders from their own countries, MS violated the minimum harmonisation standard from Article 2(3) of the ADR Directive according to which MS may maintain or introduce rules that go beyond and not restrict those laid down by the Directive.[51] Moreover, a poor formulation of Article 5(1) on access to ADR entities and procedures is often incorrectly interpreted as a limitation of procedural jurisdiction of ADR bodies only to "those" cross-border disputes despite the fact that the ADR Directive is not amending the already existing MS' rules of procedure of various ADR bodies. At the end of the day, the criteria and standards introduced by the ADR Directive are in some MS not applicable to out-of-court disputes between domestic consumers and foreign traders to the detriment of the consumers. This is in direct conflict with the goal of the ADR Directive ensuring that "*consumers have access to high-quality, transparent, effective and fair out-of-court redress mechanisms no matter where they reside in the Union.*"[52] It is also in direct conflict with the recitals of its preamble according to which the ADR Directive "*should allow traders established in a Member State to be covered by an ADR entity which is established in another Member State*"[53] and "*should establish quality requirements of ADR entities, which should ensure the same level of protection and rights for consumers in both domestic and cross-border disputes*".[54]

These arguments demonstrate that the ADR mechanisms will not be able to extinguish the role of the courts in the enforcement of consumer protection law in the EU.[55] As seen, the implementation of the ADR Directive resulted in the adoption of various MS' laws transposing the Directive and therefore did not reduce the level of legal fragmentation or the number of available ADR mechanisms across the MS. As an example, in Croatia the ADR procedures before the Courts of Honour of the Croatian Chamber of Economy and of the Croatian Chamber of Trades and Crafts are regulated by their own Ordinances,[56] the mediation is subject to the

---

solutions, such as the German model, which circumvented the whole issue by omitting the distinction between domestic and cross-border disputes and applying the standards from the ADR Directive to *consumer disputes* in general. See Gesetz zur Umsetzung der Richtlinie über alternative Streitbeilegung in Verbraucherangelegenheiten und zur Durchführung der Verordnung über Online-Streitbeilegung in Verbraucherangelegenheiten, BGBl. Jahrgang 2016 Teil I Nr. 9 vom 19. Februar 2016.

[51]Accordingly, MS are allowed to expand the scope of their national laws transposing the ADR Directive also to disputes explicitly excluded from its scope of application or to adopt and maintain provisions on procedures for the out-of-court resolution of disputes between traders or disputes initiated by traders against consumers. See recital 16 and Art. 2(2)(a) ADR Directive.

[52]Art. 2(3) ADR Directive.

[53]Recital 26 ADR Directive.

[54]Recital 38 ADR Directive.

[55]The legal doctrine is sharing this view; see Eidenmüller and Fries (2016), p. 113; Rühl (2015), p. 431; Cortés (2015), pp. 114–141.

[56]Ordinance of the Court of Honour of the Croatian Chamber of Economy (*Pravilnik o Sudu časti pri Hrvatskoj gospodarskoj komori*) OG Nos. 66/06, 114/06, 129/07, 8/08, 74/15 and 6/18; Ordinance of the Court of Honour of the Croatian Chamber of Trades and Crafts (*Pravilnik Suda časti Hrvatske obrtničke komore*) OG No. 22/17.

Mediation Act and its by-law,[57] while the arbitration is regulated by the Arbitration Act.[58] Regarding the consumer protection law, which has been harmonised with the EU *acquis,* further provisions on ADR can be found in the Consumer Protection Act, Consumer Credit Act, Insurance Act, Payment System Act etc.[59] Moreover, the use of ADR mechanisms is *not mandatory* and does not exclude the jurisdiction of courts in most of the MS.[60] An exception is the French legal system, where a hurried implementation of the ADR Directive in 2016 resulted in the introduction of an obligatory mediation procedure before judicial proceedings on consumer protection.[61] Another exception exists under the German law, where Section 15a(1) of the Introductory Act to the German Code of Civil Procedure foresees an option for state governments to institute obligatory out-of-court conflict resolution for specific civil matters.[62] Furthermore, decisions brought by ADR entities are not necessarily binding[63] and can usually be enforced within the judicial proceedings by the courts. The rulings of ADR bodies are therefore again subject to the judicial control within the court proceedings as seen in the CJEU landmark cases on consumer protection *Mostaza Claro*[64] and *Asturcom Telecomunicaciones.* Here, the CJEU confirmed the duty of national courts responsible for the enforcement to examine *ex officio* the unfairness of arbitration clauses,[65] even once the out-of-court proceeding had finished and the arbitral award issued by an arbitral tribunal had become final.[66]

---

[57]Mediation Act (*Zakon o mirenju*) OG No. 18/11 and Ordinance on Mediation (*Pravilnik o mirenju*) OG No. 142/11.

[58]Arbitration Act (*Zakon o arbitraži*) OG No. 88/01.

[59]See Mišćenić (2019), pp. 189–222.

[60]Under the Danish Act No. 524 of 29 April 2015 on consumer complaints ("lov om alternativ tvistløsning i forbindelse med forbrugerklager (forbrugerklageloven)") it is not mandatory for consumers to use the ADR system. Under Art. 10 of the Cyprus Law 78 (I) 2011, out-of-court settlement of consumer disputes is non-mandatory. See *EC Evaluation Study*. . ., *op. cit.*, Strand II, Consumer ADR.

[61]Ordinance n°2015-1033 du 20 August 2015 and Decree n°2015-1382 du 30 October 2015, Art. L. 612-1 Code de la Consommation, modified by the Ordinance of 14 March 2016.

[62]Section 15a(1) Gesetz betreffend die Einführung der Zivilprozessordnung, zuletzt geändert durch Art. 1 G v., 21.6.2018, I 863 concerning claims under the value of 750 EUR. According to the results of *EC Evaluation Study*. . ., *op. cit.*, Strand II, Consumer ADR 11 States have enacted such laws, however, without practical success.

[63]*EC Evaluation Study*. . ., *op. cit.*, Strand II, Consumer ADR confirmed that in most of the MS' the ADR entities cannot issue binding decisions, but parties can reach a settlement in the form of an enforceable title, i.e., notarial deed, court settlement or an arbitration award.

[64]Judgment of 26 October 2006, C-168/05, *Mostaza Claro,* EU:C:2006:675, para. 40.

[65]Judgment of 27 June 2000 in the joined cases C-240/98 to C-244/98, *Océano Grupo and Salvat Editores,* EU:C:2000:346.

[66]CJEU case *Asturcom Telecomunicaciones*, para. 60: "(. . .) *a national court or tribunal hearing an action for enforcement of an arbitration award which has become final and was made in the absence of the consumer is required, where it has available to it the legal and factual elements necessary for that task, to assess of its own motion whether an arbitration clause in a contract concluded between a seller or supplier and a consumer is unfair, in so far as, under national rules of procedure, it can carry out such an assessment in similar actions of a domestic nature.*"

4 The Role of MS' Courts in the Application of the EU Consumer Protection Law

Regarding the role of the courts in the application of consumer protection law, this is acknowledged by both the EU legislation and CJEU case law interpreting the *acquis*. Apart from the EU Directives on consumer protection, which deal with the enforcement of substantive rights of consumers only sporadically by referring to courts or administrative proceedings[67] or by requesting efficient protection of consumer rights guaranteed by the respective Directive (*effet utile*),[68] there are several specific EU Directives focusing on consumer redress proceedings. Among the most important ones is the Directive 2009/22/EC on injunctions for the protection of consumers' interests[69] enabling entities, who have a legitimate interest, to pursue action on behalf of consumers for an infringement that harms the collective interests of those consumers. There are also other EU law instruments facilitating the enforcement of consumer rights such as the Brussels Ibis Regulation, European Enforcement Order Regulation, European Payment Order Regulation or European Small Claim Regulation, which are relevant for cross-border disputes.[70] Regarding pure domestic B2C disputes, there are still national procedural rules of MS that are applicable and due to which the procedural autonomy of MS is to be respected. According to the CJEU case law, it was not the intention of EU law "*to create new remedies in the national*

[67]Such as Article 7 UCTD or Articles 11 to 12 UCPD referring to courts or other competent administrative bodies' proceedings.

[68]Various manifestations of the "effet utile" include also the rule usually contained in EU Directives requesting from MS to introduce effective, proportionate and dissuasive sanctions for infringements of the national provisions adopted pursuant to the relevant Directive. Under Art. 23 of the Directive 2008/48/EC of the European Parliament and of the Council of 23 April 2008 on credit agreements for consumers and repealing Council Directive 87/102/EEC, OJ L 133, 22.5.2008, pp. 66–92: "The penalties provided for must be effective, proportionate and dissuasive."

[69]Directive 2009/22/EC of the European Parliament and of the Council of 23 April 2009 on injunctions for the protection of consumers' interests, OJ L 110, 1 May 2009, pp. 30–36.

[70]Regulation (EU) No 1215/2012 of the European Parliament and of the Council of 12 December 2012 on jurisdiction and the recognition and enforcement of judgments in civil and commercial matters, OJ L 351, 20.12.2012, pp. 1–32; Regulation (EC) No 1393/2007 of the European Parliament and of the Council of 13 November 2007 on the service in the Member States of judicial and extrajudicial documents in civil or commercial matters (service of documents), and repealing Council Regulation (EC) No 1348/2000, OJ L 324, 10.12.2007, pp. 79–120; Council Regulation (EC) No 1206/2001 of 28 May 2001 on cooperation between the courts of the Member States in the taking of evidence in civil or commercial matters, OJ L 174, 27.6.2001, pp. 1–24; Regulation (EC) No 805/2004 of the European Parliament and of the Council of 21 April 2004 creating a European Enforcement Order for uncontested claims, OJ L 143/15, 30.4.2004; Regulation (EC) No 1896/2006 of the European Parliament and of the Council of 12 December 2006 creating a European order for payment procedure, OJ L 399, 30.12.2006, pp. 1–32; Regulation (EC) No 861/2007 of the European Parliament and of the Council of 11 July 2007 establishing a European Small Claims Procedure, OJ L 199, 31.7.2007, pp. 1–22; Council Directive 2002/8/EC of 27 January 2003 to improve access to justice in cross border disputes by establishing minimum common rules relating to legal aid for such disputes, OJ L 26/41, 31.1.2003.

courts to ensure the observance of Community law other than those already laid down by national law".[71] Consequently, despite the various EU mechanisms guaranteeing the enforcement of consumer rights, disputes of consumers as private individuals are still mostly governed by national civil procedure rules that could potentially affect and undermine the effectiveness of the consumers' rights protection. There are plenty of reasons for this assumption at the level of each MS. As proven in a recent European Commission Study on Enforcement from February 2018,[72] the rules of MS' civil law procedures differ significantly regarding the jurisdiction of individual courts (i.e., courts having jurisdiction over consumer disputes), formal requirements for bringing a case, types of available legal actions, parties' representation, legal aid, time limits applicable to procedural steps of the action, taking of evidence, right to appeal and review, as well as regarding the enforcement of judgments or other enforcement titles such as arbitration awards, notarial deeds etc. As an example, one could mention the recent *Pula Parking* case in which the Croatian domestic rules on enforcement on the ground of the so-called "trustworthy" document (in this case the unpaid parking bill) contradicted the rules of the Brussels Ibis Regulation.[73] The CJEU concluded that notaries "*do not fall within the concept of 'court' within the meaning of that regulation*", which requires from competent MS' "courts" to deliver a certificate for enforcing the judgment cross-border.

However, since the MS national procedural laws are subject to the procedural autonomy of MS,[74] by relying on the above-presented general requirement of the effectiveness of EU law the CJEU developed two special principles setting boundaries and limitations to the procedural autonomy of MS. Furthermore, on the ground of the principles of equivalence and effectiveness, the CJEU case law established certain requirements for the procedural protection of consumer rights deriving from EU law. These concern in particular the duty of MS courts and potentially of other enforcement bodies to monitor and apply consumer protection law of their own motion, i.e., *ex officio*. *Ex officio* control belongs to the procedural mechanisms that can be utilised within the MS' national legal systems for promoting a more effective enforcement of consumer protection law.

---

[71] Judgment of 13 March 2007, C-432/05, *Unibet*, EU:C:2007:163, para. 40; judgment of 7 July 1981, C-120/78, *Rewe-Zentral v Bundesmonopolverwaltung für Branntwein* EU:C:1979:42, para. 44. For more information see Arnull (2011), p. 54.

[72] *European Commission Evaluation Study of the Impact of National Procedural Laws and Practices on the Free Circulation of Judgements and on the Equivalence and Effectiveness of the Procedural Protection of Consumers under EU law*, JUST/2014/RCON/PR/CIVI/0082, February 2018, Strand I Mutual Trust and Free Circulation of Judgments, available at: https://publications.europa.eu/en/publication-detail/-/publication/531ef49a-9768-11e7-b92d-01aa75ed71a1/language-en.

[73] Judgment of 9 March 2017, C-551/15, *Pula Parking*, EU:C:2017:193.

[74] CJEU case *Duarte Hueros*, para. 31: "*(...) in the absence of European Union legislation, the procedural rules governing actions for safeguarding the rights that individuals derive from Directive 1999/44* ***fall within the internal legal order of the Member States by virtue of the principle of procedural autonomy of those Member States***."

4.1 Principles of Effectiveness and Equivalence in the EU Consumer Protection Law

It would actually be wrong to conclude that the principles of equivalence and effectiveness as developed by the CJEU are limited to MS' procedural laws. As confirmed by the CJEU case law especially in the field of consumer protection, these two principles operate also at the level of MS' substantive law rules and MS have to comply with their requirements to achieve the ***full effect*** of EU law. In the famous *Brasserie du Pêcheur* case,[75] where the CJEU examined the substantive law rules on damage compensation based on the yardstick of the principles of equivalence and effectiveness, it stressed an "*obligation on national courts to ensure the full effectiveness of Community law by guaranteeing effective protection for the rights of individuals (...)*".[76] National courts and eventually other enforcement bodies can achieve this obligation by applying national rules that "*must not be less favourable than those governing similar domestic actions (principle of equivalence) or such as to make it in practice impossible or excessively difficult to exercise the rights conferred by European Union law (principle of effectiveness)*".[77]

The focus of the CJEU case law defining the two principles is nonetheless on the MS' procedural law rules. The CJEU requires from MS' courts and tribunals to evaluate on a case-by-case basis whether national procedural rules contradict the requirements of the principles of equivalence and effectiveness. For example, in the *Asturcom Telecomunicaciones* case dealing with the unfairness of the arbitration clause the CJEU concluded that "*in accordance with the principle of equivalence, the conditions imposed by domestic law under which the courts and tribunals may apply a rule of Community law of their own motion must not be less favourable than those governing the application by those bodies of their own motion of rules of domestic law of the same ranking*"[78] and imposed the duty to determine this on the national court, "*which alone has direct knowledge of the detailed procedural rules governing actions in the field of domestic law, to consider both the purpose and the essential characteristics of domestic actions which are claimed to be similar*".[79] However, while the principle of equivalence is rarely disputed in consumer protec-

[75]Judgment of 5 March 1996, joined cases C-46/93 and C-48/93, *Brasserie du Pêcheur SA v Bundesrepublik Deutschland* and *The Queen v Secretary of State for Transport, ex parte: Factortame Ltd and Others*, EU:C:1996:79.

[76]*Ibid.*, para. 72.

[77]CJEU case *Duarte Hueros*, para. 31; judgment of 3 October 2013, C-472/11, *Banif Plus Bank*, EU:C:2013:88, para. 26; CJEU case *Banco Español de Crédito*, para. 46; CJEU case *Aziz*, para. 53; CJEU case *Asturcom Telecomunicaciones*, para. 38 and many others.

[78]CJEU case *Asturcom Telecomunicaciones*, para. 49.

[79]*Ibid.*, para. 50.

tion law cases,[80] the principle of effectiveness affects MS' procedural laws significantly. The CJEU case law sets criteria that must be examined to assess whether the principle of effectiveness has been respected and which include "*the role of the provision in the procedure, its progress and its special features, viewed as a whole, before the various national bodies*".[81] It was by applying these criteria that the CJEU has decided that the Spanish procedural rules on *res iudicata* and *ne bis in idem* do not comply with the EU principle of effectiveness since they make "*the enforcement of the protection which Directive 1999/44 seeks to provide to those consumers excessively difficult, if not impossible*".[82] Under Spanish procedural law in the case at hand, the consumer was not able to submit another action concerning a dispute between the same parties and in the same dispute matter (*ne bis in idem*) once the national court had already ruled on the non-conformity of goods (*res iudicata*). Since Ms. Duarte Hueros submitted an action requesting the rescission of the sale contract, which was denied to her because the defect of goods was minor, she lost her right to other legal remedies available under Directive 99/44/EC on sale of goods.[83] The CJEU argued that "*in those circumstances, it must be held that such procedural rules are liable to undermine the effectiveness of the consumer protection intended by the European Union legislature in so far as* ***they do not allow the national court to recognise of its motion the right of the consumer to obtain an appropriate reduction in the price of the goods****, even though that consumer is not entitled to refine his initial application or to bring a fresh action to that end*".[84] This judgment, which has been hotly disputed by both the legal doctrine and practice, could have serious consequences on MS' procedural laws.[85] Not only do the principles of *ne bis in idem* and *res iudicata* belong to the common principle of MS' procedural laws, these principles usually can also be subject to exceptions under which the renewal of a proceeding is to be allowed. Moreover, one cannot but question whether this negligent or, in this case, "ignorant" consumer[86] should be rewarded for not using all procedural options, such as legal aid, and for not requesting the enforcement of other legal remedies that are at his disposal. Should the MS' courts violate another key principle of procedural law, which is *non ultra petita,* to guarantee to the consumer the enforcement of rights arising under the EU law that he is not even asking for?

---

[80]CJEU case *Duarte Hueros*, paras. 32 and 33: "*As regards the principle of equivalence, it must be noted that the documents before the Court do not point to anything that is capable of raising doubts that the Spanish procedural legislation does not comply with that principle. Indeed, it is apparent from those documents that* ***that legislation applies regardless of whether the law on which the consumer has based his application is European law or national law****.*"

[81]*Ibid.*, para. 34, by referring to the CJEU case *Banco Español de Crédito,* para. 49 and case *Aziz,* para. 53.

[82]*Ibid.*, para. 41.

[83]Directive 1999/44/EC of the European Parliament and of the Council of 25 May 1999 on certain aspects of the sale of consumer goods and associated guarantees, OJ 1999 L 171/12.

[84]CJEU case *Duarte Hueros,* para. 39.

[85]See Mišćenić (2016), p. 135.

[86]On various images of the consumer in EU law, see: Leczykiewicz and Weatherill (2016), p. 1.

The question has already been answered by the CJEU's case law on the *ex officio* application of EU law,[87] which justifies a limitation of national procedural rules "*in exceptional cases where the public interest requires its intervention*".[88] However, in *Duarte Hueros*, there is no mention of the "*public interest*" argument and the CJEU justifies such limitations because of particularly rigid procedural requirements for presenting both the principal and alternative claim at the same time. Moreover, the consumer is often unaware of, or does not appreciate, the extent of his rights[89] and finally is unable to anticipate the outcome of the competent court's analysis of the legal characterisation regarding the lack of conformity in the goods.[90] It is needless to explain that these arguments can be associated with every other individual trying to solve a dispute in a national civil law proceeding. Despite the fact that the consumer is a weaker party *vis-à-vis* the trader and therefore needs to be protected by consumer law guaranteeing consumer rights, the question remains whether the consumer is also a weaker party in MS' civil law proceedings enforcing his rights.

4.2 **Ex officio** *Application of the EU Consumer Protection Law*

The above presented *Duarte Hueros* case has brought forward the following key question of the EU consumer protection law enforcement: *How far should the ex officio application of consumer protection law go*? To answer this question, one should start from the beginning by referring to key CJEU cases, which are the basis of the duty for MS' courts to apply consumer protection law of their own motion.[91] To the landmark cases interpreting the legal consequences of unfairness under Article 6(1) UCTD and establishing the *ex officio* duty for MS' courts to examine the unfairness of contract terms belongs *Océano Grupo and Salvat Editores,* dealing with the prorogation clauses in B2C sales contracts of encyclopaedias. It was here

[87]See *infra*, title 4.2.

[88]Regarding this point, see judgment of 17 December 2009, C-227/08, *Martín Martín,* EU: C:2009:792, paras. 19 and 20: "(. . .) *Community law does not, in principle, require national courts to raise of their own motion an issue concerning the breach of provisions of Community law,* ***where examination of that issue would oblige them to go beyond the ambit of the dispute defined by the parties themselves and rely on facts and circumstances other than those on which the party with an interest in application of those provisions has based his claim*** *(. . .) That limitation on the power of the national court is justified by the principle that, in a civil suit, it is for the parties to take the initiative, and that, as a result, the court is able to act of its own motion only in exceptional cases where the public interest requires its intervention*" by referring to the judgment of 14 December 1995, C-430/93, *van Schijndel and van Veen* EU:C:1995:441, para. 21 and judgment of 7 June 2007, joined cases C-222/05 to C-225/05 *van der Weerd and Others,* EU:C:2007:318, para. 35.

[89]CJEU case *Duarte Hueros,* para. 38.

[90]*Ibid.*, para. 40.

[91]For more see: Law (2018), p. 283 *et seq.*

that the CJEU established for the first time that a consumer is the "*weaker party*" in B2C relations[92] and that the aim of Article 6 UCTD would never be achieved if the consumer himself was about to raise the unfairness of contract terms during the proceeding.[93] Nonetheless, the CJEU also established that the consumer is a "*weaker party*" in civil law procedures. The MS' procedural law rules enable individuals to defend themselves or require legal representation in such proceedings.[94] It is the view of the CJEU that both scenarios are bad for the consumer, who either ends up not invoking the unfairness because of the lack of legal knowledge or restrains from the action because of the high costs of legal representation and procedural costs. It therefore emphasised that "*effective protection of the consumer may be attained only if the national court acknowledges that it has power to evaluate terms of this kind of its own motion*".[95] In cases that followed, such as *Mostaza Claro* and *Asturcom Telecomunicaciones*, the CJEU raised Article 6 UCTD to the level of a *public policy* rule[96] and relieved the *ex officio* duty of courts to examine unfair contract terms by adding the pre-condition of having at their disposal the legal and factual elements necessary for that task.[97] The CJEU's jurisprudence manifested itself in the procedural laws of MS, as well as, for instance, in the conclusions of the Croatian Supreme Court establishing the *ex officio* duty of ordinary courts to examine the unfairness of contract terms only if the claimant has submitted the traders' standard contract terms

---

[92]CJEU case *Océano Grupo and Salvat Editores*, para. 25: "*As to the question of whether a court seised of a dispute concerning a contract between a seller or supplier and a consumer may determine* ***of its own motion*** *whether a term of the contract is unfair, it should be noted that* ***the system of protection introduced by the Directive is based on the idea that the consumer is in a weak position vis-à-vis the seller or supplier****, as regards both his bargaining power and his level of knowledge.*"

[93]*Ibid.*, para. 26.

[94]According to the results of the *EC Evaluation Study*. . ., *op. cit.*, Strand II, Part I in most of the MS' the general rules of civil law proceedings apply when it comes to legal representation, meaning that the consumer is subject to the same procedural rules as any other individual during the proceeding. In some countries, as Belgium, the parties can defend themselves (Art. 728 of the Belgian Judicial Code), while in others the legal representation is requested when the value of dispute exceeds a certain amount (§ 27 of the Austrian ZPO). In many MS, legal representation is not obligatory (Bulgaria, Czech Republic, Croatia, Denmark, Estonia, Finland etc.). On the other hand, German procedural rules require legal representation by an attorney (Sec. 78 para. 1 of the German ZPO).

[95]CJEU case, *Océano Grupo and Salvat Editores,* para. 26.

[96]CJEU case *Mostaza Claro,* para. 38: "*The nature and importance of the* ***public interest*** *underlying the protection which the Directive confers on consumers justify, moreover, the* ***national court being required to assess of its own motion whether a contractual term is unfair****, compensating in this way for the imbalance which exists between the consumer and the seller or supplier.*" See also CJEU case *Asturcom Telecomunicaciones*, para. 52: "*(. . .) in view of the nature and importance of the* ***public interest*** *underlying the protection which Directive 93/13 confers on consumers,* ***Article 6 of the directive must be regarded as a provision of equal standing to national rules which rank, within the domestic legal system, as rules of public policy***".

[97]See judgment of 4 June 2009, C-243/08, *Pannon GSM,* EU:C:2009:350: "*The national court is required to examine,* ***of its own motion****, the unfairness of a contractual term* ***where it has available to it the legal and factual elements necessary for that task.***" See order of 21 November 2002, C-76/10, *Pohotovosť,* EU:C:2010:685, CJEU case *Banco Español de Crédito*, para. 46 and many others.

together with an action.[98] The development of this *ex officio* duty in consumer protection law has gone far beyond of what was expected initially. At one point, the CJEU established this duty even in not necessarily *inter partes* proceedings, such as payment order proceedings,[99] despite the fact that in many other cases it accentuated the importance of the *audi alteram partem* principle in national civil law proceedings.[100]

For most MS' courts, the establishment of the *ex officio* duty regarding unfair contract terms is not actually an issue because unfair contract terms are invalid[101] and the nullity is generally observed *ex officio* by courts in MS' civil law proceedings.[102] This conclusion can be supported by the results from the abovementioned *EC Study on Enforcement of Consumer Protection Law* confirming the awareness of courts and other enforcement bodies of this important duty. What is however unclear to the majority of courts across the Union is *whether they are obliged to apply consumer protection law of their own motion, and if the answer to this question is positive, on the basis of which legal ground*? To our knowledge, MS' procedural rules do not contain a rule explicitly obliging courts or other enforcement bodies to apply consumer protection law of their own motion. The result is that in many MS consumer protection law, with the exception of the rules on unfair contract terms, is not applied *ex officio*. There are, however, MS, such as Austria and Italy, in

[98]Conclusions of the Supreme Court of the Republic of Croatia, No. Su-IV-155/16 of 12 April 2016: "*In cases when this doesn't follow from factual allegations of the parties, i.e. when there is no explicit statement of parties in respect of nullity of certain general standard contract term, the court must ex officio (when it has general standard contract terms at disposal), evaluate whether provisions of general standard contract terms are invalid, i.e.* ***in case when this doesn't follow from factual allegations and there are no general standard contract terms available in the proceeding file, the court is not obliged to evaluate nullity (preclusion) of certain provision of general standard contract terms ex officio****, and the adequacy of the claim shall in this case be decided upon the rules on the burden of proof.*"

[99]For example, the Opinion of Advocate General *Trstenjak* delivered on 14 February 2012 was not followed by the CJEU in the case *Banco Español de Crédito*. The AG concluded that the UCTD is to be interpreted to the effect that it does not require a national court, in the context of a national order for payment procedure, to give a ruling of its own motion and *in limine litis* on whether a term concerning interest on late payments in a consumer credit agreement is not binding, provided the assessment of whether that term is unfair can be transferred, in accordance with the national procedural rules, to an *inter partes* procedure to be initiated through an appeal brought by the debtor, in which the national court is given the opportunity to obtain the legal and factual elements necessary to conduct such an assessment.

[100]See judgment of 21 April 2016, C-377/14, *Radlinger and Radlingerová*, EU:C:2016:283, para. 71: "(. . .) *provided always that the principle of audi alteram partem has been complied with* (. . .)".

[101]Article 6(1) UCTD stipulates a duty for MS to lay down that unfair terms used in B2C contracts *"as provided for under their national law"* shall not be binding on the consumer and *"that the contract shall continue to bind the parties upon those terms if it is capable of continuing in existence without the unfair term"*.

[102]E.g., under Art. 327(1) of the Croatian Obligations Act, OG Nos. 35/05, 41/08, 125/11, 78/15 and 29/18, the court monitors the nullity *ex officio* and every interested party can invoke nullity. Under Art. 36(3) of the Italian Consumer Code nullity operates only for the benefit of the consumer and may be ascertained *ex officio* by the court with regard to the unfair contract terms.

which consumer protection law is observed and applied on the ground of the fundamental principles of procedural law, such as *iura novit curia*. In other MS, e.g., Croatia,[103] Denmark[104] and again Italy,[105] this duty can also emanate from the general principles of laws requiring an *ex officio* observance of provisions of *mandatory nature*, i.e., also those on consumer protection. The EU consumer protection directives regularly contain the rule prohibiting the waiver of consumer rights and therefore changing the nature of many consumer protection rules from *ius dispositivum* to *ius cogens*.[106] Such an approach can be supported when applying by analogy the conclusions of the CJEU in other cases, such as *van Schijndel and van Veen*, in which the Court held that "*where, by virtue of domestic law, courts or tribunals must raise of their own motion points of law based on binding domestic rules which have not been raised by the parties, such an obligation also exists where binding Community rules are concerned* (...)".[107] Only in a few MS, such as Portugal, does the duty of the courts and possibly other enforcement bodies to an *ex officio* application of consumer protection law rely on the CJEU case law on *public policy rules*. It was not only in the jurisprudence on unfair contract terms that the CJEU recognised the importance of the mandatory provisions of Article 6 UCTD for public interest and public policy, but also in other cases dealing with off-premises contracts, the non-conformity of goods or provisions of credit agreements, where the CJEU concluded that MS' courts are obliged to monitor certain rules arising from EU Directives of their own motion. In relation to the violation of the pre-contractual information duty of the trader to inform the consumer about his fundamental right of withdrawal from the off-premises contract, the CJEU requested from MS' courts to monitor this rule of public interest of their own motion.[108] The request of the CJEU in the *Martín Martín* case was put forward despite the fact that the consumer had "*at no stage, pleaded that the contract was void before the competent national*

---

[103]Under the Croatian Civil Procedure Act, the *ex officio* control represents an obligation for the judge. The *ex officio* duty of courts to monitor the parties' dispositions that are contrary to mandatory rules and public morality in civil proceedings (Art. 3(3)) encompasses an *inter alia ex officio* control of the parties' dispositions that are contrary to the mandatory rules of consumer protection law.

[104]Under Section 338 of the Danish Administration of Justice Act, the courts have a general obligation to apply ex officio "*mandatory rules that cannot be waived*".

[105]Under Art. 143(1) of the Italian Consumer Code, the rights of consumers as acknowledged by this Act may not be waived and any agreement in breach of this legal provision is invalid.

[106]For example, under the title Imperative nature of the Directive, Art. 25 CRD regulates "*If the law applicable to the contract is the law of a Member State, consumers may not waive the rights conferred on them by the national measures transposing this Directive. Any contractual terms which directly or indirectly waive or restrict the rights resulting from this Directive shall not be binding on the consumer.*"

[107]CJEU case *van Schijndel and van Veen*, para. 13.

[108]CJEU case *Martín Martín,* para. 27: "*(...) the obligation to give notice of the* ***right of cancellation*** *laid down in Article 4 of the Directive* ***plays a central role in the overall scheme of that directive, as an essential guarantee (...) for the effective exercise of that right and, therefore, for the effectiveness of consumer protection sought by the Community legislature.***"

courts".[109] The CJEU concluded that *the court is able to act of its own motion only in exceptional cases where the public interest requires its intervention* and concluded that Article 4 of Directive 85/577/EEC *does not preclude a national court from declaring, of its own motion, that a contract falling within the scope of that directive is void on the ground that the consumer was not informed of his right of cancellation* (...).[110] In the *Faber* case,[111] the CJEU came to the conclusion that Article 5(3) of Directive 1999/44/EC must be regarded as a norm equivalent to the national rules of public policy "*that is to say, as a rule which may be raised of its own motion by the national court*".[112] The case concerned the so-called "*six-month presumption*" rule according to which the burden of proof on the conformity of goods is reversed to the seller during the first six months.[113] This deadline is soon to be prolonged in favour of the consumers to two years under Article 8(3) of the proposed Online Sales Directive,[114] what also means a longer period for the MS' courts regarding their *ex officio* duty. The CJEU case law interpreting the provisions of the Consumer Sales Directive continues to remain relevant and applicable to the corresponding provisions of the forthcoming Directive.[115] On the other hand, in the case *Radlinger and Radlingerová*, the CJEU established the *ex officio* duty of MS' courts to examine the creditor's compliance with the duty to inform a consumer about the information to be included in the credit agreement under Article 10(2) of Directive 2008/48/EC.[116] However, not only the creditor's compliance with the "*full and mandatory harmonisation*" rules of this Directive[117] is to be observed by MS' courts *ex officio*. What is more, the MS' courts are obliged to guarantee the principle of effectiveness by applying adequate legal consequences under their national laws, which satisfy the requirements of Article 23 of the Directive demanding that the penalties for the infringement of the national provisions should be dissuasive (*effet utile*).[118]

The presented CJEU case law is very often at odds with the MS' procedural rules and practice. MS' courts are still puzzled with the nature of consumer protection law

---

[109] *Ibid.*, para. 18.

[110] *Ibid.*, para. 37.

[111] CJEU case *Faber*, para. 65.

[112] *Ibid.*, para 49.

[113] Art. 5(3) of the Consumer Sales Directive.

[114] Amended proposal for a Directive of the European Parliament and of the Council on certain aspects concerning contracts for the online and other distance sales of goods, amending Regulation (EC) No 2006/2004 of the European Parliament and of the Council and Directive 2009/22/EC of the European Parliament and of the Council and repealing Directive 1999/44/EC of the European Parliament and of the Council, COM/2017/0637 final—2015/0288 (COD).

[115] Recital 15. The amended Online Sales Directive Proposal of 31 October 2017 extends the material scope of the proposed Directive from distance sales contracts also to face-to-face sales and, in contrast to the original, by its Article 21 proposes repealing the Consumer Sales Directive.

[116] CJEU case *Radlinger and Radlingerová*, para. 102.

[117] *Ibid*, 61. As well as the judgment of 18 December 2014, *CA Consumer Finance SA*, C-449/13, EU:C:2014:2464, para 21.

[118] *Ibid.*, para. 102.

rules as transposed from EU Directives. For example, in *Belgium* initially existed a clear distinction between consumer protection rules as "protective rules" from "*ordre public* rules", which did not encompass consumer protection law.[119] The court practice however changed this view and nowadays the *ex officio* application concerns the whole body of law.[120] The same solution exists in Germany, where the whole body of law is applied *ex officio*. In *Cyprus*, the *ex officio* control of consumer protection law is not established although some authors plead for the *ex officio* application of consumer protection law as public order rules. The *Bulgarian* legal doctrine and practice refer to CJEU case law on UCTD and *ex officio* control.[121] The *Czech Republic* does not require the *ex officio* application of consumer protection law. Despite the fact that *Croatian* courts have the legal background for an *ex officio* application of consumer protection law, in practice they are not aware of its mandatory nature. The exception is the *ex officio* control of unfair contract terms, where the first collective redress proceeding on unfair terms in CHF credit agreements demonstrated an observance of the CJEU case law to a certain extent.[122] Such an understanding exists also in *Estonia*, where the *ex officio* control of unfair contract terms is confirmed by domestic case law.[123] With the exception of unfair contract terms, *Finish* courts are now aware of the *ex officio* application of consumer protection law. In countries such as France the legislation does oblige the courts regarding unfair contract terms,[124] but the issue of an *ex officio* application of consumer protection law lacks clear regulation. There are doubts whether the rules satisfy the conditions of public policy rules. On the other hand, some MS, such as *Greece* and *Hungary*, struggle even with the *ex officio* control of unfair contract terms. Greek courts are not certain about the form of nullity to be applied to unfair contract terms (absolute or relative), while for the Hungarian judges the *ex officio* control is a strange concept. *Malta's* national law does not address the issue nor does it place any obligation on courts to apply consumer protection law *ex officio*. Explicit regulation in this respect does not exist in the Netherlands, but the courts seem to follow CJEU's case law. After many interventions of the CJEU, the *Spanish* procedural rules were amended to comply with the UCTD completely and the *ex*

[119]de Wulf (2016), p. 181.

[120]Cour de cassation de Belgique, 14 *Avril* 2005, n° C.03.0148.F/1.

[121]Iosifov (2013), p. 191 *et seq.*

[122]More on this issue: Mišćenić (2018b), pp. 127–159.

[123]Case law of the Estonian Supreme Court: Case of 18 January 2006, No. 3-2-1-155-05 para. 19; Case of 12 March 2008, No. 3-2-1-2-08; Case of 17 June 2008, No. 3-2-1-56-08; Case of 23 March 2011, No. 3-2-1-2-11; Case of 15 November 2010, No. 3-2-1-100-10; Case of 29 May 2012, No. 3-2-1-64-12; Case of 11 February 2014, No. 3-2-1-150-14.

[124]Under Article R632-1 of the Code de la Consommation modified by Decree n°2016-884 of 29 June 2016 "*(...) the judge may raise of its own motion the dispositions of the present code. The judge shall of its own motion strike out an abusive provision after having consulted the parties*".

officio control of unfair contract terms is explicitly guaranteed.[125] This is not the case though with the rest of consumer protection law that is still not considered by Spanish judges containing public policy rules.[126]

5 Concluding Remarks

There are various consumer protection enforcement mechanisms across the MS, but not all of them are *effective* as required by Union law.[127] Among those most promoted is the ADR, whose role became particularly attractive with the introduction of the European ADR/ODR regulation enabling online dispute resolution.[128] However, this new EU legislation, regardless of its appeal, has not brought significant improvements to the enforcement of consumer rights.[129] Many out-of-court bodies do not offer "*online*" dispute resolution and require the presence of the parties and their representatives during the proceedings instead. Although the new ADR rules demand *expertise*, *independence* and *impartiality* of the staff working in ADR bodies, the latter can be formed as private dispute resolution bodies and thus bringing all these criteria into question. Through the introduction of common standards for ADR bodies all around the Union, the ADR Directive has not managed to lower the level of legal fragmentation or to diminish the variety of out-of-court procedures within the MS. They all continued to exist and operate by their own rules to which new laws transposing the standards and criteria from the ADR Directive were added. In some aspects, the misinterpretation of ADR Directive rules even managed to lower the level of consumer protection by excluding the venue for B2C disputes between domestic consumers buying from foreign traders in quite a number of MS. Overall, the ADR system suffers from too many flaws to be able to ensure "*effective legal protection in the fields covered by Union law*",[130] including consumer protection law.[131] The question remains, however, whether judicial protection

[125]The source of the cited case law and literature on the MS is the above mentioned *EC Evaluation Study. . ., op. cit.*, Strand II, forthcoming in the publication The Impact of National Procedural Laws and Practices on the Equivalent and Effective Procedural Protection of Consumers under EU Consumer Law, Hart/Beck/Nomos, 2018.

[126]Judgments of the Supreme Court of 5 May 2008, núm. 317/2008, ES:TS:2008:1726, of 30 April 2012, núm. 260/2012, ES:TS:2012:2869 and of 22 April 2015, núm. 265/2015, ES:TS:2015:1723 confirm the approach of the Spanish courts that allow the assessment of the nullity of a contract of its own motion only exceptionally, in cases of contract terms that are notoriously illegal or contrary to the moral or public policy.

[127]More to the issue of effectiveness and enforcement of consumer law in the recent book edited by Micklitz and Saumier (2018), p. 1 *et seq.*

[128]See, for example, Creutzfeldt (2016), pp. 169–175.

[129]On the shortcomings of the ADR system see Loos (2016), pp. 61–80.

[130]Article 19(1) TEU.

[131]Serious doubts as to the improvement of the consumer protection enforcement by the ADR/ODR regulation are also expressed by Eidenmüller and Fries (2016), p. 113.

can guarantee the same. Procedural law rules that enjoy the protection of the Member States procedural autonomy have been so often measured against the yardstick of the CJEU's principles of effectiveness and equivalence.[132] In the area of consumer protection, even the most fundamental principles of procedural laws, such as *res iudicata, ne bis in idem* or *non ultra petitem*, have been limited to guarantee the full effectiveness of EU law. However, despite the CJEU case law raising the consumer protection rules to the level of public policy rules on so many occasions, the national courts seem to be reluctant to the idea of an *ex officio* application of consumer protection law.[133] The provisions of the MS' consumer protection laws are undoubtedly of a mandatory nature and thus should be observed by the MS' courts. The CJEU case law makes the distinction between mandatory and public policy rules, thereby confirming that not all of the rules of the consumer protection *acquis* are rules "*of equal standing to a national rule which ranks, within the domestic legal system, as a rule of public policy*".[134] Nonetheless, it seems that there is a disguised intention of the CJEU to create an interpretation equalising all of consumer protection law with the public policy rules. The rulings in cases such as *Océano Grupo and Salvat Editores, Duarte Hueros* or *Faber* all share a common reasoning and are based on the concept of the "*weak consumer*",[135] who, because of the low level of knowledge and ignorance of the law, "*will not rely on the legal rule that is intended to protect him*".[136] If the *right* argument for an *ex officio* application of the EU consumer protection law transposed into Member States laws is actually a weak position of the consumer rather than the principle of effectiveness, then consumer protection law is to be applied *ex officio* always. In other words, if the principle of effectiveness depends upon the position of the consumer *vis-à-vis* the "*business*", but also *vis-à-vis* the relevant enforcement procedure, its application will without a doubt always results in an *ex officio* application of consumer protection law.

It is no secret that the Union is faced with numerous problems when it comes to effective enforcement of consumer rights. From "Fitness Check" to "New Deal for Consumers", the European Commission is trying to come up with better and more favourable legislative solutions that would guarantee more effectiveness in

[132]See in particular Pavillon (2007), p. 737 *et seq.*

[133]On effectiveness of MS justice systems see Communication from the Commission to the European Parliament, the Council, the European Central Bank, the European Economic and Social Committee and the Committee of the Regions—The 2017 EU Justice Scoreboard European Commission, COM(2017) 167.

[134]CJEU case *Faber*, para. 56.

[135]CJEU case *Martín Martín*, para. 28: "*Such a provision, therefore, comes under the public interest justifying (...) a positive intervention by the national court in order to compensate for the imbalance between the consumer and the trader in the context of contracts concluded away from business premises.*"

[136]CJEU case *Radlinger and Radlingerová*, para. 65.

enforcement of consumer protection law across the Union.[137] A recent result of these efforts is the so-called Proposal of a Directive on better enforcement and modernisation of the EU consumer protection rules[138] that would eventually amend four Directives with the goal of enforcement improvement. However, it is highly unlikely that this new piece of EU legislation in the field of consumer protection will or actually can affect judicial enforcement of consumer rights. Even the Commission acknowledges that "*The effective enforcement of existing EU law is just as important as the work devoted to developing new legislation*".[139] At the end of the day, it is not about providing more or even new remedies to consumers, but rather about remedying in more efficient and consistent way Union-wide. Law deprived of its proper enforcement is law deprived of its own purpose.

References

Arnull A (2011) The principle of effective judicial protection in EU law: an unruly horse? Eur Law Rev 36(1):51–70

Cauffmann C (2016) Critical remarks on the ADR Directive. In: Cauffmann C, Smits J (eds) The citizen in European private law: norm-setting, enforcement and choice. Intersentia, pp 155–160

Cortés P (2015) A new regulatory framework for extra-judicial consumer redress: where we are and how to move forward. Leg Stud 35(1):114–141

Creutzfeldt N (2016) Implementation of the consumer ADR Directive. J Eur Consum Mark Law (1):169–175

de Wulf V (2016) L'office du juge en matière de contrats destinés aux consommateurs. In: Verdure C (ed) Contrats et protection des consommateurs. Anthemis, pp 181–206

Eidenmüller H, Fries M (2016) Against false settlement: designing efficient consumer rights enforcement systems in Europe. In: Micklitz H-W, Wechsler A (eds) The transformation of enforcement: European economic law in global perspective. Hart Publishing, Oxford, pp 87–114

Heinze C (2009) Effektivitätsgrundsatz. In: Basedow et al (eds) Handwörterbuch des Europäischen Privatrechts, Volumen I. Mohr Siebeck, pp 337–341

Inchausti FG (2014) Specific problems of cross-border consumer ADR: what solutions? Zeitschrift für das Privatrecht der Europäischen Union (GPR) (4):197–208

[137]These are two main European Commission policy evaluations including among others national reports from various MS checking the effectiveness of EU consumer protection law in practice. For more information see http://ec.europa.eu/newsroom/just/item-detail.cfm?item_id=59332 and http://ec.europa.eu/newsroom/just/item-detail.cfm?item_id=620435 (last visited: 25 July 2018).

[138]Proposal for a Directive of the European Parliament and of the Council amending Council Directive 93/13/EEC of 5 April 1993, Directive 98/6/EC of the European Parliament and of the Council, Directive 2005/29/EC of the European Parliament and of the Council and Directive 2011/83/EU of the European Parliament and of the Council as regards better enforcement and modernisation of EU consumer protection rules, COM(2018) 185 final—2018/0090(COD), Brussels, 11.4.2018.

[139]Communication from the Commission to the European Parliament, the Council, the European Economic and Social Committee and the Committee of the Regions, Commission Work Programme 2018, An agenda for a more united, stronger and more democratic Europe, COM (2017) 650 final, Strasbourg, 24.10.2017.

Iosifov I (2013) Neravnopravnite klauzi v konteksta na zapovednoto proizvodstvo. Nauchni trudove na Rusenskia Universitet 52(7):191–195

Law S (2018) The transformation of consumer law in times of crisis: the ex officio control of unfair contract terms. In: Uzelac A, van Rhee CH (eds) Transformation of civil justice, unity and diversity. Springer, pp 283–307

Leczykiewicz D, Weatherill S (eds) (2016) The images of the consumer in EU law: legislation, free movement and competition law. Hart Publishing

Loos MBM (2016) Consumer ADR after implementation of the ADR Directive: enforcing European consumer rights at the detriment of European consumer law. Eur Rev Priv Law (1):61–80

Mak C (2014) Rights and remedies. Article 47 EUCFR and effective judicial protection in European private law matters. In: Micklitz H-W (ed) The constitutionalization of European private law. Oxford University Press, pp 236–258

Micklitz H-W, Saumier G (eds) (2018) Enforcement and effectiveness of consumer law. Springer

Mišćenić E (2016) Legal risks in development of EU consumer protection law. In: Mišćenić E, Raccah A (eds) Legal risks in EU law: interdisciplinary studies on legal risk management and better regulation in Europe. Springer, pp 135–163

Mišćenić E (2018a) Protection of consumers on the EU digital single market: virtual or real one? In: Viglianisi Ferraro A, Jagielska M, Selucka M (eds) The influence of the European legislation on national legal systems in the field of consumer protection. Cedam, Kluwer Law International, pp 219–246

Mišćenić E (2018b) Uniform interpretation of Article 4(2) of UCT Directive in the context of consumer credit agreements: is it possible? Revue du droit de l'Union européenne (3):127–159

Mišćenić E (2019) Croatian consumer protection law: from legal approximation to legal fragmentation. Studia Iuridica Toruniensia, Part I, XXII:189–222

Pavillon C (2007) ECJ 26 October 2006, Case C-168-05 Mostaza Claro v. Centro Movil Milenium SL – the unfair contract terms directive: the ECJ's third intervention in domestic procedural law. Eur Rev Priv Law:737–748

Rühl G (2015) Alternative and online dispute resolution for (cross-border) consumer contracts: a critical evaluation of the European legislature's recent efforts to promote competitiveness and growth in the internal market. J Consum Policy 38(4):431–456

van Duin A (2017) Metamorphosis? The role of Article 47 of the EU Charter of Fundamental Rights in cases concerning national remedies and procedures under Directive 93/13/EEC. J Eur Consum Mark Law (EuCML) 6(5):190–198

Weber F (2015) Is ADR the superior mechanism for consumer contractual disputes? - An assessment of the incentivizing effects of the ADR Directive. J Consum Policy (38):265–285

The Democratic Deficit of the EU: Two Schools Under One Roof

Adnan Mahmutovic and Nermina Memic-Mujagic

Contents

1 The Theoretical Debate

After nearly three decades of academic discussion, the EU continues to find itself at a democratic crossroads, facing on one hand a polemical understanding of those who support the thesis on democratic deficit, and on the other those who insist almost in aspirational terms that the EU is democratic to the extent it could or should be.[1] As time passed, these two opinions or viewpoints have developed a virtual system of

[1] Sementilli (2012), p. 6.

A. Mahmutovic (✉)
Prince Mohammad Bin Fahd University, Khobar, Kingdom of Saudi Arabia
e-mail: amahmutovic@pmu.edu.sa

N. Memic-Mujagic (✉)
University of Sarajevo, Sarajevo, Bosnia and Herzegovina

Z. Meškić et al. (eds.), *Balkan Yearbook of European and International Law 2019*,
Balkan Yearbook of European and International Law (2020) 2019: 155–172,
https://doi.org/10.1007/16247_2019_9, Published online: 5 December 2019

different arguments supporting and opposing the main idea. These eventually morphed into two more or less distinct schools of thought.

The first we call the Democratic Deficit School (DDS), which represents the thesis of the existence of a democratic deficit in the EU; as a factor significantly slowing down the continuation of the integration process, and which undermines the credibility and legitimacy of the EU as a supranational beast. Andreas Follesdal and Simon Hix[2] are, among others, representatives of this school.

The second, or Non-Conformist School (NSC), with Andrew Moravcsik[3] and Giandomenico Majone[4] as main protagonists, opposes the previous thesis. They criticize the existence of a democratic deficit in the EU, stressing that a democratic deficit can be part of the *specificum* of the institutional architecture of the Union, but that its significance has been overcome.[5]

This article focuses on the issue of the EU democratic credentials through the prism of these two schools of thought. It delineates that these two schools are not mutually conflicting in all viewpoints, but rather that certain congruencies can be identified, i.e., they both take the democratic deficit as a starting point in the discussion. Thus, while they retain variant interpretations, both have contributed significantly to this discussion. We utilize these two arguments to explain our position in favor of the concept of an EU democratic deficit paradigm, based on the realities of the existing institutional architecture, and the often-competing priorities of member states as well as supranational and intergovernmental visions.

2 Democratic Deficit School

Within the framework of the Democratic Deficit School, one can perceive different arguments that relate to the problem of the EU democratic deficit.[6] In fact, it may be said that all arguments suggest two main aspects. The first aspect relates to questioning the legitimacy of the most important supranational institutions, or democracy in the broader sense, from a normative-theoretical point of view, as well as analysis of debates on the problem. The second aspect focuses on the specific relationship between citizens and the EU, as well as the consequences resulting from the citizens' confidence or lack thereof in the political and legal institutions affecting political life in the EU. In fact, here the arguments are mostly related to the lack of popular support, common *res publica*, and the political people—*demos*. Therefore,

[2]Follesdal and Hix (2006).

[3]Moravcsik (2008), pp. 331–340.

[4]Majone (1998), pp. 5–28.

[5]Sementilli (2012), p. 17.

[6]Boyce (1993), pp. 458–477; Warleigh and Warleigh-Lack (2003), p. 10.

discussion about the democratic deficit of the EU generally gives primacy to two fundamental aspects—institutional[7] and socio-psychological.[8]

2.1 The Institutional Aspect of the Democratic Deficit

The institutional aspect underlines the existence of the EU's democratic deficit because of transferring sovereignty powers from the popularly elected institutions at the national level, enjoying direct democratic legitimacy via the regulatory powers of the Council. Arguably, executive powers are transferred from the national level to that of the EU with no adequate increment of national democratic oversight over ministers at the national level, and parliamentary scrutiny at the supranational level.[9] As some pointed out that insufficient parliamentary control over EU decisions is the original sin of the democratic deficit.[10] It gives the impression that the popularly elected institutions at both levels do not properly check the Council. Therefore, the EU's democratic deficit becomes visible in both the horizontal and vertical distribution of powers because of the lack of a constitutionally fixed balance between the Council, the European Parliament, and the Commission, which is a characteristic of the relations between national and supranational levels.

In the literature, there is an evident criticism of the dominance of supranational executive power at the expense of parliamentary influence.[11] This means national parliaments have no sufficient power to deal with EU affairs, while the function of the European Parliament is still not well structured. Thus, governments can ignore the national parliaments when voting in Brussels, and also may be outnumbered in the Council.[12] This situation affects the representative function that, in the west, mostly is entrusted to parliaments as institutions with direct democratic legitimacy. As a direct consequence of this situation, EU citizens are not able to affect the key policy framework and decisions at a supranational level.

The analysis of the institutional aspect of the democratic deficit has shown two main arguments. The first suggests the democratic deficit is primarily the result of its *sui generis* institutional architecture, while the other suggests the deficit as a consequence of the present technocracy.

---

[7]Stavridis (2006), pp. 4–5.

[8]Crombez (2003), pp. 101–120.

[9]Stavridis (2006), p. 4.

[10]Lord (2013), p. 236.

[11]Craig and De Búrca (2003), p. 168; Raunio (1999), pp. 180–202.

[12]Stavridis (2006).

2.1.1 Democratic Deficit Is the Result of sui generis Institutional Architecture

The first argument of Democratic Deficit School emphasizes the horizontal aspect, i.e., democratic deficit, as a manifestation of a somewhat deeper problem referring to the question of democratic foundations of the EU and its institutions. This aspect focuses on the power disparity among the *Holy Trinity* of the EU institutional architecture: The Council, Parliament and Commission. In this context, some argue that the EU is probably the most complex political-legal project ever attempted[13] and consequentially the biggest challenge of democracy today.[14] Certain "democratic loopholes" may be observed within institutional architecture where institutions fall short of general principles of democracy; for example, how members are nominated and elected, the low turnout for European elections, the procedures by which decisions are made, openness and transparency, accountability, the European Court of Justice makes law rather than interpreting it, and generally speaking how power is distributed and exercised. It seems this institutional framework is best suited for intergovernmental cooperation rather than traditional power-sharing arrangements. The power is allocated to main institutions such as the Council and the Commission, which are not directly accountable to EU citizens. The Council has long been criticized for being secretive and the Commission for being appointed rather than directly elected. The two combine legislative and executive powers, and the European Parliament, the only institution whose members are elected by popular vote, has a relatively diminished role except for the ordinary legislative procedure that it shares with the Council. Arguably, the Council is made of consecutive ministers but performing the legislative role, and the Commission mainly stands for the executive branch but with legislative initiative power. The two primarily tend to overregulate and encroach in the life affairs of the Union's citizens, while a directly elected institution such as a Parliament may not subject them to democratic oversight covering all areas of politics, including sanctions.[15] In spite of the Parliament being the natural focus of efforts to democratize the EU, and in spite of its achievements in legislative powers, it still lacks democratic legitimacy.

The institutional dimension of the democratic deficit could be defined as a consequence of attempts to align multiple interests that have caused an inherent institutional imbalance, or structural problems in the organization of the decision-making process within the EU. Due to the lack of a traditional separation of powers, openness, transparency, popularity and accountability, as important elements of the democratic system, the institutions of the EU are considered less democratic than the national institutions.[16]

---

[13]Chryssochoou (1997), p. 2.

[14]Katz (2001), p. 2.

[15]Maurer (2004), p. 56.

[16]Chryssochoou (2000), p. 10.

Contrary to the above-mentioned discussion, some attribute the democratic deficit, not to EU institutions, but to their Member States. They see the democratic deficit as a natural consequence of the democratic deficit of EU member states.[17]

2.1.2 Democratic Deficit Is the Result of Present Technocracy

The interests and preferences of EU's citizens are neglected because unelected and non-accountable technocrats mostly govern the EU; or democratic deficit occurs because of reliance on technical capacities. In this respect, the second problem of the legitimacy input is seen in the great influence of technocrats on the decision-making process, especially with regard to the role of comitology of the Directorate Generals in the Commission, and the COREPER in the case of the Council.[18] The two, assisted by a large number of expert committees drawn from the appropriate sectors in the Member States, have a significant role in drafting new legal solutions. The EU appears as the ultimate consequence of this condition, drawing its democratic deficit from a large number of committees that are not accountable to anyone, and which work in secret and without public oversight.[19] It should be noted that because of this secrecy, it is not possible to know the attitudes and opinions of all the participants in the decision-making process within the Council and the Commission.[20] The evident secrecy represents an obstacle to openness and transparency as important elements of the democratic legitimizing of European governance. According to an estimate published at the end of the 1990s, nine tenths of all decisions adopted at Union level were created by a large number of closed committees composed of technocrats and government representatives of Member States.[21]

Our observation concerning the second argument of the institutional dimension has shown the democratic deficit because of the lack of openness, transparency and accountability of the supranational institutions towards the Union's citizens. It could be said that the issue of legitimacy, because of this deficiency, is associated with the discrepancy between the powers transferred to the regulatory authorities and the control of the elected national parliaments and the European Parliament with impeccable democratic credentials over them.[22]

[17]Innerarity (2015), pp. 173–174.
[18]Craig and De Búrca (2003), p. 168.
[19]Paley (2002), pp. 469–470.
[20]Ballmann (2002), pp. 551–574.
[21]Stein (2001), pp. 489–534.
[22]Dilek (2011), p. 244.

2.2 The Socio-Psychological Aspect of the Democratic Deficit

Unlike the first main argument, which questions the legitimacy input of the EU and its institutions as the cause of democratic deficit, the second one points out that the Union's democratic deficit is a result of poor governance or shortcomings in legitimacy output; that is to say, the lack of the link between voter preference and policy outcome, essentially the citizen's assessment of the relevance and quality of the institution's performance in Brussels as well as their support for and interest in the cause. This is a socio-psychological aspect of the democratic deficit.[23] It is referred to as socio-psychological because it implies the individual feelings of citizens of the Union and their connection to the European institutions.

Hence, democratic deficit occurs because decisions made by the EU institutions do not reflect the interests of the majority of its citizens—*government for the people*, as an important element of democratic representation. Notwithstanding that citizens' interests and preferences may be different in nature or even mutually exclusive, they still lie at the heart of democracy; and the definition of political systems as democratic or undemocratic depends on satisfying those interests.

In a democratic system, there is a strong correlation between the citizens and the institutions that can be defined as the arena of democratic representation. One of the main questions raised within this arena is to what extent the people can control the performance of the leaders to whom power has been delegated. However, before that, citizens need to have the opportunity to make their own choice on policy options offered by political subjects through the process of deliberation and contestation. In fact, the opportunity is given to the voters through European elections but the absence of a European dimension makes them second-order affairs. This can be seen as a consequence of no visible link between democratic elections and output. Normally, the government will be accountable for whatever happens during its term in office. We see that this option is not available in the Union.[24] The second-order elections problem was addressed with the so-called *Duff proposal*; to elect twenty-five members of the European parliament on transnational lists, in a pan-European district. Some studies have shown that certain improvements are likely to be expected in that respect.[25] The pan-European district has become popular thanks to the qualification of the European Parliament as composed of representatives of the Union's citizens made by article 14.2 TEU—The Lisbon Treaty,[26] instead of representatives of the peoples of the Member States brought together in the Community previously made by article 189 ECT—the Nice Treaty. The pan-European district proposal has opened door for the discrepancy between the preference of EU citizens and the outcomes made by non-elected technocrats to be reduced. However, some further improvements are needed to establish a European electoral agenda.

---

[23]Bellamy and Castiglione (1997), pp. 421–445.

[24]Anell (2018), pp. 6–64.

[25]Bol et al. (2016), pp. 525–545.

[26]See: Article 223(1) TFEU.

There are also authors who suggest developing a standard EU parliamentary democracy where supranational parties will fight to be put in charge in a two chamber EP with a "Prime Minister of Europe" or contest for additional seats through Europe-wide lists to create vital space for political contestation.[27]

At this point, the Union's citizens cannot have an effective influence on the decision-making process in the EU and therefore they do not feel part of that process. Their feelings are best seen in the percentage of voters in EP elections, which is in a state of permanent decline.[28] Indeed, decision-making process in Brussels is both opaque and confusing to most citizens and decisions are often such that even experts struggle to comprehend them. Therefore, it transpires that decisions are not made in the citizens' interests, but primarily in the interests of unabashed elitists, multinational companies, corporations, lobbyists, or the interests of certain political groups. The incomprehensibility of the regulations passed in Brussels can be interpreted as a classic violation of one of the key principles of lawmaking in a democratic society, i.e., that regulations must be available to citizens and written in a form understandable to the layperson. The incomprehensibility of the regulations could jeopardize legal certainty of a democratic society because they represent a message that cannot be read by average citizens, thereby posing the question to whom the message was even addressed. This may not be justified by an argument that ignorance of the law is not excuse, as that is not caused by subjective considerations; rather, it is an objective format far from the reach of ordinary citizens.

This democratic deficit is closely linked with the previous argument, which focuses on the weakness of institutional design and the role of technocrats. Namely, due to the lack of accountability, as well as openness and transparency of the institutions towards the citizens of the Union, they are not significantly interested in what is happening in the EU. Citizens are showing less and less willingness to accept and support a "passive government of irresponsible elites".[29] Given that most of the debates that precede decision-making in the EU are held behind closed doors, little information is available to the European public. It does not change the course, but it arguably merely attenuates the rate at which the citizens are democratically plundered.

The insufficiency of social legitimization, besides undermining current achievements, may harm the future of the project of European integration. The socio-psychological dimension of the democratic deficit exposes the inability of the EU to establish a democracy modelled on states, as on the supranational level, there are no social assumptions on which democratic rule is based: collective identity and European demos.[30] This is, by far, one of the main causes of limited prospects of citizens' participation in the process of decision-making and the lack of distributive

[27]Lee (2014), p. 9.

[28]Gagatek (2010), pp. 3–33.

[29]Arnull and Wincott (2002), p. 7.

[30]Stavridis (2006).

justice.[31] The EU has no demos but multiple citizenships of its citizens—"demoi." As some argued: "If there is no demos, there can be no democracy".[32] Indeed, with no demos it will be hard to achieve some of the essentials of democratic coexistence: recognition, public legitimacy, solidarity, popularity, etc.

In summing up on the two aspects of legitimacy, one can say both forms are important, but there is a question of priority. Considering the arguments, a little priority is given to input legitimacy over output one, in particular, because, in our opinion the former determines the latter. However, it is certain that regardless of their differentiation, these two dimensions of the democratic legitimacy demonstrate a certain degree of interconnectedness, which in most of the academic literature on the EU's democratic deficit is evident in the fact that research relies on two equally important points: the legislative process and the public's role within it.[33] Arguably, the socio-psychological dimension of the democratic deficit may be caused by the complexity of the institutional structure, and the lack of the balance of power among the Union's institutions and the decision-making process of the EU. The perception of a socio-psychological democratic deficit of the EU most often stems from the perception of how the process of supranational decision-making takes place, or the possibility of citizen participation in the process.[34]

2.3 The Concept of a Standard Version

In the absence of single meaning, some authors try to identify a Standard Version of democratic deficit, which will include a set of widely-used arguments. The first attempt was made by Joseph Weiler who highlighted the need for standardized access to democratic deficit based on a set of different arguments.[35] One of the most cited types, offered by Simon Hix, is based on the expansion of Weiler's arguments. Hix lists five basic constructs on which the concept of democratic deficit in the EU is based[36]:

1. The integration process has led to a strengthening of the executive, and to the weakening of the national parliamentary control
2. The European Parliament is too weak
3. There are no "European" elections
4. The EU is too distant from its citizens who do not understand it
5. The result of the above factors is a so-called policy drift

[31]Grimm (1995), pp. 282–302.

[32]Weiler and Weiler (1999), p. 337.

[33]Crombez (2003), pp. 101–120.

[34]Crombez (2003).

[35]Sementilli (2012).

[36]Follesdal and Hix (2006), p. 177.

By analyzing the first construct, we see that the institutions of the executive branch mostly make the decisions in the EU.[37] According to this construct, the main problem is the fact that there is a shift of power from the democratic parliamentary systems at national level to the executive-centered systems at the EU level. Unlike Member States, where government ministers are typically accountable to voters through parliaments, the existing institutional architecture of the EU still provides an unparalleled position to the ministers of the Member States represented in the Council, and politically nominated Commission officials, which elude the supervisory mechanisms of national parliaments. Thus, when the ministers sit in Brussels, its members, otherwise representatives of the executive branch of government, become the legislative power. The subordinated ministers, at once become superior to their national parliaments (due to the supremacy of the EU law over national law). This situation leads to the policy-making at the European level to be dominantly controlled by consecutive ministers who can simply ignore the vote of national parliaments.[38] In addition, the decisions are usually made in small, closed diplomatic committees such as COREPER, which is beyond any parliamentary control.[39]

The second construct centers on the fact that regardless of the strengthening of the role of the European Parliament, which has been achieved by gradual reform from the Maastricht Treaty to the Lisbon Treaty, there has not been a significant offset of the democracy deficit that ensued with the loss of control by national parliaments. Notwithstanding that the Ordinary legislative procedure over a time has been extended, the legislative procedures in which the Parliament has only limited powers are still significantly present.

In the third construct, the presence of the democracy deficit is attributed to the absence of real European elections. EU citizens are not in a position to vote on EU policies except at periodic referendums on membership in the EU or the revision of the constitutional treaties. Elections for the European Parliament do not have a real European dimension. They neither feature primarily European issues and candidates at the European level, nor encourage debate on the future direction of EU policies. European elections are not well publicized by the media, which preview European Parliament elections as an event of peripheral importance. The absence of a European dimension, in part, is caused by the lack of European political parties.

The fourth construct shows that the EU is too distant from its citizens in institutional and psychological terms, due to which it is incomprehensible to them. The institutional aspect of distance implies a lack of the aforementioned electoral control over the Council and the Commission, while the socio-psychological aspect pertains to the deficit in communication between the citizens and the institutions of the EU, which is evident in comparison to communication with the local democratic institutions to which citizens are accustomed. Too much diversity leads to a lack of

[37]Raunio (1999), pp. 180–202.

[38]Follesdal and Hix (2006), p. 534.

[39]Hayes-Renshaw and Wallace (1997), pp. 135–138.

understanding and an inability to identify with such a complex system and with predominantly technocratic policy-making processes.

Finally, the fifth construct, notes that the EU, due to the previously described shortcomings, adopts policies not supported by the majority of citizens in the Member States. It is often the case that governments of the Member States at the supranational level advocate policies that cannot be realized domestically, where they are limited by parliaments, courts and non-corporate structures of interest groups. This is the case, for example, with the support for the development of the neoliberal regulatory framework for a single European market, monetary union, subsidies given to farmers through a common agricultural policy, etc. In this sense, it can be said that the process of European integration produces a sort of policy shift from the ideal voter preferences in the Member States.

In addition, Hix often states that the presence of the democratic deficit is a consequence of the absence of a competitive approach of European parties to political leadership, or the lack of public importance in creating policies in the EU. In this sense, Hix pleads the case that the EU is democratic in the procedural sense, but in the substantive sense, the Union is closer to enlightened despotism than democracy. He sees a way out of the existing situation in accumulating more competitive spirit in the political process at EU level. Further, it follows from Hix's arguments that the basic problem of the democratic deficit of the EU lies in the fact of change in political oversight from a democratic parliamentary system of governance at the national level to an executive-centralized system of governance on the supranational level. In such a system, the institutions representing the executive branch of the government are not accountable to the one of legislative, and their decisions are most often non-transparent and generally, they do not consider the preferences of the citizens of the EU, rather taking into account the interests of the Member States.

3 The Non-Conformist School

We have previously pointed out that the dominant point of view in academic literature presumes that the EU is facing a democratic deficit, while fewer authors claim that this is in fact a mythological argument based on incorrect analogy.[40] Andrew Moravcsik and Giandomenico Majone are among the most prominent representatives of this school.

---

[40]Moravcsik (1993), pp. 473–524.

3.1 The EU as an International Organization

Andrew Moravcsik is the most significant author of those who deny the existence of the EU's democratic deficit. He criticizes proponents of the democratic deficit, because in their viewpoints they assess the EU in accordance with the utopian model of democracy instead of reasonable, *realistic and modern governance criteria.*[41] It follows from a reasonable criterion that the EU is not a state, but an international organization that the individual Member States have joined with the main purpose of achieving common goals.[42] In his opinion, the normative justification of the political authority of the EU follows from the performance of the organization itself and in particular to the extent that it guarantees results that cannot be achieved by the individual approach of the Member States. The democratic deficit argument is pointless because the decision on achieving common goals is made by the representatives of the democratically elected governments of the Member States that enjoy full democratic legitimacy.[43] Each of these representatives was elected democratically in an EU member state to represent the citizens of those states at the level of economic cooperation. Real power is not centralized on the supranational level—rather, it is in the hands of government representatives of the Member States, who are the most accountable participants of the Union's political life. It is completely incorrect to insist on democratic accountability of the supranational level when such a level does not possess real power. Accountability is sought from those who have the power to create the political, legal and social conditions, and that they are not supranational, but national representatives.

Therefore, one cannot say that there is a gap between the interests of the democratically elected member state governments and the final results of EU policies. This is the reason why the EU cannot be labelled as an undemocratic creation.[44] Moreover, Moravcsik believes that the EU itself has contributed to democracy because it has made national governments more accountable to their citizens, because the ministers' activities are not only controlled in the Member States, but also in the wider, European context.

Responding to Hix's concept of democratic deficit, Moravcsik states his arguments. First, in the context of the argument that the integration process has brought to the strengthening of the executive at the expense of legislative branch, Moravcsik points out that national ministers are equally accountable to citizens at the national and at the European level due to which they are subjected to the oversight of national media that regularly inform citizens on the decisions made in Brussels.[45] Other than that, the introduction of the "early warning mechanism" enables national parliaments

[41]Moravcsik (2002), pp. 603–624.

[42]Moravcsik (1993), Ibid.

[43]Moravcsik (2002), p. 603.

[44]Hiks (2007), p. 179.

[45]Moravcsik (2008), pp. 331–340.

to object the Commission's proposals if they consider that the principle of subsidiarity has been breached.

Secondly, the argument that the European Parliament is too weak cannot be accepted because the most significant *democratic input* on the supranational level in the past two decades, i.e., from the Treaty of Maastricht, has been achieved through continuous strengthening of the legislative powers of the European Parliament, as well as when electing members of the Commission. In support of these claims, the case of the resignation of the Jacques Santer Commission is often pointed out. France and Germany opposed the resignation, but the European Parliament emerged as the winner of this crisis.

Thirdly, responding to the argument that institutions should ensure a greater possibility of citizen participation, Moravcsik states that questions on the Union are simply not important enough for voter participation.[46]

Commenting on the standard argument about the distance between the citizens and the Union, he says that is a continental-level characteristic of international organizations that they are distant from individual citizens.[47] However, as he states, the decision-making process at the European level is more transparent than at the national level where citizens and those who reside in the EU have a greater possibility of access to documents of the Union's institutions.

Fourthly, rejecting the argument that the EU adopts policies not supported by the majority of citizens, Moravcsik points out that the decisions, in accordance with the "checks and balances" principle, are always supported by consensus or qualified majority.

In addition, Moravcsik offers an interesting opinion, that it is incorrect to compare and evaluate the democratic legitimacy of the institutions in the "real world" with democratic legitimacy in international institutions. In other words, it is hard to find common parameters that could be used to compare the democratic legitimacy of international organisations with an ideal system of democracy. Democracy was not originally created for international organizations so that each questioning of democracy in the context of international organizations varies from the normative model. Instead, we must ask ourselves whether international institutions achieve democracy in the "real world" at all, which has mostly been achieved through already existing advanced societies faced with restrictions of public information and interest, overregulation, the credibility of convictions and the related consensus. This author points out that if a reasonable criterion for assessing democratic governance is adopted, widespread criticism of the democratic legitimacy of the EU is unsubstantiated by valid empirical evidence. Therefore, the EU shows no sign of a lack of legitimacy.

On the contrary, its accountability, according to Moravcsik, is manifested through the accountability of directly elected representatives in the Parliament, but also

[46]Ibid.

[47]Ibid.

through the accountability of the highest-level elected officials in the European Council.[48]

Moravcsik concludes that the search for new channels of democratic legitimization is not necessary for at least two reasons.

Firstly, the EU, as the product of intergovernmental cooperation, is a pragmatically efficient, normatively attractive and politically stable creation and fully meets the requirements of the Member States.[49]

Secondly, the increase in opportunities for citizen participation in the decision-making process does not necessarily lead to a greater legitimization of the process. In fact, the decline in interest of voters in the elections for the European Parliament appears as the fact according to which a greater space for democratic legitimization established by constitutional treaties becomes unused. As the cause of this condition, Moravcsik highlights the nature of the tasks performed by the EU, which are mainly technical and elite-driven with meaningful powers.

3.2 The EU as a Regulatory Agency

The works of *Giandomenic Majone*[50] are central to the framework of the Non-Conformist School on democratic deficit. In his normative and theoretical standpoints, Majone presumes that the EU is basically a supranational *regulatory state*[51] or even a *regulatory agency* whose basic goal is the creation of effective results of regulatory policy and whose jurisdiction is delegated to the European level.[52] According to his understanding, the EU can be compared with national regulatory agencies such as Telecom.[53] The basic characteristics of the regulatory state model is that it sees institutions as a means of achieving certain goals, and not as a goal itself.[54]

If we analyze Majone's starting point, we can conclude that he emphasizes the economic aspect of European integration more than others. Despite Majone's admission that the democratic character of the Member States is sufficient to legitimize the intergovernmental, but not the supranational component of the EU, he conceptualizes the legitimacy of supranational components based on the successful referral to the EU as a regulatory state. Therefore, for Majone, the legitimacy of the EU depends on the successful fulfillment of the EU's functions as a regulatory body. Majone does not see the problem of democratic deficit as much as that of

[48]Moravcsik (2002), Ibid.
[49]Moravcsik (2006), pp. 219–241.
[50]Follesdal and Koslwoski (1998), p. 54.
[51]Misita (2007), p. 204.
[52]Majone (1998), pp. 5–28.
[53]Majone (1993).
[54]Misita (2007), p. 191.

'credibility crisis'.[55] Legitimacy should be exempt from the need to find political majority and to be the object of political disputes. In other words, Majone stresses the "procedural legitimacy".[56] It actually implies the successful delegation of specific functional tasks, which may be performed more efficiently and more robustly at the supranational level.[57] As long as that is guaranteed, Majone does not see any further need for further legitimizing the EU.[58]

Comparing with Hix's concept of democratic deficit, we can note that Majone does not consider that the increase in competencies and the strengthening of the role of the Parliament may lead to a decrease of the democratic deficit, but that the strengthening of the Parliament position would improve the so-called majority or "Westminster" model that leads to the tyranny of the majority By presenting his own specific viewpoints, Majone concludes that the process of EU integration itself is a non-majority and the de-politicization of European policy is the price for the preservation of national sovereignty.[59] In this context, Majone emphasizes the Commission as the most important supranational institution that with its characteristic capacities strives to protect the Treaty-defined interests of the Union. For Majone, technocrats in the Commission, the Council and EU agencies will most likely better protect the citizens' interests than the majority in the European Parliament.

3.3 Final Touches

Considering the main arguments of Majone's and Moravcsik's school, one can conclude on the resistance to the democratic deficit school as a product of their specific understanding of the EU.[60] In fact, in understanding democratic legitimacy they highlight a functional, or the so-called *output* dimension of legitimacy, that is, decisions taken by the deputies must satisfy most of those they represent, while completely leaving aside the *input* dimension. This is surprising, and by all accounts an exception. Hence, besides the output dimension, which represents the quality of the legislation and decisions, Scharpf points out the input dimension that he claims represents the quality of participation in the process of law and decision-making.[61] The denial of *input* dimensions of democratic legitimacy is questionable, because even the weakest models of liberal democracy would agree that democracy is always

[55]Majone (2002), pp. 375–392.
[56]Misita (2007), p. 191.
[57]Wiesner (2008), pp. 96–122.
[58]Follesdal and Koslwoski (1998), p. 77.
[59]Majone (1998), Ibid.
[60]Wiesner (2008), Ibid.
[61]Scharpf (1999), pp. 261–288.

in need of an *input* dimension.[62] However, why are *Majone* and *Moravcsik* leaving the *input* dimension aside? This is because they do not see the EU as a supranational democratic order for which the *input* dimension of legitimacy is necessary, but they see it as a regulatory state or an international organization, thereby arguing that EU policymaking procedures are enough of a justification for its intergovernmental character and balancing authority between multiple institutions and levels of governance. Therefore, as Moravcsik states, the existence of a democratic deficit is argued by those who express federal aspirations about the future of the EU. In this way, the debate on democratic deficit fits perfectly into the debate on federalism-intergovermentalism.[63]

4 Conclusion

Our analysis has examined the emergence of two broad schools of thought about the democratic credentials of the European Union gleaned from selected literature spanning from 1993 to 2018. The schools of thought, for this paper, are termed the Democratic Deficit School and the Non-Conformist School. The main divergence between these two schools lies not in their specific understanding of democracy, but rather in their incongruent conceptualizations about supranational organizations and the status of intergovernmental relations. The specific outcomes and differences in each, can be traced to the evolution of the aforementioned concepts in each school.

The discussion of the main arguments brought to light some of the categorical weaknesses of the non-conformist approach. The principle weakness lies in the failure to recognize a shift from negative to positive integration forces within the EU, which has been achieved over recent decades. The integration process began by removing obstacles to economic cooperation among its member states. However, it soon became apparent that such activities required certain national government functions to migrate to a supranational level. Consequently, EU institutions have slowly grown in power and stature, increasingly affecting the life of its citizens. With the migration of various nation-state functions, questions about EU's democratic legitimacy have surfaced in the public arena and in its agenda.

The non-conformist approach has greater credence in examining the initial stages of the integration process where it was limited, primarily, to economic cooperation between member states. In these circumstances, with effective policies bringing about desired results, this was sufficient for legitimization. Nowadays, the integration process, with its visible elements of a supranational democratic order, is too pervasive to simply label the EU as a functional, regulatory regime. This becomes abundantly evident in the growing ascendancy of EU law over the national laws.

[62] Ibid.

[63] Ash (2002).

Most of the work of non-conformists draws on technocratic, utilitarian criteria for establishing EU legitimacy, while conformists subscribe to liberal democratic ones. The former embody economic considerations, while the latter focus on political processes. The persisting dynamic of the integration with the multiple interests of conflicting visions will, eventually, pave the path for a legalization process within the EU.

One critique of the Democratic Deficit School argument revolves around the question of whether the EU is being unduly reified due to its sui generis structure, but also the influence of technocrats in the decision-making process within key EU posts. This paper contends that the EU should not be seen as embodying the ideal of democratic representation. Instead, the EU approximates a prosthetic form of governance, i.e., a regulatory regime that does not require a popular mandate for legitimacy.

The EU is not a state, but rather, it approximates a hybrid with its unique, sui-generis, a polity multi-level governance legal entity that can be thought of as a laboratory for testing the prospects and perspectives of democracy to exist outside the framework of the nation-state. Although the EU falls well short of democratic legitimacy in many areas, similarly, it is unreasonable to expect greater democratic accomplishments, at this time. This viewpoint is clearly backed up by recent developments where Member States are crucial actors in resolving various EU crises, when EU bodies have been unable to effectively respond.

This, notwithstanding, the EU merits greater recognition for democratic legitimacy, having achieved greater efficiencies and demonstrated its capabilities in the political arena. Although, currently, there is no viable political solution, the construction of EU political authority is aimed at achieving actual democratic representation. In turn, this presupposes the establishment of mechanisms for democratic oversight, transparency and accountability. In the absence of these mechanisms, the distance between the policymakers and citizens will continue to grow. Herein, lies the core argument on the democratic deficit of the EU.

References

Anell L (2018) A democratic future for the European Union. Available at: http://arenaide.se/wp-content/uploads/sites/2/2018/02/rapport-a-democratic-future.pdf

Arnull A, Wincott D (eds) (2002) Accountability and legitimacy in the European Union. Oxford University Press on Demand

Ash T (2002) The EU's future: the federalism/intergovernmentalism debate. Retrieved: http://www.kentlaw.edu/faculty/bbrown/classes/IntlOrgSp07/CourseDocs/VITheEU'sFuture_FederalismorIntergovernmentalism.pdf (January 2018)

Ballmann A, Epstein D, O'halloran S (2002) Delegation, comitology, and the separation of powers in the European Union. Int Organ 56(3):551–574

Bellamy R, Castiglione D (1997) Building the Union: the nature of sovereignty in the political architecture of Europe. Law Philos 16(4):421–445

Bol D, Harfst P, Blais A, Golder S, Laslier J-F, Stephenson L, Van der Straeten K (2016) Addressing Europe s democratic deficit: an experimental evaluation of the pan-European district proposal. Eur Union Polit 17(4):525–545. First Published February 14, 2016
Boyce B (1993) The democratic deficit in the European Community. Parliam Aff 46(4):458–478
Chryssochoou DN (1997) Democracy and European integration theory in the 1990s. ESCA-USA conference Seattle Washington
Chryssochoou DN (2000) Democracy in the European Union. IB Tauris
Craig P, De Búrca G (2003) EU law: text, cases, and materials. Oxford University Press
Crombez C (2003) The democratic deficit in the European Union: much ado about nothing? Eur Union Polit 4(1):101–120
Dilek K (2011) The problem of "democratic deficit" in the European Union. Int J Humanit Soc Sci 1 (5):244
Follesdal A, Hix S (2006) Why there is a democratic deficit in the EU: a response to Majone and Moravcsik. JCMS: J Common Mark Stud 44(3):533–562
Follesdal, Koslwoski (1998) Democracy and the European Union. Springer-Verlag, Berlin
Gagatck W (2010) The 2009 Elections to the European Parliament. Country Reports. European University Institute
Grimm D (1995) Does Europe need a constitution? Eur Law J 1:282–302
Hayes-Renshaw, Wallace (1997) The Council of Ministers. Macmillan Press, Basingstoke and London
Hiks S, Radić I, Mihajlović M, Ateljević V, Međak V (2007) Politički sistem Evropske unije. Službeni glasnik
Innerarity D (2015) The inter-democratic deficit of the European Union: the governance of Europe's economic, political and legal transformation, pp 173–174
Katz RS (2001) Models of democracy: elite attitudes and the democratic deficit in the European Union. Eur Union Polit 2(1):53–79
Lee D (2014) The European Union's democratic deficit and options for EU democracy in the 21st century. EU Centre in Singapore, Working Paper No. 22
Lord PH (2013) The European Union: parliamentary wasteland or parliamentary field? In: Crum B, Erik Fossum J (eds) Practices of interparliamentary coordination in international politics: the European Union and beyond. ECPR Press, Colchester, pp 235–250
Majone G (1993) The European Community: an 'Independent Fourth Branch of Government?'
Majone G (1998) Europe's 'democratic deficit': the question of standards. Eur Law J 4(1):5–28
Majone G (2002) The European Commission: the limits of centralization and the perils of parliamentarization. Governance 15(3):375–392
Maurer A (2004) Doprinos parlamenata u procesu približavanja EU. Politička misao: časopis za politologiju 40(2):54–87
Misita N (2007) Osnovi prava Evropske unije, drugo izmijenjeno i dopunjeno izdanje. Pravni fakultet, Sarajevo
Moravcsik A (1993) Preferences and power in the European Community: a liberal intergovernmentalist approach. JCMS: J Common Mark Stud 31(4):473–524
Moravcsik A (2002) Reassessing legitimacy in the European Union. JCMS: J Common Mark Stud 40(4):603–624
Moravcsik A (2006) What can we learn from the collapse of the European constitutional project? Politische Vierteljahresschrift 47(2):219–241
Moravcsik A (2008) The myth of Europe's 'democratic deficit'. Intereconomics 43(6):331–340
Paley J (2002) Toward an anthropology of democracy. Annu Rev Anthropol 31(1):469–496
Raunio T (1999) Always one step behind? National legislatures and the European Union 1. Gov Oppos 34(2):180–202
Scharpf FW (1999) Legitimacy in the multi-actor European polity. In: Organizing political institutions. Scandinavian University Press, pp 261–288
Sementilli L (2012) A 'democratic deficit' in the EU. The reality behind the myth. University of Brussels

Stavridis S (2006) Why the EU's constitutionalization and parliamentarization are worsening the existing democratic deficit in European foreign and defence policies. JMWP No. 59.06, February 2006

Stein E (2001) International integration and democracy: no love at first sight. Am J Int Law 95 (3):489–534

Warleigh A, Warleigh-Lack AJF (2003) Democracy in the European Union: theory, practice and reform. Sage

Weiler JH, Weiler K (1999) The Constitution of Europe: 'Do the new clothes have an Emperor?' and other essays on European integration. Cambridge University Press

Wiesner C (2008) Democratic legitimacy, democratisation and democratic identity of the European Union-old questions, new challenges. Redescriptions: Yearbook of Political Thought, Conceptual History and Feminist Theory, pp 96–122

Some Private International Law Aspects of European Economic Migration

Jasmina Alihodžić

Contents

1 Introduction

Migration with an international element must be viewed with regard to its territorial and temporal scope as emphasised by *King*. In a territorial sense, the national border crossing is necessary for the realisation of international migrations. Although not very complicated at first glance, this question in practice is much more complex, and it is necessary to observe it from the aspect of the "openness" of the boundaries towards migration. For example, there is a clear difference between the internal borders within the European Union and the external borders of the Schengen area. Given the temporal component of migration, and to be statistically measurable and different from other forms of mobility (for example, tourism), the migration timeframe is considered to be 1 year in the country of destination.[1] In addition, in

[1]King (2012), pp. 7–9.

J. Alihodžić (✉)
Faculty of Law, University of Tuzla, Tuzla, Bosnia and Herzegovina
e-mail: jasmina.altumbabic@untz.ba

Z. Meškić et al. (eds.), *Balkan Yearbook of European and International Law 2019*,
Balkan Yearbook of European and International Law (2020) 2019: 173–194,
https://doi.org/10.1007/16247_2019_10, Published online: 5 December 2019

relation to the above, there are significant differences noted in the scholarship. Migration is considered the movement of workers who have signed 1-year employment contracts, but also in the case of long-term arrangements lasting from 5 to 10 years, or those with a tendency to become permanent. On the other hand, seasonal migrations, which do not exceed the threshold of 1 year, are vital for certain economic sectors, such as agriculture, tourism and construction of the country of destination.[2] Migration further differs in whether it involves a movement between only two countries, the country of origin and the country of destination or, on the way to the country of destination, the migrant is retained for a certain period in the so-called transit countries.[3] In addition to the established division to internal and international, temporary and permanent, and legal and illegal migrations, some authors also point to the existence of a dichotomy between voluntary and forced migrations, while distinguishing economic migrants and refugees.[4] Economic migration, according to Trachtman is a result of demand and supply. Namely, present value of life opportunities in the country of origin, including cost of migration presents total cost to the potential migrant. On the other hand, present value of life opportunities in the country of destination is the benefit to the potential migrant. Whenever the benefit exceeds the cost, the potential migrant will probably wish to migrate.[5] However, the aforementioned division on voluntary and forced migrations seems to be simplified, especially if one considers that armed conflicts in one country can also cause economic destruction to it, which is a catalyst for the migration of the population from that area, while considering the above-mentioned conceptual dichotomy, such category of migrants are not considered a category to enjoy legal protection in the country of destination under the provisions of the Convention relating to the Status of Refugees.[6] Furthermore, armed conflicts are inextricably linked to the (non)functioning of the state apparatus, which causes a strong interconnection of economic and political factors as the cause of migration of the population from a certain area. In addition to the mentioned migration divisions, which can be considered typical given the current practice, in the era of globalisation and the new world order, new forms of population movement appear, which, given their basic characteristics, can be considered as migrations. So today, we can talk about migration for the purposes of family reunification, residential tourism, reproductive tourism, marital migration, student migration, migration because of retirement conditions, brain drain, etc.[7]

---

[2]Ibid.

[3]Bosnia and Herzegovina as well as other countries from Western Balkan region can be considered transit countries on the road to the EU for most of the migrants coming from war-affected areas of the Middle East.

[4]Sales (2007), p. 47. Hagen-Zanker (2008).

[5]Trachtman (2009), p. 8.

[6]UN General Assembly, *Convention Relating to the Status of Refugees*, 28 July 1951, United Nations, Treaty Series, vol. 189, p. 137, available at: https://www.refworld.org/docid/3be01b964.html [accessed 7 May 2019].

[7]On types and reasons for migrations see in: Vukorepa (2018), pp. 85–92.

The regulation of the status of economic migrants in the EU, as well as the legal protection of these persons, depends on the appropriate application of private international law instruments. In the first part of the paper, the concept and legal framework of economic migration in the EU are analysed, pointing in particular to legal instruments that implement EU immigration and integration measures in relation to third-country nationals. The second part of the paper points to the necessity of interaction between private international law instruments and migration law. The third part of the paper is concerned with the recognition of foreign public documents and the recognition of foreign court decisions as instruments of private international law necessary to regulate the status of economic migrants in the EU. However, the role of private international law instruments is not exhausted with the aforementioned functions, so in this part of the article touches upon the rules of jurisdiction and applicable law that will be applied in case of a dispute based on an individual employment contract concluded by an employee who is a third country national with an EU employer. The author emphasises that there are no international mechanisms to regulate these issues in a comprehensive manner, and propose concrete solutions to the possible regulation of various aspects of private international law, which would improve the status of migrants from third countries at the EU level.

2 Economic Migration in the European Union

Economic migrants are, from the perspective of the European Union, considered third-country nationals who are allowed formal access to the EU.[8] Given the possibility and the right to move within the EU, their status vary considerably from the position of EU citizens moving or living in a Member State other than their country of origin. Although most third-country nationals enjoy rights that are equal to the rights of nationals of the Member State in which they reside, their movement within the EU is significantly limited. To regulate the status of migrants, the EU migration policy is based on two pillars[9]: *immigration measures*, which regulate entry, stay, employment, return, deportation of immigrants, and *integration measures*, which aim to regulate the way immigrants are included in the country of destination. In this regard, the EU has taken a number of steps towards the establishment of a legal framework that would enable migrants with a residence in the EU to exercise certain rights (equal working conditions, employment opportunities, equal access to goods and services, education, and integration into society in general).[10] It is worth mentioning that there is no such instrument at the EU level

[8]Mügge and van der Haar (2016), p. 84.

[9]Vukorepa (2018), pp. 93–94.

[10]Council Directive 2000/43/EC of 29 June 2000 implementing the principle of equal treatment between persons irrespective of racial or ethnic origin, *OJ L 180, 19.7.2000, pp. 22–26.* Council

granting the rights to *all workers* who are third-country nationals legally employed in the EU territory. Instead, a number of legal provisions provide for the protection and equal treatment of *certain categories* of third-country nationals.[11]

The legal framework for regulating the entry, residence and work of third-country nationals in EU Member States is incorporated in the provisions of Articles 77–80 of the Treaty on the Functioning of the EU,[12] which regulates border control, asylum and immigration. In addition, by the entry into force of the Lisbon Treaty,[13] the EU Charter on Fundamental Rights[14] has become part of the primary EU law and contains a number of provisions that can be considered relevant for the protection and equal treatment of workers.

Article 15 of the Charter provides that everyone has the right to work and to perform a freely chosen or accepted occupation. Every citizen of the Union can freely seek employment, work and exercise the right to a business establishment and to provide services in each Member State. Third-country nationals allowed to work within the national borders of the Member States are entitled to working conditions equivalent to those enjoyed by EU citizens. The Charter further provides that within the scope of application of the Treaty and without prejudice to any of their special provisions, any discrimination based on nationality shall be prohibited.[15] Besides, there is the Council Regulation 859/2003[16] that constitutes an application of the Regulation 1408/71 and the Regulation 574/72, both comprising coordination rules applicable to third country nationals legally resident in the EU. It is important to

---

Directive 2000/78/EC of 27 November 2000 establishing a general framework for equal treatment in employment and occupation, *OJ L 303, 2.12.2000, pp. 16–22.* EU has also adopted Common Basic Principles for Immigrant Integration Policy, known as "EU Zaragoza Integration Indicators". Third–country Nationals in the European Union, Indicators of immigrant Integration 2015: settling in (2015). OECD/European Union, https://www.oecd-ilibrary.org/docserver/9789264234024-17-en.pdf?expires=1537788002&id=id&accname=guest&checksum=27452592D2EC6E9FDF30305785C6EA9E. See also Regulation (EU) No 604/2013 of the European Parliament and of the Council of 26 June 2013 establishing the criteria and mechanisms for determining the Member State responsible for examining an application for international protection lodged in one of the Member States by a third-country national or a stateless person 180/31.

[11]Commission Staff Working Document accompanying document to the Proposal for a Council Directive on a Single application procedure for a single permit for third country nationals to reside and work in the territory of a Member State and on a common set of rights for third country workers legally residing in a Member State, SEC (2007) 1408, Brussels, 23.10.2007.

[12]Consolidated version of the Treaty on the Functioning of the European Union, *OJ C 326, 26.10.2012, pp. 47–390.*

[13]Treaty of Lisbon amending the Treaty on European Union and the Treaty establishing the European Community, signed at Lisbon, 13 December 2007, *OJ C 306, 17.12.2007, pp. 1–271.*

[14]EU Charter on Fundamental Rights, Official Gazette of the EU, No. 2007/C 303/01.

[15]Article 21, paragraph 2 of the Charter.

[16]Council Regulation (EC) No 859/2003 of 14 May 2003 extending the provisions of Regulation (EEC) No 1408/71 and Regulation (EEC) No 574/72 to nationals of third countries who are not already covered by those provisions solely on the ground of their nationality, *OJ L 124, 20.5.2003, pp. 1–3.*

emphasise that provisions of these regulations are applicable to third-country nationals provided that person concerned is already legally resident in the territory of the EU and has links only with a third country and a Member State.[17] To approximate the legal status of third-country nationals who holds a long-term residence permit to that of Member States' nationals, the Council adopted the Directive 2003/109/EC,[18] which incorporates a section on the treatment of long-term residents, including: access to employment and self-employment, education and vocational training, recognition of professional diplomas, certificates and other qualifications, social security, social protection and social assistance, tax benefits, access to goods and services, freedom of association and affiliation and membership of an organisation representing workers or employers and free access to the entire territory of the Member State concerned.[19]

A number of directives that are relevant for economic migrants from third countries have been adopted, among others: directives aimed at facilitating the migration of certain desirable groups such as students,[20] scientists,[21] highly skilled workers,[22] seasonal workers,[23] the transfer of management staff, experts and trainees within the enterprise,[24] directive on the issuance of a unique residence permit,[25] a directive laying down sanctions and measures for employers who employ illegal immigrants,[26] and others. Bearing in mind the character and structure of the adopted legal instruments, a conclusion can be drawn on the aspiration of the EU to address a

---

[17]Commission Staff Working Document accompanying document to the Proposal for a Council Directive on a Single application procedure for a single permit for third country nationals to reside and work in the territory of a Member State and on a common set of rights for third country workers legally residing in a Member State, SEC (2007) 1408, Brussels, 23.10.2007.

[18]Council Directive 2003/109/EC of 25 November 2003 concerning the status of third country nationals who are long-term residents, *OJ L 16, 23.1.2004, pp. 44–53.*

[19]Article 11 (1) of the Directive 2003/109/EC.

[20]Council Directive 2004/114/EC of 13 december 2004 on the conditions of admission of third-country nationals for the purposes of studies, pupil exchange, unremunerated training or voluntary service, *OJ L 375, 23.12.2004, pp. 12–18.*

[21]Council Directive 2005/71/EC of 12 October 2005 on a specific procedure for admitting third-country nationals for the purposes of scientific research, *OJ L 289, 3.11.2005, pp. 15–22.*

[22]Council Directive 2009/50/EC of 25 May 2009 on the conditions of entry and residence of third-country nationals for the purposes of highly qualified employment, *OJ L 155, 18.6.2009, pp. 17–29.*

[23]Directive 2014/36/EU of the European Parliament and of the Council of 26 February 2014 on the conditions of entry and stay of third-country nationals for the purpose of employment as seasonal workers, *OJ L 94, 28.3.2014, pp. 375–390.*

[24]Directive 2014/66/EU of the European Parliament and of the Council of 15 May 2014 on the conditions of entry and residence of third-country nationals in the framework of an intra-corporate transfer, *OJ L 157, 27.5.2014, pp. 1–22.*

[25]Directive 2011/98/EU of the European Parliament and of the Council of 13 December 2011 on a single application procedure for a single permit for third-country nationals to reside and work in the territory of a Member State and on a common set of rights for third-country workers legally residing in a Member State, *OJ L 343, 23.12.2011, pp. 1–9. See more in:* Groenendijk (2015), pp. 547–561.

[26]Directive 2009/52/EC of the European Parliament and of the Council of 18 June 2009 providing for minimum standards on sanctions and measures against employers of illegally staying third-

problem of the demographic deficit, as well as the issue of the shortage occupations, which especially refers to highly qualified persons, by selective immigration policy.[27] To exercise rights of economic migrants or workers from third countries governed by the abovementioned instruments, it is necessary that these persons have residence in the territory of a Member State.[28]

Provisions on equal treatment of third-country workers are also contained in Association, Partnership and other Agreements between the EU and third countries aiming to provide certain minimal rights to migrant workers originating from a limited number of countries.[29] Article 47 of the Stabilisation and Association Agreement with Bosnia and Herzegovina, for example, reads: "(a) treatment accorded to workers who are nationals of Bosnia and Herzegovina and who are legally employed in the territory of a Member State shall be free of any discrimination based on nationality, as regards working conditions, remuneration or dismissal, compared to nationals of that Member State".

Workers from third countries with whom the EU has not concluded specific agreements, which fall into one of the categories governed by the aforementioned legal instruments, may refer to the provisions on employment opportunities as well as the equal treatment clauses in the Directive, provided that the employer or the future employer is a national or other public authority.[30] The EU Court of Justice has on several occasions taken the view that directives cannot create an obligation for individuals.[31] Private employers, natural or legal persons, cannot be directly bound by the directive. Obligation based on the rights prescribed by the directive may arise for these persons, only based on a national regulation that implements the relevant directive in national legislation.[32] In accordance with the practice of the EU Court of Justice,[33] the authorities of the Member States, including the courts, shall interpret the national legislation in such a way as to comply to the greatest extent possible with EU law.[34] In relation to the rights of migrant workers and because these rights

---

country nationals, *OJ L 168, 30.6.2009, pp. 24–32* On these instruments see more in: Vukorepa (2018), p. 95. Groenendijk (2010), p. 18.

[27]Vukorepa (2018), p. 95.

[28]Commission Staff Working Document accompanying document to the Proposal for a Council Directive on a Single application procedure for a single permit for third country nationals to reside and work in the territory of a Member State and on a common set of rights for third country workers legally residing in a Member State, SEC (2007) 1408, Brussels, 23.10.2007.

[29]These are, for example: Association Agreements signed with Tunisia (1995) and Morocco (1996), a Stabilisation and Association Agreements with FYROM and Bosnia and Herzegovina, Partnership and Cooperation Agreement (PCA) with Russia, ACP Partnership Agreement, etc.

[30]Groenendijk (2010), p. 18.

[31]More on the Directive as a secondary legal source of EU Law in: Kaczorowska (2013), pp. 278–279. Alihodžić (2012), pp. 73–78.

[32]ECJ, 152/84 (Marshall I), ECR 1986, 723, from 26.2.1982.

[33]ECJ, C-212/04 (Adeneler), ECR 2006, I- 6057, from 4.7.2006.

[34]The directive is an act that should be transposed into national laws. However, in certain cases the Court of Justice recognises the direct effect of directives to protect the rights of individuals.

are mainly regulated by directives, one may notice that there is a huge variation between the sectoral legislation (intra-corporate transferees, seasonal workers, single permit holders, blue card holders) granting rights to migrant workers.[35] As Member States have the possibility to implement or apply legislation based on directives differently, sometimes overlapping with other secondary legislation, the aforementioned issue becomes more complex, having in mind the purpose of directives to ensure equal employment opportunities as well as equal treatment of third country nationals. However, the principle of effectiveness, applied by the EU Court of Justice, has an aim to promote effective enforcement of EU law within the legal systems of the Member States. In the EU Court of Justice decision C-579/13[36] from June 4, 2015 it is stated that Article 11 (1) of Directive 2003/109 guarantees to third-country nationals who have acquired the status of a person with long-term residence equal treatment such as treatment enjoyed by nationals of that Member State. The question referred to the European Court of Justice is whether the obligation of civil integration, which manifests itself in proving the written and oral knowledge of the language and society of a Member State, can be imposed on third-country nationals with long-term residence, without having the same obligation for nationals of that Member State. In other words, does the application of the civil integration measure prescribed by national legislation violate the principle of equal treatment under Article 11 of the Directive?[37] The opinion of the European Court of Justice is set out in paragraph 41 of the decision under which the principle of equal treatment requires that in comparable situations different treatment is not practiced, and that different situations are not treated in the same way, unless such treatment is objectively justified.

The principle of non-discrimination must not be called into question by the way in which civil integration measures apply. Since the basic purpose of the Directive is to integrate third country nationals with a long-term residence in a Member State, this Directive is not contrary to a national legislation that prescribes the obligation of civil integration, provided that the modalities of its implementation do not jeopardise the attainment of the objectives of the Directive.[38] In this decision, the European Court of Justice applied the principle of harmonious interpretation that requires national law to be interpreted in the light of directive.[39]

Therefore, the Court laid down in its case law that a directive has direct effect when its provisions are unconditional and sufficiently clear and precise and when the EU country has not transposed the directive by the deadline. ECJ, 41/74 (van Duyn) ECR 1974, 1337, from 4.12.1974. Swedenborg (1998), p. 22.

[35]Kochenov and van den Brink (2015), p. 88.

[36]C-579/13, ECLI:**EU**:C:2015:369, from 4.6. 2015.

[37]Point 38, C-579/13, ECLI:EU:C:2015:369, from 4.6. 2015.

[38]Point 57, C-579/13, ECLI:EU:C:2015:369, from 4.6. 2015.

[39]Craig and De Burca (2011), p. 200.

3 Interaction Between Private International Law and Migration Law

Although in the context of EU law, private international law and migration law fall within the area of freedom, justice and security[40]; there is no single approach to regulating a matter whose solution depends on the application of one or other rules. Namely, each of these legal areas has its own rules and almost no connection exists between them. However, given the increasing international mobility, that is, the global migration of the population, and the difficulties encountered by the judiciary and other authorities in the EU Member States when applying the mechanisms of private international law to resolve the status of migrants, it seems necessary to establish additional mechanisms that would bridge the gap between these disciplines.[41]

Adoption of the private-legal perspective in this sense would mean that in the context of migration, the focus shifts from the state's interest to the interests of the migrant as an individual. In the context of resolving issues in relation to the status of migrants, EU Member States mainly focus on the distribution of a burden of care and the prevention of abuse, and subsequently approach this problem from a distance, keeping in focus almost exclusively statistical indicators.[42] On the other hand, consideration of the interests of migrants and their families requires much more concrete approach. Private International Law has specific tools and methods that can prove to be very effective in the context of managing international or European migration.[43] In this context, it is of particular importance to overcome the traditional dichotomy between public and private rights.

4 Private International Law Instruments Regulating the Status of Migrant Workers in the EU

The function of private international law instruments in the context of regulating the status of migrant workers must be observed depending on the nature of the issue and the timeframe when this issue arises before the competent authorities of the EU Member State. Its interaction with migration law is emphasised especially in the area of registration and recognition of facts and documents (documents, court decisions), which govern the regulation of the personal status of migrants, including migrant workers from third countries in the EU.

---

[40] Article 67 Consolidated version of the Treaty on the Functioning of the European Union, *OJ C 326, 26.10.2012, pp. 47–390.*

[41] Eechkout (2015).

[42] Private International Law in a Context of Increasing International Mobility: Challenges and Potential (2017). Directorate General for Internal Policies of the Union.

[43] Van Den Eechkout (2017).

International migration involves the resolution of many private law issues, including, but not limited to, the protection of children, marital and/or family relationships and their impact on family reunification, the recognition of foreign diplomas, etc. In this context, recognition of foreign public documents and judicial decisions is of crucial importance. Namely, there are situations when the registration and recognition of the personal status of migrant workers under the PIL rules appear as a prerequisite for acquiring a specific migrant status. For example, the recognition of a marriage concluded in the country of origin or a decision to divorce a marriage or marriage certificate issued in the country of origin has a decisive influence on the issue of migrant status, such as the approval of a visa or residence permit, family reunification, etc. For the issuance of a residence permit for the purpose of employment, it is necessary that the foreign diploma on certain profession is recognised in the country of destination,[44] usually with an apostille certificate attached to it.[45] However, the role of private international law instruments is not exhausted by resolving the status of migrant workers in the EU. Namely, after obtaining a residence and work permit under the regulations of the EU Member States, migrant workers can find themselves in a situation where the EU employer has disputed their rights guaranteed by the aforementioned EU law instruments. Disputes arising out of individual employment contracts of third country nationals may be dealt with by means of an alternative way to obtain the support and protection of professional associations against the discriminatory conduct of the employer or to contact the Ombudsman or Equal Treatment Committee with the competencies to conduct an independent investigative procedure. In this sense, these institutions are considered an attractive and effective legal remedy for the protection of third-country workers' rights, which are guaranteed by EU legislation on equal treatment.[46] The above is valid if there is a violation of the rights of workers from third countries by private employers, natural or legal persons, and public authorities that appear in the role of the employer. However, third-country workers still have the possibility to seek protection of their rights before ordinary courts, if the employer does not agree with the opinion of the Ombudsman or the Equal Treatment Committee.[47]

[44]Article 11 (1) of the Directive 2003/109/EC.

[45]The legalisation of foreign public documents at the international level is regulated by the Hague Convention of 5 October 1961 Abolishing the Requirement of Legalisation for Foreign Public Documents.

[46]See f.n. 21, 25 i 26. of this paper.

[47]Groenendijk (2010), p. 22.

4.1 Recognition of Foreign Public Documents/Court Decisions with the Function of Regulating the Status of Migrant Workers in the EU

It has already been emphasised that the regulation of the migrant status of third-country nationals in the EU (residence permit, work permit, family reunification, etc.) depends on the prior recognition of relevant documents (public documents/ court decisions), or legal facts that were created/issued in the country of origin. In this context, the recognition of foreign court decisions or public documents (e.g., diploma on acquired professional qualifications, decision on divorce, marriage certificate, etc.) as an instrument of procedural private international law arises as a prerequisite for regulating migrant status.

Legal and other facts in the procedure, in cases with an international element, are proven by foreign public documents. Such a document is obtained through international legal assistance channels or is presented by the party itself. One of the requirements for a foreign public document to be accepted by the competent authority in the country of destination is legalisation, or verification of the authenticity of a public document. This is a procedure in which the authenticity of the signature of the person who signed the document and the seal placed on it is confirmed for the needs of international traffic.[48] Regarding the recognition of court decisions from third countries in the EU, it has to be stated that the rules of the regulations applicable in the territory of the EU will not be applied,[49] but the national laws of the individual Member States that regulate specific matter. In some Member states, the signed bilateral or multilateral agreements in force between respective Member States and the third country or country of origin from which the migrant arrives may have priority in application in relation to the national legislation of a Member State.[50] However, it happens that, in an effort to regulate migrant status in the EU, third-country nationals use fraudulent actions with regard to documents, issued in the country of origin, to prove their status. The latter can be considered as a reason why some Member States have adopted particularly restrictive laws regarding the fulfillment of conditions for obtaining residence or work permits in those countries, as well as regulating other issues of migrant status.[51]

[48]F.n. 28. See also Muminović (2006), pp. 136–139.

[49]Several regulations governing the recognition and enforcement of court decisions, important for the subject of this paper, are in force in the EU. It is worth mentioning EU Regulation No. 1215/ 2012 on Jurisdiction, Recognition and Enforcement of Judgments in Civil and Commercial Matters (Brussels I Recast), Regulation EC No. 2201/2003 concerning Jurisdiction, Recognition and Enforcement of Judgments in Matrimonial Matters and the Matters of Parental Responsibility (Brussels II a), Regulation EC No. 4/2009 on Jurisdiction, Applicable law, Recognition and Enforcement of Decisions and Cooperation in Matters relating to Maintenance Obligations, etc.

[50]More on the status of international agreements in: Rosas (2011), pp. 1304–1345. Mohay (2017), pp. 151–164. Alihodžić (2015), pp. 91–105.

[51]Macniven (2012).

Alternative methods of proofing are not always available, so migrant workers can face the inability to prove the accuracy of their civil status data. In practice, this can endanger the unity of the family, or lead to the violation of the right to respect for family life, which is guaranteed by Article 8 of the European Convention on Human Rights.[52] Since this is a very complex and sensitive issue, it is necessary to adopt an innovative and practical approach that would allow the destination countries (EU Member States) an effective means of protection against abusing the documents proving the status of migrants, without neglecting the rights guaranteed by the European Convention on Human rights. In this sense, there are several possible models of action.

The optimum approach would be to achieve EU cooperation with countries of origin in the context of the adoption of rules on the circulation of public documents. However, when it comes to the likelihood of establishing this kind of cooperation or concluding bilateral agreements between the EU and the countries of origin, one should bear in mind that the countries of origin are highly heterogeneous.[53] To achieve international cooperation, it is necessary that the performance of the activities of presenting public documents by the public administration bodies in the countries of origin takes place smoothly or at a satisfactory level. A model for establishing cooperation with third countries in the field of circulation of public documents could be the Regulation No. 2016/1191 of the European Parliament and of the Council of 6 July 2016 on promoting the free movement of citizens by simplifying the requirements for presenting certain public documents in the European Union and amending Regulation (EU) No 1024/2012.[54] The provision of Article 14 of this Regulation prescribes the procedure in cases where there is a reasonable doubt as to the authenticity of a public document or its certified photocopy.[55] Thus, if an EU Member State authority has reasonable doubts as to the authenticity of a public document (a birth certificate for example), it may, through

[52] Van Dijk and van Hoof (2001), pp. 459–509.

[53] In some countries, for example, to get a birth certificate, people have to wait for the authorities to come to their village, and enter data, which happens twice a year. Consequently, in the birth records only the month of January or the month of June is recorded as the month of birth, leaving room for doubt or fraud, or opens a dilemma as to whether a person is a minor or not, which entails other legal consequences, for example the need to appoint a guardian to the person, etc. Similar problems may arise in situations where migrants come from countries that use another era to calculate time (e.g., Persian calendar). Cited according to: Private International Law in a Context of Increasing International Mobility: Challenges and Potential (2017). Directorate General for Internal Policies of the Union, p. 13.

[54] *OJ L 200, 26.7.2016, pp. 1–136. See also*: Private International Law in a Context of Increasing International Mobility: Challenges and Potential (2017). Directorate General for Internal Policies of the Union.

[55] Article 14 states:

Requests for information in cases of reasonable doubt

1. Where the authorities of a Member State in which a public document or its certified copy is presented have a reasonable doubt as to the authenticity of that public document or its certified copy, they shall take the following steps to dispel their doubt:

the information system or the competent central authorities, request a statement from the authorities that issued the document.

Based on the abovementioned provision of Article 14 of the Regulation No. 2016/1191, and having in mind the satisfactory functioning of the authorities in charge of civil status registers, this kind of cooperation might be achieved between the EU and the Balkan countries that have functional mechanisms for achieving international cooperation and from which a large number of economic migrants arrive to the EU.[56] Regarding Bosnia and Herzegovina, for example, the role of the central authority in the realisation of the services described above could be assumed by Migration Service Centers[57] operating within the Employment Bureau or other authorities/

(a) check the available models of documents in the repository of IMI as referred to in Article 22;
(b) if a doubt remains, submit a request for information through IMI:

   (i) to the authority that issued the public document or, where applicable, to the authority that made the certified copy, or to both; or
   (ii) to the relevant central authority.

2. A reasonable doubt as to the authenticity of a public document or its certified copy as referred to in paragraph 1 may relate, in particular, to:

   (a) the authenticity of the signature;
   (b) the capacity in which the person signing the document acted;
   (c) the identity of the seal or stamp;
   (d) the document having been forged or tampered with.

3. Requests for information made under this Article shall set out the grounds on which they are based.
4. Requests for information made under this Article shall be accompanied by a copy of the public document concerned or of its certified copy, transmitted electronically by means of IMI. Such requests and any replies to those requests shall not be subject to any tax, duty or charge.
5. The authorities shall reply to requests for information made under this Article within the shortest possible period of time and in any case within a period not exceeding 5 working days or 10 working days where the request is processed through a central authority.

In exceptional cases where the time limits referred to in the first subparagraph cannot be adhered to, the requested authority and the requesting authority shall agree upon an extension of the time limit.

6. If the authenticity of the public document or of its certified copy is not confirmed, the requesting authority shall not be obliged to process them.

[56]Private International Law in a Context of Increasing International Mobility: Challenges and Potential (2017). Directorate General for Internal Policies of the Union, p. 13.

[57]The establishment of Migration Service Centres is supported by the Migration for Development in the Western Balkans (MIDWEB) project led by the International Organization for Migration (IOM) in partnership with the Migration, Asylum, Regional Initiative for Refugees (MARRI), the German Federal Office for Migration and Refugees and the Vienna Institute for International Economic Studies (WIIW), and is funded by the European Commission's IPA 2009 multi-beneficiary program 2. In addition to providing information on work opportunities and studying abroad, visa procedures, work and residence permits, access to health care and education abroad and other information that can be useful for economic migration, the Network of Migration Service Centres, among other things, aims to promote regular migration to EU countries, and capacity building of public services

services designated by the competent authorities in BH (the Ministry of Foreign Affairs, as member of the Coordination Body for Migration and Asylum).

In addition, a bilateral agreement should establish a system of control over employment agencies dealing with recruiting workers from the aforementioned countries. Another way of overcoming the aforementioned problem is the adoption of an international convention within the framework of the Hague Conference on Private International Law,[58] which would regulate the diverse and complex issues of economic migration. The basis of the problem lies in the fact that there is a deep gap from the economic and security point of view, between the countries of origin and the countries of destination of the migrants. If there is a clear intention to solve the problem "in the root,"[59] international cooperation between countries of origin of economic migrants and destination countries (EU Member States) is necessary. Currently, there is no such type of cooperation at the international level. The regulation of private international law aspects of economic migration through intergovernmental cooperation should be based on the following[60]:

First, it is necessary to establish a balance between the right of every person to a dignified life in the country of origin and his fundamental right to freedom of movement. In other words, the conventions should clearly reflect the view that migrations are justified only if they are the result of free choice rather than economic pressure;

Secondly, the convention provisions must recognise the interest of the countries of origin not to lose the highest quality population (the so-called brain drain), i.e., leaving an economically active and qualified part of the population, which in the long run can have a negative impetus to the economic and demographic development of the country of origin;

Thirdly, destination countries have an interest in introducing special measures to limit influx of migrants, but in that sense, it is necessary to achieve co-operation with countries of origin in terms of creating preconditions for the return of these persons to the country of origin;

Finally, economic migrants, countries of origin, as well as countries of destination have a common interest to regulate a system of control over agencies/intermediaries engaged in employment of migrants.

According to opinion of some authors, the Convention on International Adoption[61] can serve as a model for the adoption of a convention, which would comprehensively regulate the complex issues of economic migration. Following the model

in the context of the policy and potential of labour migration of countries in the region. www.bih.iom.int/labour-migration, access to page 20.9.2018.

[58]On the role of the Hague conference on PIL see in: Alihodžić (2012), op. cit, pp. 56–61. Schulz (2007), p. 940.

[59]Van Loon (2002).

[60]Ibid.

[61]The Hague Convention of 29 May 1993 on Protection of Children and Co-operation in Respect of Intercountry Adoption. https://www.hcch.net/en/instruments/conventions/specialised-sections/intercountry-adoption, access to page 25.8.2018.

of this instrument, the basic premise of the future Convention is that every person, if possible, should find employment in the country of origin. Subsequently, international economic migrations would be acceptable only if such an undertaking would be unsuccessful. Furthermore, the convention should establish a link between seemingly unrelated areas: the migration and legal protection of economic migrants.

The Convention should establish a system of central authorities that would coordinate international economic issues with economic migrants. Finally, the convention would necessarily have to establish a system of control over intermediaries in employment. Bearing in mind that the number of economic migrants in the EU Member States is on the rise, a multilateral approach seems to be an optimal solution. These issues go beyond the framework of traditional understanding of private international law, but the methods and instruments of this legal discipline are certainly indispensable when it comes to regulating migration issues internationally.

4.2 International Jurisdiction Rules and the Law Applicable to Individual Employment Contracts in relation to European Economic Migration

If third-country employees need to protect their rights arising from individual employment contracts concluded with employers with headquarters in the EU, before the courts of the EU Member States, it is necessary to consider private international law instruments that contain jurisdiction rules and the law applicable for international disputes between employees and employers. Regulation Brussels I Recast (EU) No. 1215/2012[62] and Regulation Rome I (EC) No. 593/2008[63] contain special provisions for determining the courts of the Member States with international jurisdiction in disputes related to individual employment contracts and for determining the law applicable to employment contracts.

Regarding the application of the EU instruments mentioned above to third-country nationals, two situations should be distinguished: *first*, when an employee who is a third-country national act as a prosecutor, and the other when this person appears in the defendant's role.

If a claimant, an employee of a third country, alleging a breach of his obligations arising from an individual employment contract, sues an employer with a seat in an EU Member State, the international jurisdiction of the court shall be determined

[62]Regulation (EU) No 1215/2012 of the European Parliament and of the Council of 12 December 2012 on jurisdiction and the recognition and enforcement of judgments in civil and commercial matters, *OJ L 351, 20.12.2012, pp. 1–32. More on the Regulation see in:* Radončić and Meškić (2013), pp. 46–55.

[63]Regulation (EC) No 593/2008 of the European Parliament and of the Council of 17 June 2008 on the law applicable to contractual obligations (Rome I), *OJ L 177, 4.7.2008, pp. 6–16.*

under the provisions of the Brussels I Recast Regulation.[64] The Brussels I Recast Regulation has taken on the connecting factors established to determine the place where disputes related to individual employment contracts can be initiated. Amendments to the rules on jurisdiction for individual employment contracts that followed with the entry into force of the revised Regulation relate, *inter alia*, to the possibility of applying these rules in the proceedings against an employer domiciled outside the EU, and that an employee may sue several employers as adjudicators before the courts of the Member State in which one of them has domicile.[65] Under the provisions of the Brussels I Recast Regulation, an employee may sue the employer:

- In the place where the employer has his/her domicile, or in the place where the employer has a branch, agency or other establishment[66]
- In the place where or from which the employee regularly performs his work or before the court of the last place where he worked,[67] or
- In the event that an employee usually does not perform his work in only one country, in the place where the business which engaged the employee is or was situated.[68]

The Regulation does not provide for an autonomous definition of the domicile of a natural person, and in the context of the application of the rules where the domicile occurs as a connecting factor, a differentiated approach may be reached in its definition, since the provision of Article 62 of the Regulation refers in that regard to the national provisions of the Member States. This can lead to the fact that a particular person—an employer—is domiciled in more than one country.[69] This, however, will not be the case with determining the seat of legal entities, since Article 63 of the Regulation gives the autonomous definition of that concept, according to: the statutory headquarters, the central administration and the main place of business. If the employer has no domicile in a Member State, but has a branch, agency or other establishment in it, it shall be deemed to have domicile in that Member State for the purpose of determining international jurisdiction. In support of the above, there is a judgment of the EU Court of Justice in *Mahamdia C-154/11* case.[70] The Regulation also does not provide an interpretation of the concept of a place where an employee

[64]From 10 January 2015, the Brussels I Regulation Recast replaced Regulation 44/2001/EC. The Brussels I Recast Regulation applies to proceedings initiated on 10 January 2015 or later, while Regulation 44/2001/EC continues to apply to proceedings initiated before that date. More on rules on the international jurisdiction of courts for individual employment contracts under Regulation EC No 44/2001 see in: Alihodžić (2011), pp. 193–213.

[65]Article 20 (1), article 21 (1) (b) (i), article 21 (2) of the Brussels I Recast Regulation.

[66]Article 20 (1) and (2) Regulation Brussels I Recast.

[67]Article 21 (1) (b) Regulation Brussels I Recast.

[68]Article 21 (1) (b) ii Regulation Brussels I Recast.

[69]Esplugues Mota and Palao Moreno (2007), p. 333.

[70]Mahamdia, C 154/11, from 19 July 2012. In paragraph 52 of this decision, the Court stated that, in regard to individual employment contract concluded by the embassy on behalf of the sending State, the embassy would be deemed to be "establishment" in terms of designing international jurisdiction

habitually performs his/her work. The application of the said rule on the international jurisdiction of a court of a Member State according to the place of habitual work necessarily requires the definition of the term "habitual", especially in situations where the employee performs work activities in several places. In the *Mulox case* of 1993, the EU Court of Justice concluded that the definition of "habitual work" is closely related to the need to avoid the multiplication of courts which might possibly have jurisdiction in a specific case, thereby preventing the adoption of incompatible court decisions, and facilitates mutual recognition and enforcement in the Member States other than the state in which the decision in question was brought.[71] In this regard, it is necessary to distinguish the business activity of the employee that is "regular". In the aforementioned decision, the Court concluded that the place of performance of the work is the place where, or from where the employee "principally" fulfills his legal obligations towards the employer.[72] Later on, the word has been replaced by the term habitual work. It is considered that employees habitually carry out work in the place where they have established an effective center of their business activities, and from where they fulfill the essential part of their obligations towards the employer.[73] The Brussels I Recast Regulation has extended the jurisdiction of the courts of the Member States to labor disputes against an employer who is domiciled outside the EU. The intention of the EU legislator was to provide additional protection to the employee as a weaker party to the contract.[74] Accordingly, an employee who regularly carries out his work in a Member State, regardless of his domicile, can rely on the aforementioned jurisdiction rule and sue an employer who has his domicile in a third country before a court of the Member State in which he regularly performs his work.

However, if an employee, a third-country national, appears in the role of the respondent, two situations should be distinguished. Firstly, if this person has domicile in the EU, the employer can sue him only in the Member State in which he has domicile.[75] On the contrary, third-country employees who do not have their residence in the EU, and who appear in the defendant's role, do not fall under the "Brussels regime". An employer who has domicile in a Member State will rely on the national rules of international jurisdiction in that case. This will often include exorbitant grounds of jurisdiction. Additionally, referring to the provision of Article 6 in conjunction with the application of Article 20 of the Regulation aims to prevent

---

of a court of a Member State, when the function carried out by an employee falls under the exercise of public authority.

[71]Mulox IBC Ltd. v. Hendrick Geels, C -125/92, 1993, ECR I-4075, point 21.

[72]Mulox, point 26.

[73]Cf. Article 5 (1) of San Sebastián Convention with Article 19 (2) (a) of Regulation 44/2001 and Article 21 (1) (b) Brussels I Recast Regulation. More on the interpretation of this concept in: Alihodžić (2011), pp. 202–203.

[74]Galič (2016), p. 124.

[75]Article 6 Brisel I Recast Regulation.

the "reflexive effect" of the Regulation, or the application of protective rules on jurisdiction, in favor of employees from third countries.[76]

Regarding the law applicable to individual employment contracts, the relevant choice of law rules in EU law are contained in the Rome I Regulation.[77] Although this regulation starts from the party autonomy as the basic mechanism for determining the applicable law for contracts in general, when it comes to individual employment contracts, this principle is limited in such a way that the choice of law cannot have the effect of depriving employees of protection guaranteed by provisions that cannot be derogated from by an agreement based on law that, if not selected, would be applicable under paragraphs 2, 3, and 4 of Article 8 of the Rome I Regulation.[78]

If the parties have not chosen the law that will be applicable to an individual employment contract, the contract is subject to the law of the country in which, or from which an employee normally performs his work based on a contract.[79] If the applicable law cannot be determined in this way, the contract is subject to the law of the country in which the place of business is located. The Regulation provides for the possibility that none of the aforementioned laws referred to in Article 8 of the Rome I Regulation will be applied, if it is clear from all the circumstances of the case that the contract is closely related to the law of another State.[80] Issues that fall within the scope of the regulation in respect of individual employment contracts relate, *inter alia*, to: interpretation, enforcement, consequences of breach of obligations, including compensation of damages, and ways of termination of obligations and the consequences of the nullity of the contract.

Given the number of Western Balkan citizens who might appear in the role of employees in EU Member States and the efforts of individual Member States to encourage economic migration from these countries in some sectors, the establishment of international cooperation in this area appears as an imperative.

In this regard, it should be emphasised that Member States have lost the possibility of entering into bilateral relations with third countries or international organisations in those areas that are, within the EU, regulated by EU legislative acts.[81]

However, Member States have been given the option, in certain sectors, to conclude agreements with third countries under prescribed conditions, if there is a particular interest in it.[82] This is made possible by the Regulations 664/2009[83] and

---

[76]Galič (2016), p. 126.

[77]See. f.n. 48.

[78]Hoek (2014), pp. 157–162.

[79]Article 8 paragraph 2 Rome I Regulation.

[80]Article 8 paragraph 4 Rome I Regulation.

[81]Alihodžić (2010), pp. 73–91.

[82]Ibid.

[83]Council Regulation (EC) No 664/2009 of 7 July 2009 establishing a procedure for the negotiation and conclusion of agreements between Member States and third countries concerning jurisdiction, recognition and enforcement of judgments and decisions in matrimonial matters, matters of parental responsibility and matters relating to maintenance obligations, and the law applicable to matters relating to maintenance obligations, *OJ L 200, 31.7.2009, pp. 46–51.*

662/2009.[84] As can be seen from the title and content of the Regulation 662/2009, the possibility of international cooperation (concluding a bilateral agreement) between the Member States and third countries in the part relating to the choice of law for individual employment contracts is envisaged. We believe that the above model could serve as an inspiration for the conventional regulation of not only the rules of the applicable law, but also the rules on jurisdiction and the recognition and enforcement of foreign court judgments, thus allowing third-country employees to also apply protection rules on jurisdiction over this type of contract, regardless of their domicile.

5 Concluding Remarks

Economic, political, cultural, religious, educational and other reasons generate the movement of the population from the traditionally economically poor countries of origin to the more economically prosperous countries of Western Europe, the members of the EU.

International migration and the realisation of the status of migrant workers in the EU implies prior regulation of a number of issues that fall within the scope of private international law, such as the recognition of different types of public documents or court decisions, which prove a certain status, or are necessary for obtaining a residence permit in EU Member State. Sometimes ascertaining such a status will be difficult because of a doubt about the authenticity of the document presented to the authorities of the destination country. Private International Law has specific instruments and methods that enable more effective management of international economic migration in the context of the regulation of these issues.

The role of private international law mechanisms is also important when it comes to determining the jurisdiction of the courts and the applicable law in a situation where a dispute arises between third-country employee and EU employer. At the EU level, regulations have been adopted that regulate the abovementioned issues within the EU. Bearing in mind the external competence of the EU and potentials of European Private International Law instruments, it is necessary to consider optimal forms of international cooperation, which would aim to improve the status of migrant workers from third countries. One solution envisages the possibility of concluding a bilateral agreement between the EU and a third country following the provisions of the Regulation 2016/1191, which would apply to the rules on the circulation of public documents necessary for regulating the status of migrants in the EU. Another possibility is the conventional regulation of this issue within the

[84]Regulation (EC) No 662/2009 of the European Parliament and of the Council of 13 July 2009 establishing a procedure for the negotiation and conclusion of agreements between Member States and third countries on particular matters concerning the law applicable to contractual and non-contractual obligations *OJ L 200, 31.7.2009, pp. 25–30.*

framework of the Hague Conference on Private International Law. Conventional solutions should therefore strike a balance between the interests of the countries of origin and the countries of destination of economic migrants, in particular with regard to controlling the outflow of a qualified part of the population into EU Member States.

When it comes to the protection of economic migrants—third-country employees based on an individual employment contract concluded with an EU employer, instruments of European Private International Law relating to the rules of international jurisdiction of courts and applicable law are of decisive importance.

Migrant workers will be subject to different rules of private international law, depending on whether they appear in the role of the claimant or the respondent. International jurisdiction of the courts will be designated according to Brussels I Recast Regulation, provided that an employee, a third country national, appears as a claimant in a dispute. If a third country national appears in a dispute as a respondent and has no domicile in an EU Member State, national rules on jurisdiction will be applied. Subsequently, protective rules on jurisdiction envisaged by the Brussels Regime will not be applied in the later case. Thus, considering possibility of cooperation in the form of bilateral agreements would certainly contribute to the protection of economic migrants regardless of their domicile.

It turns out from the above that the existing instruments of private international law are not sufficient to respond to the needs of the protection of economic migrants in the EU.

In addition, when it comes to the need to simplify the conditions related to the circulation of public documents, as well as the establishment of a system of control over employment agencies and other issues related to the rights of economic migrants, we consider the optimal solution to be the adoption of a new international convention to regulate these issues comprehensively.

References

Alihodžić J (2010) Uticaj vanjske nadležnosti Evropske unije na sklapanje međunarodnih ugovora država članica u oblasti međunarodnog privatnog prava – osvrt na Uredbu EZ br. 664/2009 i njen značaj za BiH. Anali Pravnog fakulteta u Zenici 6:73–91

Alihodžić J (2011) Pravila o međunarodnoj nadležnosti kod pojedinačnih ugovora o radu u pravu Evropske unije i Bosne i Hercegovine. In: Collection of Papers, IX Private International Law Conference: Recent Trends in European Private International Law – Challenges for the national legislation of the South East European countries, Praven fakultet "Justinijan Prvi", Skopje, pp 193–211

Alihodžić J (2012) Razvoj evropskog međunarodnog privatnog prava: pravci reforme zakonodavstva u Bosni i Hercegovini. OFF-SET, Tuzla

Alihodžić J (2015) Nekoliko napomena o odnosu izvora međunarodnog privatnog prava u Evropskoj uniji i Bosni i Hercegovini, Zbornik radova sa X Savjetovanja iz oblasti građanskog prava, Udruženje sudija Republike Srpske, pp 91–103

Craig P, De Burca G (2011) EU law, text, cases and materials. Oxford University Press, Oxford

Eechkout V (2015) The instrumentalization of private international law: Quo Vadis? Rethinking the 'neutrality' of private international law in an era of globalization and Europeanization of private international law. In: Bergé JS et al (eds) Boundaries of European private international law/Les frontières de droit international privé européen/Las fronteras del derecho internacional privado europea/Bruylant, Bruxelles, pp 387–406
Esplugues Mota C, Palao Moreno G (2007) Jurisdiction over individual contracts of employment. In: Magnus U, Mankowski P (eds) Brussels I regulation, European commentaries on private international law. European Law Publishers, Sellier, pp 326–345
Galič A (2016) Jurisdiction over consumer, employment, and insurance contracts under the Brussels I regulation recast. Aust Law J 2:122–134. www.austrian-law-journal.at
Groenendijk K (2010) Equal treatment of workers under EU law and remedies against violations by employers. Online J Free Mov Work Eur Union 1:16–22
Groenendijk K (2015) Equal treatment of workers from third countries: the added value of the Single Permit Directive. ERA Forum 16(4):547–561
Hagen-Zanker J (2008) Why Do People Migrate? A Review of the Theoretical Literature, Maastricht Graduate School of Governance Working Paper No. 2008/WP002. Available at SSRN: https://ssrn.com/abstract=1105657 or https://doi.org/10.2139/ssrn.1105657
Hoek A (2014) Private international law: an appropriate means to regulate transnational employment in the EU. Erasmus Law Rev 3:157–169
Kaczorowska A (2013) European Union law. Routledge/Taylor and Frances Group, London/New York
King R (2012) Theories and typologies of migration: an overview and a Primer. Malmö Institute for Studies of Migration, Diversity and Welfare (MIM): Willy Brandt Series of Working Papers in International Migration and Ethnic Relations
Kochenov D, van den Brink M (2015) Pretending there is no Union: non-derivative quasi-citizenship rights of third-country nationals in the EU. In: Thym D, Zoeteweij-Turhem M (eds) Rights of third country nationals under EU association agreements: degrees of free movements and citizenship. Brill/Nijhoff, Leiden/Boston, pp 63–100
Macniven D (2012) Fraud with respect to civil status. http://www.europarl.europa.eu/RegData/etudes/note/join/2012/462499/IPOL-JURI_NT(2012)462499_EN.pdf
Mohay A (2017) The status of international agreements concluded by the European Union in the EU legal order. Pravni vjesnik 33(3.4):151–164
Mügge L, van der Haar M (2016) Who is an immigrant and who requires integration? Categorizing in European policies. In: Garces-Mascarenas B, Penninx R (eds) Integration processes and policies in Europe (contexts, levels and actors). IMISCOE, Springer, pp 77–90
Muminović E (2006) Procesno međunarodno privatno pravo. Pravni fakultet Univerziteta u Sarajevu, Sarajevo
Radončić Dž, Meškić Z (2013) Uredba (EU) br. 1215/2012 Evropskog parlamenta i Savjeta od 12. decembra 2012. godine o nadležnosti, priznanju i izvršenju sudskih odluka u građanskim i trgovačkim predmetima. Nova pravna revija, br.1:46–55
Rosas A (2011) The status in EU law of international agreements concluded by EU Member States. Fordham Int Law J 34(5):1304–1345
Sales R (2007) Understanding immigration and refugee policy, contradictions and continuities. Bristol University Press
Schulz A (2007) The accession of the European community to the Hague conference on private international law. Int Comp Law Q 56(4):939–949
Swedenborg J (1998) Horizontal direct effect of directives. Juridiska Fakulteten Lund
Third-country Nationals in the European Union, Indicators of immigrant Integration 2015: settling in (2015) OECD/European Union. https://www.oecd-ilibrary.org/docserver/9789264234024-17-en.pdf?expires=1537788002&id=id&accname=guest&checksum=27452592D2EC6E9FDF30305785C6EA9E
Trachtman JP (2009) The international law of economic migration: toward the fourth freedom. W.E. Upjohn Institute for Employment Research, Kalamazoo, Michigan

Van Den Eechkout V (2017) Private international law in an era of globalization: "Neutral" private international law!? I could be brown, I could be blue, I could be violet sky. Available at SSRN: https://ssrn.com/abstract=3034231 or https://doi.org/10.2139/ssrn.3034231

van Dijk P, van Hoof GJH (2001) Teorija i praksa Evropske konvencije o ljudskim pravima. Müller, Sarajevo

van Loon H (2002) The Hague Conference on Private International Law: Current Problems and Perspectives. Available at: www.ehu.eus/cursosderechointernacionalvitoria/ponencias/pdf/2002/2002_1.pdf

Vukorepa I (2018) Migracije i pravo na rad u Evropskoj uniji. Zbornik Pravnog fakulteta u Zagrebu 68(1):85–120

The manufacturer's authorised representative in the EU is Springer Nature Customer Service Centre GmbH, Europaplatz 3, 69115 Heidelberg, Germany. If you have any concerns regarding our products, please contact ProductSafety@springernature.com

Printed and bound by CPI Group (UK) Ltd, Croydon, CR0 4YY
28/09/2026
02224083-0011